Labor Income Share

Saumik Paul

Labor Income Share

Understanding the Drivers of the Global Decline

palgrave
macmillan

Saumik Paul
Newcastle University
London, UK

ISBN 978-981-15-6859-6 ISBN 978-981-15-6860-2 (eBook)
https://doi.org/10.1007/978-981-15-6860-2

This Palgrave Macmillan imprint is published by the registered company Springer Nature Singapore Pte Ltd.
The registered company address is: 152 Beach Road, #21-01/04 Gateway East, Singapore 189721, Singapore

Acknowledgments

This book is an outcome of roughly four years of work on labor income share. It would not have been completed without the support and contribution of many people. I sincerely thank Cristiano Perugini for introducing me to this topic. Cristiano was a visiting scholar at Hitotsubashi University back in 2017. I had a series of idle chats in between intense discussions with Cristiano and Kyoji Fukao that later helped me formulate the idea of writing this book. In 2018, the Asian Development Bank Institute hosted a conference on "Labor Income Share in Asia: Conceptual Issues, Drivers, and Policy Considerations." The proceedings of this conference were published in 2019 as a book volume edited by Gary Fields and me. Working with Gary during this time has helped to shape up many parts of this book. I thank (in alphabetical order) Robert Chirinko, Mitali Das, Marta Guerriero, Kyoji Fukao, Dibyendu Maiti, Debdullal Mallick, Naoyuki Yoshino, and other conference participants at the Asian Development Bank Institute for their feedback on my work.

Parts of Chaps. 4, 5, and 6 have been presented in various seminars and conferences. I am grateful for the comments I received from Cristiano Antonelli and Fabio Berton at the University of Turin; Davide Fiaschi and Angela Parenti at the University of Pisa; Raffaele Miniaci and Maria Laura Parisi at the University of Brescia; Silvia Marchesi and Tania Masi at the University of Milano-Bicocca; Cristiano Perugini, Fabrizio Pompei, and Francesco Venturini at the University of Perugia; Francesco Pastore at the University of Campania Luigi Vanvitelli; Atanu Ghoshray, John Sessions, and Wessel Vermeulen at Newcastle University; Praveen Kujal and Michela Vecchi at Middlesex University; and other seminar participants at the

University of Brescia, University of Pisa, University of Perugia, University of Milano-Bicocca, University of Campania Luigi Vanvitelli, Middlesex University, and Newcastle University. Chapters 3, 4, 5, and 7 involved a large amount of data work. My sincere thanks (in alphabetical order) to Hironobu Isaka, Saloni Lakhia, Abdelbari Lakhim, Yoko Oishi, Ken Suzuki, and Liam Thomas for excellent research assistance. Liam has also provided timely support in editing some of the chapters.

I thank my colleagues at Hitotsubashi University, the Asian Development Bank Institute (Tokyo), and Newcastle University (UK) for their encouragement and support. My gratitude to Silvia Marchesi for hosting me at the University of Milano-Bicocca in 2019, where the bulk of this book was drafted. My sincere thanks go to Gabrielle Cimenilli and Asier Mariscal for providing many helpful comments on my paper on "Capital-Skill Complementarity and Labor Income Share," and Tim Gindling and Daniel Hammermesh for their useful comments on my paper titled "Understanding the Global Decline in the Labor Income Share."

I thank my father, Dilip Paul, for his encouragement throughout. My wife Ronita and our daughters, Siya Pritha and Sayuri Radha, were happy to see me writing a book. I thank my family for their continuous encouragement and for gracefully accepting the cyclic nature of life that "downs" are as much a part of life as "ups" are, while I have been completing this book project.

Contents

List of Figures

List of Tables

CHAPTER 1

Introduction

The functional distribution of income (factor income shares) has long been a topic of concern for economists. David Ricardo's statement, published back in 1817, serves as a testimony to this fact, "*To determine the laws which regulate [this] distribution is the principal problem in political economy.*" The share of labor income has been seen to be constant. Keynes (1939) described this constancy as "the most surprising, yet best-established fact," whereas Kaldor (1956) advocated the constancy of the labor income share (LIS) as "the stylized fact" of long-term economic growth. Despite its long pedigree, the academic interest in factor income shares has had a rollercoaster ride. As Atkinson (2009) wrote "Since the 1960s, factors shares have been downplayed. The textbooks no longer give them much space." Recent years saw a comeback with a large volume of studies documenting a global decline in the labor income share. Growing concern over this trend has encouraged debate about fair distribution of personal incomes. The topic of income distribution is once again at the center of economic debates, and this book joins this discussion in a timely fashion.

The study of factor income shares plays an important role in understanding the relationship between national income and personal income and their links to overall income inequality. The global share of income going to labor is declining, coupled with the fact that a disproportionate share of this decline is found among low- and middle-skilled workers. The labor income share has been increasing for high-skilled workers and

S. Paul, *Labor Income Share*,
https://doi.org/10.1007/978-981-15-6860-2_1

declining for middle- and low-skilled workers worldwide. Several factors contribute to this secular trend. Growing skill premium, as an outcome of globalization, and an increasing complementarity between capital and skill through the advancement of technology could explain the polarization of labor income shares across the skill spectrum. If capital can be substituted with unskilled labor more readily than with skilled labor, a drop in the relative price of capital would result in a larger drop in the employment of unskilled workers compared to skilled workers. This could then lead to a decline in the share of income for unskilled labor more so than for skilled labor. Higher exposure to routinization of tasks (i.e., the automation of tasks where labor can be substituted by capital to the highest degree) has also played a key role in the polarization of wages and skill premium along the skill spectrum.

The aim of this book is threefold. First, it provides novel insights on the measurement of the labor income share. Second, it amasses recent developments in the theoretical and empirical research on the labor income share to gain a deeper insight into the drivers of the labor income share. And finally, using novel datasets it provides empirical evidence on the correlates of the labor income share at the firm, sector, and country level. Chapter 2 contains a discussion on the measurement issues and the conceptual problems related to the labor income share. Chapters 3, 4, and 5 describe trends of the labor income share at the country, sector, and firm level, respectively. Chapter 6 relates to theoretical discussions, while Chap. 7 provides empirical evidence on the drivers of the labor income share both at the country and at the sector level. Chapter 8 outlines potential areas of future research and concluding remarks are forwarded in Chap. 9.

This book contributes to the issues related to the measurement of the labor income share. The difficulties associated with the measurement of labor income share increase in the presence of self-employment, which constitutes almost half of the global workforce with their labor income being inaccurately measured. Chapter 2 discusses an extension of the adjustment framework for self-employment suggested by Gollin (2002) to a more disaggregated sector level. Allowing for self-employment rate to vary across sectors, it considers an adjustment factor composed of (1) the earnings ratio of self-employment to wage-employment and (2) the employment ratio of self-employed to wage employees. The agriculture sector shows the least correlation between the adjusted and unadjusted LIS figures suggesting that agriculture sector is a greater source of the self-employment error compared to other sectors.

Secondly, this book amasses cross-country evidence on the evolution of labor income shares at the country, sector, and the firm level. It provides a unique opportunity to compare the labor income share measures at three different levels. At the sector level (following the Groningen 10-sector classification), it puts together a dataset for a sample of 54 countries. At the firm level, I construct a dataset using the World Bank enterprise survey data for 139 countries. And, at the country level, data is compiled from the existing sources for a sample of 98 countries. Evidence at the micro level suggests that while the labor income share has decreased for low-skilled workers, this has been concurrent with an increase for high-skilled workers. Globalization leading to a growing skill premium and an increasing complementarity between capital and skill through the advancement of technology also explains the polarization of labor income shares across the skill spectrum.

Finally, this book provides novel insights into theoretical research on the labor income share. Chapter 6 forwards a theoretical framework based on the Morishima elasticity of substitution to validate the capital accumulation mechanism as a driver of the labor income share. The role of capital accumulation as a driver of declining labor income share requires capital and labor to be substitutes, which appears paradoxical in a world predominantly characterized by complementarity between capital and labor. In a nested-Constant Elasticity of Substitution (CES) framework with capital-skill, the Morishima elasticity of substitution identifies the elasticity parameters at different skill levels, and based on its properties, I derive the condition that allows capital accumulation to coexist with a declining LIS when capital and labor are complements. It refines our understanding of the global decline in LIS by highlighting the significance of the skill composition of the labor market. The relevance of capital-skill complementarity for the labor share of income can also be drawn using a two-stage production structure (Goldin and Katz 1998). In the first stage, skilled workers adopt new technologies and efficiently use capital, thus showing high capital-skill complementarity. In the second stage, unskilled workers continue the mechanical process of machine maintenance indicating a relatively low level of capital-skill complementarity. Such practices are common across both developing and developed countries and provide an important link between capital-skill substitutability and factor income shares.

I hope this book proves to be useful for academics, policymakers from government agencies, policy aides in research institutions and think tanks, and broader audiences from public and private organizations. The aim of this book is to provide technical and practical insights and help design policies to reduce inequality. I briefly discuss below the contribution that each chapter makes in this book.

Chapter 2 provides an overview of the conceptual issues in the measurement of the labor income share. It first discusses various definitions proposed to measure the labor income share and then highlights the sources of the measurement problems. The national accounting statistics do not provide accurate data for labor income as it involves both incomes earned by wage employees and income earned by self-employed. In addition, various issues stem from the accounting method of national income, treatment of intangible inputs, measurement of non-private sectors and informal sectors, and attribution of mixed income. It then extends the adjustment framework for self-employment suggested by Gollin (2002) to a more disaggregated sector level, by allowing self-employment rate to vary across sectors. The novel adjustment factor at the sector level is composed of the earnings ratio of self-employment to wage-employment and the employment ratio of self-employed to wage employees. The empirical evidence confirms that agriculture sector is a greater source of the self-employment error compared to the rest of the sectors.

Chapter 3 combines macro data from various sources including the Penn World Table (PWT) and the United Nations Industrial Development Organization (UNIDO) and showcases correlates of the labor income share for a sample of 93 countries. There is a positive correlation between the GDP per capita and the average labor income share, whereas there is a weak negative correlation between the informal sector share of GDP and average labor income share. Correlation between self-employment and average labor income share shows a similar negative relationship, but with a strong goodness of fit and clear regional patterns among the upper and lower middle-income countries. Trade measures are positively correlated with the labor income share, and the goodness of fit is higher for the upper middle-income countries relative to countries from other income groups. There is also a positive correlation between the non-agricultural export volume and the average labor income share.

Chapter 4 discusses the labor income share at the sectoral level for 53 countries. Of the 53 countries, 20 are developing countries (based on the World Bank classification), and, for a sample of 45 countries, data are available for at least five years. There is considerable variation in the labor income share estimates within each region and within each broad category of sectors both at the level and with changes over time. Overall, there is a fall in the average rate of change in the labor income share in the secondary sector and the primary sector and a rise in the same in the tertiary sector.

Chapter 5 provides some evidences on the drivers of the labor income share at the firm level using a novel firm-level dataset on the labor income share. It defines the firm-level labor income share following three alternative approaches and compares these estimates across income groups, regions, firm sizes, and ownership types. The estimates average around 0.45, with considerable variations across regions and firm characteristics. Manufacturing firms tend to have a lower labor income share as the firm size increases. Large firms in services, both foreign and state-owned, pay a higher share of income to laborers.

Chapter 6 advances a theoretical discussion on the role of elasticity of substitution and complementarity between factor inputs and skill as drivers of the labor income share. It begins with a production function to establish a relationship between production technology, factor productivity, and factor income shares. The assumption of a non-unitary elasticity of substitution (σ) between capital and labor plays a crucial role in the movement of the labor income share. The role of elasticity of substitution is discussed considering a homogeneous labor market (a production function with capital and labor) and a heterogeneous labor market (a production function with capital, skilled labor, and unskilled labor). The theoretical model is then extended to analyze the comparative statics outcomes on the labor income share.

Chapter 7 discusses empirical findings on the drivers of labor income share under three broad categories: (a) technological change and capital intensity, (b) structural transformation, and (c) institutional changes. As the burgeoning literature shows, there could be numerous channels at work within these broad categories. For example, the declining rate of unionization falls under the broad category of institutional change, and it leads to a decline in labor's bargaining power and consequently to a decline in the labor income share. However, the process of globalization or the participation of a country into the global value chain could cause a decline in the unionization rate. Moreover, the participation of global value chain is allowed by the reduction in shipping or communication cost through the technological change. At the same time, the reduction of corporate income tax rate can also be categorized under institutional change and globalization if it is implemented because of international pressure or is driven by capital mobility across nations.

Chapter 8 highlights several potential areas of research on the drivers of labor income share (LIS). These include personal income inequality, skilled emigration, remittances, and brain-gain, remittances, and negative labor supply, premature deindustrialization, firm restructuring, and globalization at the sectoral level.

References

Atkinson, A. B. 2009. "Factor Shares: The Principal Problem of Political Economy?" *Oxford Review of Economic Policy* 25 (1): 3–16.

Goldin, Claudia, and Lawrence F. Katz. 1998. "The Origins of Technology-Skill Complementarity." *Quarterly Journal of Economics,* 113 (3): 693–732.

Gollin, D. 2002. Getting income shares right. *Journal of Political Economy, 110*(2), 458–474.

Kaldor, N. 1956. "Alternative Theories of Distribution." *The Review of Economic Studies* 23 (2): 83–100.

Keynes, J. M. 1939. "Relative Movements of Real Wages and Output." *The Economic Journal* 49 (193): 34–35.

CHAPTER 2

Definition, Measurement, and Conceptual Issues

The traditional labor income share measures the degree to which income can be attributed to labor in terms of capital, labor, and production. However, only using these factors to express the labor income share gives a limited account for other relevant factors such as the high informal sector, mixed income sector, or taxes on capital and labor incomes. This measure also has conceptual issues in matters such as whether a gross or net measure best accounts for the labor income share, or determining the causes for the labor income share to shift with various arguments debating factors such as competition decline, rising information technology, intellectual property products, capital accumulation, and globalization. This chapter focuses on both discussions, first in showing the range of definitions proposed to better measure the labor income share and then by highlighting the conceptual issues in the literature related to further understanding the measure.

2.1 Definition of Labor Income Share

A number of definitions of labor income share (LIS) have been introduced, starting with the traditional understanding of labor income share described by Lübker (2007) to be "how much of national income accrues to labor." This has been utilized by the Bureau of Labor Statistics (BLS) in their equation to denote the labor income share which is the form

S. Paul, *Labor Income Share*,
https://doi.org/10.1007/978-981-15-6860-2_2

popularized through much of the literature. This is shown below for year t and sector k:

$$LIS \equiv \frac{Labor\ income_{tk}}{National\ income_{tk}}$$

In examining the components of the factors in this equation, the BLS reports several series which all have a similar methodology. For the non-farm business sector, they determine labor compensation (labor income) sector as compensation of employees excluding government wages and salaries, compensation of employees of nonprofit institutions, private compensation, farm compensation of employees, but including imputed labor compensation of self-employment (Gomme and Rupert 2004). The "value added" measure conforms to these same sectors. However, this lacks coverage of information such as intangible inputs, the attribution of mixed income, non-private, and informal sectors. Consequently, the BLS definition is inappropriate for many applications, such as to find the labor income share in developing countries where attention to self-employed income is vital. This has also given way to widespread debates concerning the high level of ambiguity of proprietor's income and indirect taxes less subsidies. For the issue with ambiguity of proprietor's income, this is addressed by the Bureau of Labor Statistics by computing an implicit wage for the sector through dividing compensation by hours worked. In assuming that the self-employed will pay themselves the same wage that they could otherwise earn in this sector, their implied labor income is this implicit wage multiplied by hours of work by the self-employed.

Gollin (2002) recognizes the importance of accurately accounting for the self-employment income and proposes three adjustment approaches for the labor income share equation, which use mixed income and the employment structure of a country in their estimation of the labor income share. He argues that income shares are approximately constant across countries when using these adjustments (ibid., p. 459). He then explains how employee compensation shares are a poor measure of labor income share, since their disparities may reflect changes in the sectoral composition of output or in the structure of employment, exclude important forms of non-wage compensation, and include rents accruing to particular skills such as returns to entrepreneurial ability (ibid., p. 463). This leads to a large understatement of labor income share in countries where self-employment is a significant proportion of the workforce. He proposes that his adjustments, listed as G1, G2, and G3 below, alleviate these concerns. CoE represents the compensation of employees, MI represents mixed income, E represents the number of wage employees, and TE represents the number of total employees.

$$LIS_{G1} = \frac{CoE + MI}{GDP}$$

$$LIS_{G2} = \frac{CoE}{GDP - MI}$$

$$LIS_{G3} = \frac{\frac{CoE}{E} \times TE}{GDP}$$

Another approach is drawn from Gomme and Rupert (2004), who assume that the portion of "ambiguous" income is the same as other the sectors. The terms and equation are given as follows:

$$Y^{l} = Y^{ul} + \text{LIS} \times Y^{al}$$

$$Y^{l} = \text{LIS} \times Y = \text{LIS} \times \left(Y^{ul} + Y^{uk} + Y^{al}\right)$$

$$\text{LIS} = \frac{Y^{ul}}{Y^{ul} + Y^{uk}}$$

where

Y : Value added; Y^{l} : Total labor income; Y^{ul} : unambiguous labor income (compensation of employees); LIS : Labor income share; Y^{al} : Ambiguous labor income (proprietors' income plus indirect taxes less subsidies); Y^{uk} : *Unambiguous capital income* (*corporate profits, rental income, net interest income* and depreciation)

Kehrig and Vincent (2017) use an alternative approach and find the components of the labor income share through census data, finding different inputs than the inputs in the Bureau of Labor Statistics model to find labor compensation and value added. The authors define labor compensation or labor costs through US census data as salarie and wages, both unemployment insurance and social security contributions netted out from wages, and voluntary labor costs such as health, retirement, and other benefits paid to the employee. The value added is measured as sales less inventory investment for final and work-in-progress, resales, material inputs, and energy expenditures. There is one missing component in the lack of purchased services, but this can be accounted for by reducing establishment level value added by the industry-year specific ratio of purchased services to value added computed from the BLS data. In order to create a consistent census sample for analyses, Kehrig and Vincent drop all observations outside the one percentile to avoid outliers driving results, which includes results with a negative value added.

The labor income share value generated by the census data significantly differs from the value computed by the BLS data by about eight percentage points (ibid.). The factors that contribute the most to this change are the exclusion of non-corporate (self-employed) compensation as part of labor compensation, the exclusion of establishments that have a negative value added, and the given method to compensate for missing purchased services which gives a higher value added factor higher, all contributing to a higher denominator and a lower labor income share (ibid.).

Other definitions measure the labor income share at the firm level. Paul and Isaka (2019) use three alternative definitions to measure firm level labor income share. They create the first by adapting the standard definition with the definition provided by Gomme and Rupert (2004) and interpret this from an aggregate to a firm level. To estimate the total factor productivity, they use the definition of capital used by the World Bank which employs data from the Enterprise Survey, though the specifications of this survey mean that the LIS here is only applicable for the manufacturing sector. Paul and Isaka (2019) then find a proxy for value added by the difference of the total annual sales of the establishment by the total annual cost of inputs. The equation is given as follows:

$$LIS_{i,t} = \frac{Compensation\ of\ employees_{i,t}}{total\ annual\ sales_{i,t} - total\ annual\ cost\ of\ inputs_{i,t}}$$

The second definition to find the labor income share for the firm level also comprises of the definition of capital provided by the World Bank. This equation captures how much of the total costs of inputs come from labor and excludes the profits of firms and capitalists. This is given as follows:

$$LIS_{i,t} = \frac{Compensation\ of\ employees_{i,t}}{compensation\ of\ employees_{i,t} + total\ cost\ of\ capital_{i,t}}$$

The third measure at the firm level follows the definition of labor share provided by Zhou (2016). There are issues such as that the definition can become unclear due to firms without any procurement showing a larger LIS than firms that do procure inputs. Also, part of the value of this labor income share definition may also include the amount of input used in production, rather than just the amount of value added allocated to labor. This is given as follows:

$$LIS_{i,t} = \frac{Compensation\ of\ employees_{i,t}}{total\ sales_{i,t}}$$

2.2 Conceptual Issues

2.2.1 Gross and Net Labor Income Share

One prominent conceptual debate is whether a gross or net LIS is more appropriate as a measure of value added, with the difference being the inclusion of capital depreciation in the net value. The gross concept includes depreciation as part of GDP, where the net concept rather uses national income to calculate LIS. Recent studies such as Karabarbounis and Neiman (2014) tend to use gross shares to examine the declining labor share. This is due to the higher accessibility of gross share data available for more countries with more years and levels of aggregation. Wakita (2006) argues that while gross LIS seems plausible for theoretical analysis, using a production function including depreciation to measure LIS is more appropriate. This is refuted by Bridgman (2014), who argues against the utility of net labor share and claims that both the inclusion of depreciation and taxes on production in the denominator of the labor share has caused economists to greatly overstate the magnitude and novelty of the labor share's decline. Karabarbounis and Neiman (2014) respond by arguing that gross and net labor shares have generally moved in the same direction and that a shift from the gross to net LIS mostly attenuates the downwards trend. Rognlie (2016) then continues this debate by showing that the concerns in Bridgman's paper are valid, particularly in its coverage of the years preceding the sample provided by the Karabarbounis and Neiman study. Also, the different results between Bridgman (2014) and Karabarbounis and Neiman (2014) can be found due to Bridgman's focus on more developed countries, his adjustments for taxes, and his consideration for magnitudes by examining percentage change instead of percentage points change.

These contrasting perspectives on gross and net labor income share provide the means for the authors to reach different conclusions on the determinants of labor income share. Karabarbounis and Neiman (2014) argue that netting out depreciation has no significant impact and consequently the high depreciation of capital is not a driver of the labor income share fall. Bridgman (2014) instead considers the shift to high depreciating capital and higher production taxes as an explanation of the falling LIS. Using data on the US Corporate Sector Labor Share from 1948 to 2011, Bridgman finds that gross labor share has not fallen due to capital owners' increased bargaining power, and that trade liberalization or other forms of increased competition can put pressure on wages without reducing labor's relative bargaining power. He concludes that at least some portion of the global decline in LIS is due to these effects and that taxes have a direct impact on LIS, to which they are implicitly attributed.

Rognlie (2016) continues on the topic by arguing that both gross and net labor income share measures have legitimacy and are particularly effective when in a single good model, where the relative price of capital and output is fixed at one and losses can be reasonably included in the production function. He moves on to suggest that deciding on the most useful measure depends on which element is considered more important to be highlighted. His paper explains how the gross value added between labor and capital more directly reflects the structure of production, where the allocation of net value rather reflects more of the ultimate command over resources that is received by labor versus capital (Rognlie 2015).

2.2.2 Labor Income Share and Competition Decline

Barkai (2016) presents an argument to address the relationship between the labor share and the capital share, where he particularly focuses on the degree to which the increasing capital share had offset the decline in the labor share. He finds that changes to preferences, technology, and relative prices can cause firms to shift from labor to capital, which creates a fall in the labor income in expense of capital income. However, he adds that these mechanisms cannot explain the observed recent fall. Instead, the data used by Barkai points to competition decline as playing a significant role in this phenomenon through an increase in industry concentration (ibid.). Barkai uses this to dispute the perception that a decrease in labor income share is efficient and explains how it rather creates large gaps in output, wages, and investment (ibid.).

2.2.3 *Labor Income Share and Information Technology*

Another driver of the labor income share is said to be the role of information technology affecting the distribution of income among factors of production. Eden and Gaggl (2015) find that ICT accumulation from the 1950s is responsible for half the decline in the LIS. Particularly, their study on the relative capital prices and depreciation rates of ICT and non-ICT capital reveals that ICT accounts for 3.3 percentage points of the 6.3 percentage points measured decline of aggregate LIS since the 1950s (ibid.).

There is a consensus that any positive effect on aggregate consumption will have adverse distributional implications, with the resulting impact on net welfare depending on the quantitative importance of each of these. Eden and Gaggl (2015) test this by employing a representative agent model with a frictionless redistribution of income to find a ballpark estimate for the overall quantitative benefits of automation. This model gives an idea of the qualitative importance of ICT contributing to output at consumption growth at each point in time since the 1950s. ICT had a low degree of significance until 1980, before growing at a rapid pace up to one third of growth in output per capita in the 2000s (ibid.). Eden and Gaggl (2015) find from these results that while ICT may have a large effect on the distribution of labor income, the effect on the distribution of income between capital and labor was only moderate. Furthermore, their research points to automation being the sole cause of the declining labor share as unlikely, and rather that only half is attributed to an increase in ICT LIS. The remaining cause is said to be due to non-ICT capital income share factors such as housing (ibid.).

2.2.4 *Labor Income and Intellectual Property Products*

Koh et al. (2016) argue that Intellectual Property Products (IPP) have driven nearly the entire observed decline of the labor income share. They first compare IPP capital to traditional capital and note the difference in the investment flow, price, and the depreciation rate. They use the IPP capital share of income to assess the evolution of IPP capital intensity from 1.6% in the late 1940s to 6.6% to 2013, showing that this increase to a more IPP capital-intensive economy reflects the secular decline in the LIS (ibid.). They then validate these results by plotting the traditional LIS against the aggregate LIS computed from the 1998 Bureau of Economic Analysis (BEA) data and the similarly defined aggregate LIS computed by Gomme and Greenwood (1995) which have IPP included. All three of these series show a trendless labor share without IPP capital, suggesting that IPP is the cause of this downward trend (ibid.).

Koh, Santaeulalia, Llopis and Zheng also use their findings to evaluate the traditional measures to find the labor income share. They consider how the long-standing aggregate Cobb-Douglas production function is consistent with the long-run behavior of the trendless traditional LIS, but not with the aggregate LIS that incorporates IPP capital. In considering this, they argue that the US model needs to explicitly consider innovators and entrepreneurial activities that generate IPP for an accurate measure of LIS (ibid.). However, these findings are not consistent with the other recent studies on this topic such as Barkai (2016) who shows that the magnitude of intellectual property is too small and increases too slowly to explain the growth of profit share. Though Koh et al. (2016) frame their focus on obstacles to assessing the returns to intellectual property, and they argue that a more intangible capital intensity means a lower LIS.

2.2.5 Evaluation of the Downward Trend in Labor Income Share

The explanations of what shifts the labor income share are far from being settled, with many of the issues identified above lacking robust evidence across countries and time. Gomme and Rupert (2004) focus on one of the major holes in the literature being the limited robustness over different measurements. While many of the common discourse discuss the implications and drivers behind the recent drop in LIS, Gomme and Rupert challenge the idea altogether that the drop in the labor income share occurred. They explain how studies tend to solely fixate on the data provided by the Bureau of Labor Statistics (ibid.). Other measures of labor income share, such as the nonfinancial corporate sector or the broad macroeconomic level show the labor income share to be near a historical average (ibid.).

Their studies show that a fall in the share of labor could be associated with a rise in the share in capital, but this is not necessarily implied (ibid.). They also suggest other possible factors such as indirect taxes less subsidies, though the paper adds that the share of nonfinancial corporate business sector remains relatively constant for the nonfinancial corporate business sector. Gomme and Rupert proceed to establish that the current fall in labor income share could be representative of the cyclical pattern where labor income share rises and falls, and the recent fall was a result of the global expansion of the economy (ibid.). Though this has been refuted in papers such as Mućk et al. (2018) where their results point to the labor share only being countercyclical in the short run, before becoming procyclical in the medium run and also diverging for the long run as well. Consequently, it is necessary to keep in mind while observing these continued debates how distant the literature currently is from a clear conclusion and consensus about what drives the labor income share.

2.3 Self-Employment and Labor Income Share

In a recent study, the International Labour Organization (ILO) begins their discussion on self-employment in labor income share by reflecting on Gollin's three approaches (ILO 2019). The paper notes that there are issues with how G1 and G2 use mixed income. Some of the problems of using mixed income include measurement issues, heterogeneity in practices in the mixed income measure of country national accounts, and a tendency to be underreported (ILO 2019, p. 7). This leaves the G3 equation with the most utility due to its coverage of labor compensation rather than mixed income. However, using the G3 measure still requires determining a ratio of average labor earnings between the self-employed and employees through some rule of thumb and is therefore still limited.

The ILO proposes an alternative approach to account for the self-employment income through their Harmonized Microdata collection. The main utility of the microdata is that it provides an alternative to rules of thumb for calculating the self-employment labor income share. The data consists of a survey including variables on labor related earnings of employees, hours worked, economic activity, and worker occupation, rural or urban residence and key demographic variables (ILO 2019, p. 10). The procedure of the test uses employee wages to impute a counter-factual wage to self-employed workers based on common observable characteristics.

Firstly, by applying the results of the microdata of household surveys in 95 different countries against the labor income share generated from rules of thumb equations, the study finds that the rules of thumb do not accurately determine the self-employment labor share of income (ILO, p. 27).

Two cases of a developed and developing country particularly exemplify this. For the United States, the G3 measure assumes that the relative wage of the self-employed is one, yet the evidence using the microdata shows that the relative wage share of the United States provided by the G3 measure would be over one (ibid.). The ILO paper explains that this is because of the self-employment premium that exists in high-income countries, which is not considered in any rule of thumb approach (ibid.).The ILO paper also shows that the rule of thumb is also weak when applied to developing countries, such as the case of India. While the rule of thumb suggests that developing countries should assume the relative wage to self-employed workers to be two-thirds of employees, this would erroneously show a self-employed labor income share of over 100% (ibid.). The ILO paper explains that these errors are created by the incidence of two concurrent factors in India, being a high share of self-employment and the large self-employment penalty (ibid.) (Fig. 2.1).

However, solely depending on the microdata for a reference of the self-employment labor income share is itself limited and needs to be accommodated by more thorough data in order to show the full picture. One limitation is that the self-employment is calculated in aggregate terms, when this is not something that every sector is affected by. Providing an accurate picture of the self-employment labor income share requires the consideration of a sector-level labor income share analysis through the following steps. First, find the different degrees to which the self-employment shares of each industry. Second, adjust the margins of each industry determined by the relative share of self-employment. Thirdly, input this

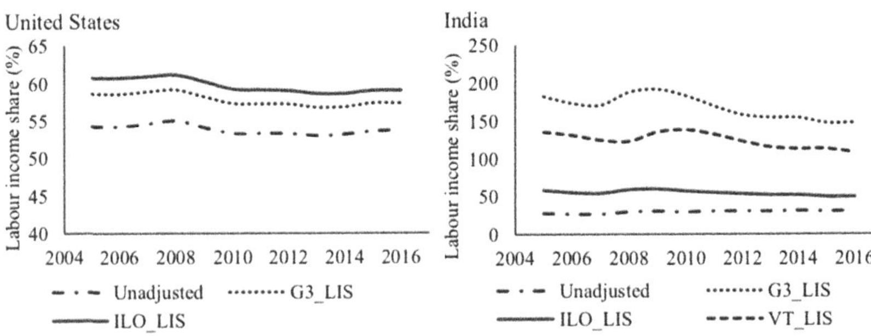

Fig. 2.1 The microdata-based adjustment versus rule of thumb (G3 and variants). (Source: International Labour Organization (ILO), 2019)

adjustment into the equation to determine the labor income share. In this chapter we will use the case of a number of countries to put this adjustment to use and make.

2.3.1 *A Conceptual Framework*

We write the aggregate labor income share (LIS_{Agr}) as a weighted sum of sectoral labor income shares in the following way

$$LIS_{Agr} = \sum LIS_i . \phi_i \tag{2.1}$$

where LIS_i and ϕ_i denote the labor income share in sector i and the share of GDP that goes to sector i, respectively. Equation 2.1 shows the aggregate labor income share as a sum of sectoral labor income shares weighted by sectoral shares of GDP. Extending the correction framework suggested by Gollin (2002) to sectoral level, we propose to adjust the labor income share at the sectoral level taking into consideration of the self-employment rates prevailing in each sector. The adjusted sectoral labor income share (LIS_i^{Adj}) can be written as a product of unadjusted sectoral labor income share (LIS_i) and the adjustment factor ($1 + \xi_i \varphi_i$).

$$LIS_i^{Adj} = LIS_i \left(1 + \xi_i \varphi_i\right) \tag{2.2}$$

The adjustment factor is composed of the proportion of average earnings between self-employment and paid employment in sector i (ξ_i) and the ratio between share of self-employed and the share of employees (or paid-employed) in sector i (φ_i). The next step is to identify ξ_i and φ_i. Unavailability of data on self-employment and employees at the sectoral level is the biggest challenge and we discuss these issues in greater detail in the subsequent sections.

2.3.2 *Identification of Earnings Ratio (ξ) Across Sectors*

At the aggregate level, adjustments to the labor income share have been carried out with various earnings ratios between self-employed and paid-employed. The European Commission's Annual Macro-economic database of the European Commission (AMECO) database provides adjusted labor income share for the European Union members and other high-income countries assuming $\xi = 1$. The International Monetary Fund uses a similar adjustment tool for its World Economic Outlook publication in 2017. Self-employment is often associated with highest level of informal activities and of the working poor (ILO 2018). The two largest categories of self-employment, own-account and contributing family work, are often associated with vulnerability and lower working and living conditions (Gammarano 2018). For instance, in a selected sample of 39 developing countries, Kapsos and Bourmpoula (2013) find that own-account workers and contributing family workers are dramatically over-represented in working poverty and extreme working poverty (corresponding to the international poverty lines), whereas employees are over-represented in economic classes above the poverty lines. Therefore, assuming the same earnings, employees will plausibly generate a strong upward bias in the labor income share in low and middle-income countries.

However, such differences are observed even among OECD countries using the ILO data. The ILO collects data on self-employment and employees based on the following definitions. Self-employment is defined as the employment of employers, workers who work for themselves, members of producers' co-operatives, and unpaid family workers. On the other hand, employed people are people aged 15 or more, who report that they have worked in gainful employment for at least one hour in the previous week or who had a job but were absent from work during the reference week.

Figure 2.2 shows a weak negative relationship between the average rate of self-employment between 2000 and 2018 and the GDP per hour worked. Aside from Italy, countries with a self-employment rate of more than 20% have a lower productivity of less than 70 GDP per hour worked. Conversely, countries with a high labor productivity tend to have low self-employment rates on average.

To identify the earnings ratio between self-employed and employees at the sectoral level we require data on wage distribution by types of employment at the sectoral level. Availability of sectoral data especially for less developed countries is scarce. Additionally, there are issues of comparability as countries follow different statistical methods to amass the information on earnings by sectors and employment types. As a second-best solution, we use data from the *Life in Transition Survey 2010* (LiTS 2010), which comprises of a sample of 39,000 respondents from 35 countries

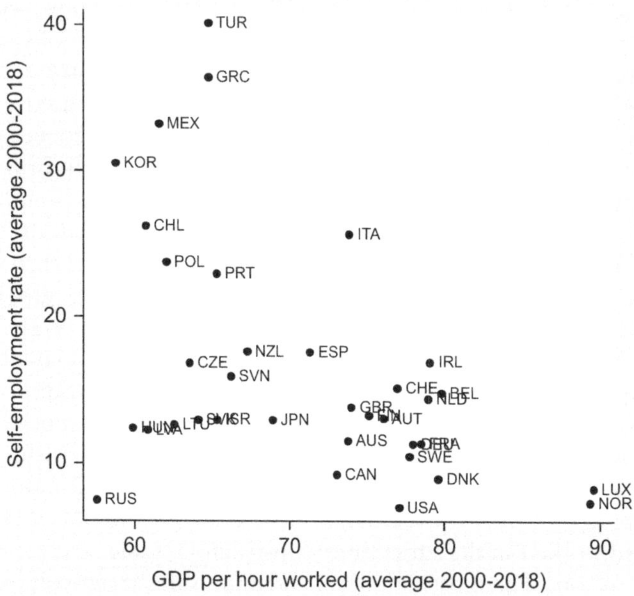

Fig. 2.2 Self-employment and productivity (GDP per hour worked) in OECD countries. (Source: Authors' calculation based on OECD database. https://data.oecd.org/. Note: Self-employment rate is averaged for the period between 2000 and 2018. GDP (in 2010 USD) per hour worked is also averaged between 2000 and 2018)

(29 transition countries, 5 western European countries, and Turkey).[1] The LiTS 2010 survey was conducted jointly by the European Bank for Reconstruction and Development (EBRD) and the World Bank.

The LiTS data provides us a consistent way to measure the ratio between self-employed and employees by sector. We combine the answers to the

[1]Albania, Armenia, Azerbaijan, Belarus, Bosnia, Bulgaria, Croatia, Czech Republic, Estonia, France, Georgia, Germany, Great Britain, Hungary, Italy, Kazakhstan, Kosovo, Kyrgyzstan, Latvia, Lithuania, Macedonia, Moldova, Mongolia, Montenegro, Poland, Romania, Russia, Serbia, Slovakia, Slovenia, Sweden, Tajikistan, Turkey, Ukraine, and Uzbekistan.

following survey questions from Sect. 2.5 on labor, education, and entrepreneurial activities, (Q 5.02) "Please list all the different jobs you have done over the past 12 months," (Q 5.06) "In what industry did you do this job?" and (Q 5.08) "In this job, did you work (self-employed/independent farmer or wage)?" Since LiTS survey did not collect data on wages or income from different sources, we had to use the information on total expenditure and savings to get a proxy measure for the monthly earnings. We combine the answers to the following survey questions: (Q2.22) "Approximately how much does your household spend on each of these items (a. Food, beverages and tobacco; b. electricity, water, gas, heating, fixed line phone; c. public transportation, fuel for car) per month?," (2.23) "At the end of a typical month, does your household have anything left over to put into savings? Approximately how much does your household save in a typical month?," and (2.24) "Approximately how much did your household spend on each of these items (a. education, b. health, c. clothing and footwear, and d. durable goods) during the past 12 months?"

Figure 2.3 shows the earnings ratio between employed and self-employed workers in the agriculture, construction, trade, and government services sectors. The most significant variation is in the agriculture sector, where the range is from Slovakia at close to zero to Sweden at close to three. Another noticeable result is Estonia's high construction ratio at around 2.7. The wholesale and retail trade sector is the most consistent with most countries between a ratio share of 1 and 2. Each country shows a lot of difference in earnings ratio between each sector. There are no clear regional patterns between the two groups of countries observed, which are Western European and transitioning countries.

Figure 2.4 shows the manufacturing, finance and real estate, transport and communication, and private services sectors. The majority of countries for each sector tend to have an earnings ratio of self-employment to wage-employment between one and two, with great diversity between sectors. Some notable observations are the high ratio for the manufacturing sector in Moldova and for the finance sector for Belarus.

Both Figs. 2.3 and 2.4 do not show any clear trends about the ratio of self-employment earnings to employment for any particular sector. The lack of similarity between sectors consequently strengthens our assertion that there is value in pursuing a disaggregated analysis to understand how the ratio of self-employment earnings differs between sectors. Consequently, a sectoral analysis of earning shares is necessary for adjusting the labor income share through self-employment.

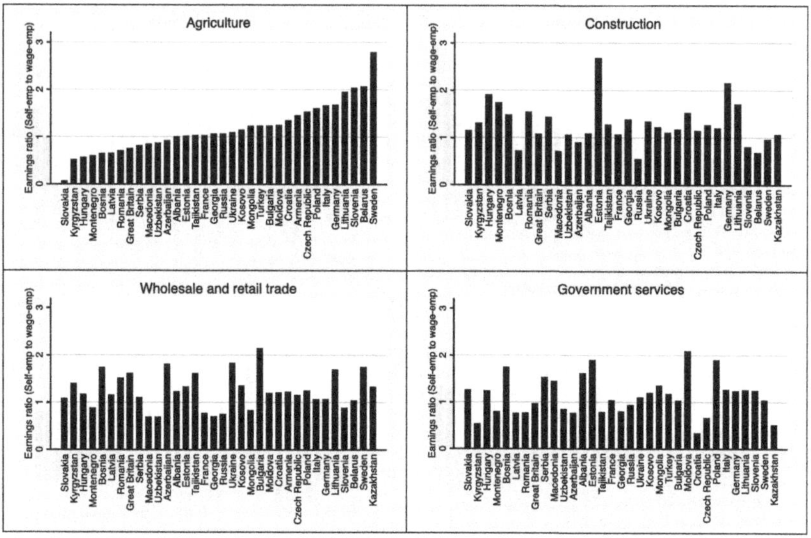

Fig. 2.3 Earnings ratio by key sectors I. (Source: Authors' calculations using Life in Transition Survey (LiTS) II data. Note: The group of countries varies across sectors because data is not available for each country-sector group. We use the same country ranking in agriculture (based on the earnings ratio) for other sectors for the sake of comparison)

2.3.3 *Identification of Employment Ratio (φ) Across Sectors*

2.3.3.1 Using Life in Transition Survey (LiTS) Data

The employment ratio in Fig. 2.5 shows further distinction between sectors. For a number of countries, particularly in Western Europe, the earnings ratio for employment is around three. For most values in the other three sectors, the employment ratio remains much lower, mostly under one. The employment ratio is at the lowest in Government services. A notable observation is the high level of both construction and trade employment ratio of the Central Asian countries Azerbaijan, Tajikistan, Uzbekistan, and Kyrgyzstan, and the fairly positive relationship of the ratio of self-employment in trade to developed countries in general.

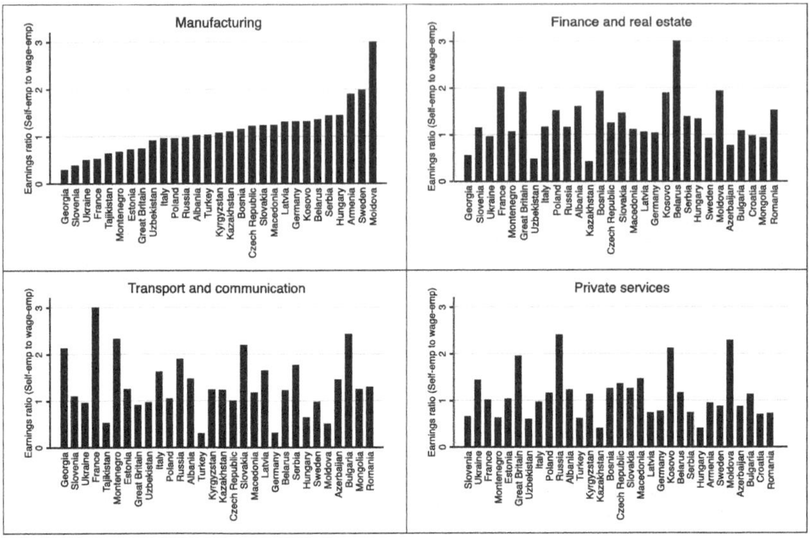

Fig. 2.4 Earnings ratio by key sectors II. (Source: Authors' calculations using Life in Transition Survey (LiTS) II data. Note: The group of countries varies across sectors because data is not available for each country-sector group. We use the same country ranking in manufacturing (based on the earnings ratio) for other sectors for the sake of comparison)

Figure 2.6 shows the same observations. The manufacturing shows nearly all countries below an employment ratio of one, aside from Tajikistan at a ratio of three. The transport and communication sector shows a trend of decreasing ratio from transitioning countries to developed European nations. Again, Tajikistan has a far greater employment ratio than the other countries in this sector. Some other transitioning Central Asian countries, Uzbekistan, and Azerbaijan also have a significantly high self-employment share in the private services sector.

Figures 2.5 and 2.6 do not show strong overall patterns between the sample of countries and the self-employment ratio. However, a number of the sectors show a clear trend of transitioning Central Asian countries with a relatively high employment ratio than developed European countries.

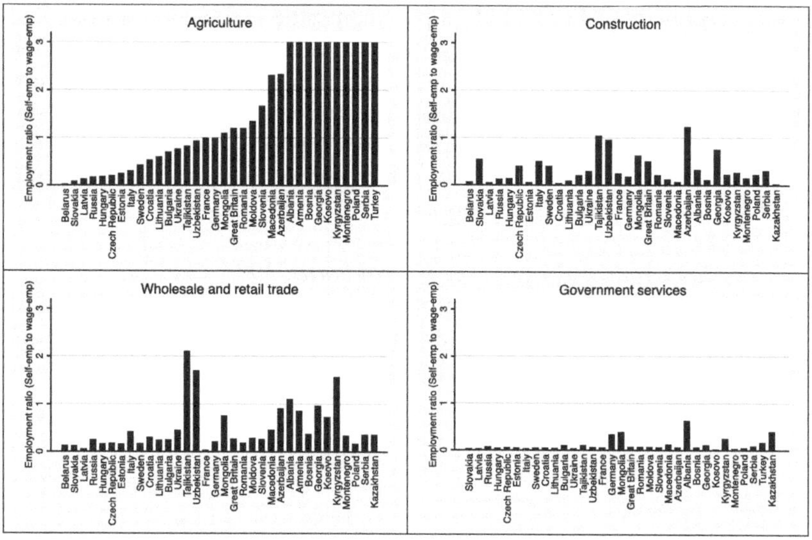

Fig. 2.5 Employment ratio by key sectors I. (Source: Authors' calculations using Life in Transition Survey (LiTS) II data)

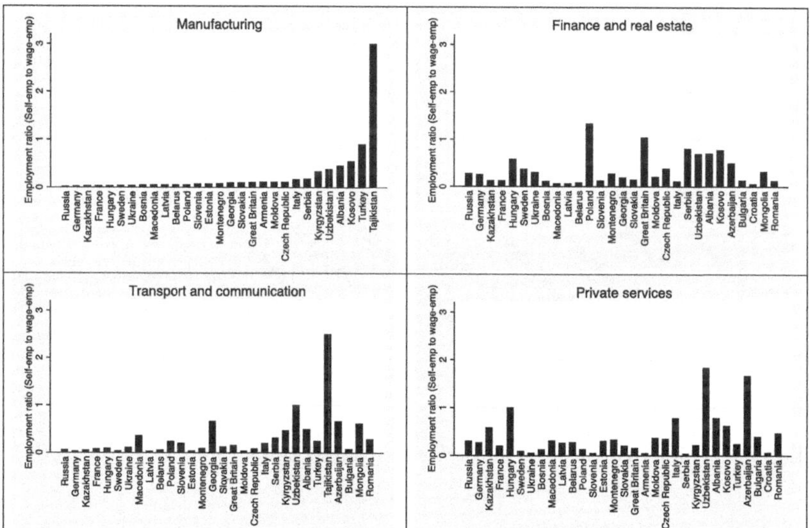

Fig. 2.6 Employment ratio by key sectors II. (Source: Authors' calculations using Life in Transition Survey (LiTS) II data)

On an aggregate scale, the self-employment ratio is the highest in agriculture, with multiple countries at an employment ratio of three and more than half over one. The smallest aggregate employment ratio in is government services. As with the data from the self-employment earnings ratio, the significant divergence between sectors supports our proposition that analyzing each sector and adjusting them accordingly to better account the labor income share is appropriate.

2.3.3.2 Employment Ratio in the United States, 2003

The US sectoral employment ratio also shows a large variance. The agriculture sector is above 0.90, where the agriculture, manufacturing, and education and health services sectors are around 0.05 (Fig. 2.7).

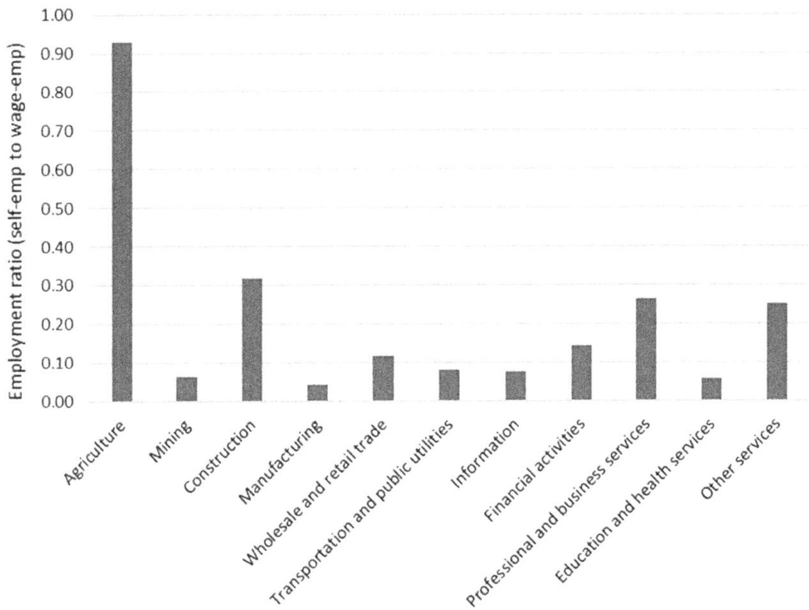

Fig. 2.7 Employment ratio in the United States, 2003. (Source: Steven 2004)

2.3.3.3 Employment Ratio in Japan, 1953–2002

Figure 2.8 is an employment ratio analysis over time for Japan from 1953 to 2003, showing us the changes in the ratio of self-employment to employed ratio as the country shifts from a developing to a developed economy. All employment shares decline, with a notable decline in both the trade and commerce sector and services sector.

We find some notable observations from the self-employment ratio of individual sectors in these particular country data. Many of the sectors show limited or no patterns. However, the set of countries in Figs. 2.5 and 2.6, in addition to the United States and Japan in Figs. 2.7 and 2.8, show a clear relationship between the level of development of a country and the self-employment ratio in the transport and communication sector. All the

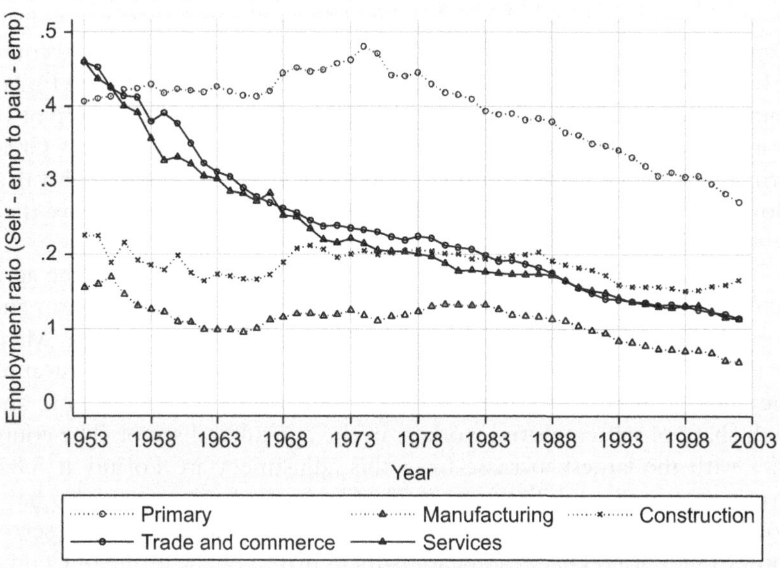

Fig. 2.8 Employment ratio by sector: trends in Japan, 1953–2003. (Source: Authors' calculations)

countries with a relatively high self-employment ratio in Fig. 2.6 are either grouped as low-income countries or they are in the lower bound of the lower middle-income country group. In Japan, this ratio has shrunken alongside Japan's continued economic growth out of development, and this is minimal in the United States. Other observations are that the employment ratios in primary and agricultural sectors are consistently the highest and that the developing Central Asian region has a high employment ratio in many of the sectors examined.

2.4 Adjusted Versus Unadjusted LIS

We calculate the adjustment factor as $(1 + \xi_i \varphi_i)$ for the 29 countries for which data is available from the LiTS database. We use our novel sectoral labor income share database (discussed in more detail in Chap. 4) as an indicator for adjusted figures, and then calculate the unadjusted figures using the adjustment factor. We calculate our novel database from 53 countries at the sectoral level generated from Groningen Growth Data Centre (GGDC) 10-Sector Database, the Socio-Economic Account (SEA), and International Labour Organization Statistics (ILOSTAT). We compare the LiTS database with our novel database through a group of 15 common countries (Bulgaria, Czech Republic, Estonia, Germany, Great Britain, Hungary, Latvia, Lithuania, Poland, Romania, Russia, Slovakia, Slovenia, Sweden, and Turkey) in both of these databases to observe their differences in adjustment.

The impact of this adjustment is the clearest when examining the agriculture sector. The adjusted agriculture sector has the highest mean and standard deviation of all the sectors at 2.57 and 1.30, respectively. Many of the 29 countries show a far greater LIS in agriculture, demonstrating the findings in Figs. 2.3 and 2.4 of the relatively high earnings ratio and high share of self-employed workers in the agricultural sector. The countries with the largest increase from this adjustment are Poland at 5.82, Armenia at 5.38, and Turkey at 4.71. The level of adjustment also has a notable impact in other sectors. The wholesale and retail trade sector shows a significant change after adjustment driven by the group of Central European developing economies in the dataset, led by Tajikistan at 4.42 and the large increases in Kyrgyzstan, Azerbaijan, Albania, Uzbekistan, and Armenia. These countries additionally drive the high adjustment in the construction and transport and communication sectors. The other three sectors, wholesale and retail trade, government, manufacturing, and finance and real estate show a much lower aggregate adjustment with a range of means from 1.13 to 1.48 and a standard deviation from 0.19 to 0.54. This exhibits the extent to which the adjustment factor can greatly vary between sectors.

Table 2.1 below compares the adjusted and unadjusted labor income share estimates on a sectoral level. We find that agriculture has the least correlation between adjusted and unadjusted LIS figures at only 0.538. The manufacturing and finance and real estate sectors show the following least correlation at 0.670 and 0.764, respectively. The rest of the sectors show a high correlation at over 0.950. All results show a statistical significance of 5%.

Figure 2.9 shows the difference between the adjusted and unadjusted labor income share and also suggests that the agriculture sector has the greatest impact from adjustment. Half of the countries in the agriculture sector graph are not closely aligned with the unadjusted labor income share line. Some other notable observations are that there is a trend of an increasing degree of adjustment for countries with higher development in the wholesale and retail trade and construction sectors. This is illustrated as countries such as Russia and Lithuania show much greater uniformity to the adjustment line than countries such as Germany and Sweden. Also, the only heavily adjusted country in the manufacturing sector is Turkey. Finally, the finance and real estate and transport and communication sectors are affected the least with no noticeable deviations from the unadjusted labor income share line.

Table 2.1 Correlation between adjusted and unadjusted LIS figures

Sectors	*Correlation between adjusted and unadjusted LIS figures*
Agriculture	0.5379*
Construction	0.9906*
Wholesale and retail trade	0.9666*
Government sector	0.9890*
Manufacturing	0.7644*
Finance and real estate	0.6702*
Transport and communication	0.9667*

Source: Authors' own calculations

* Statistically significant at 10% level

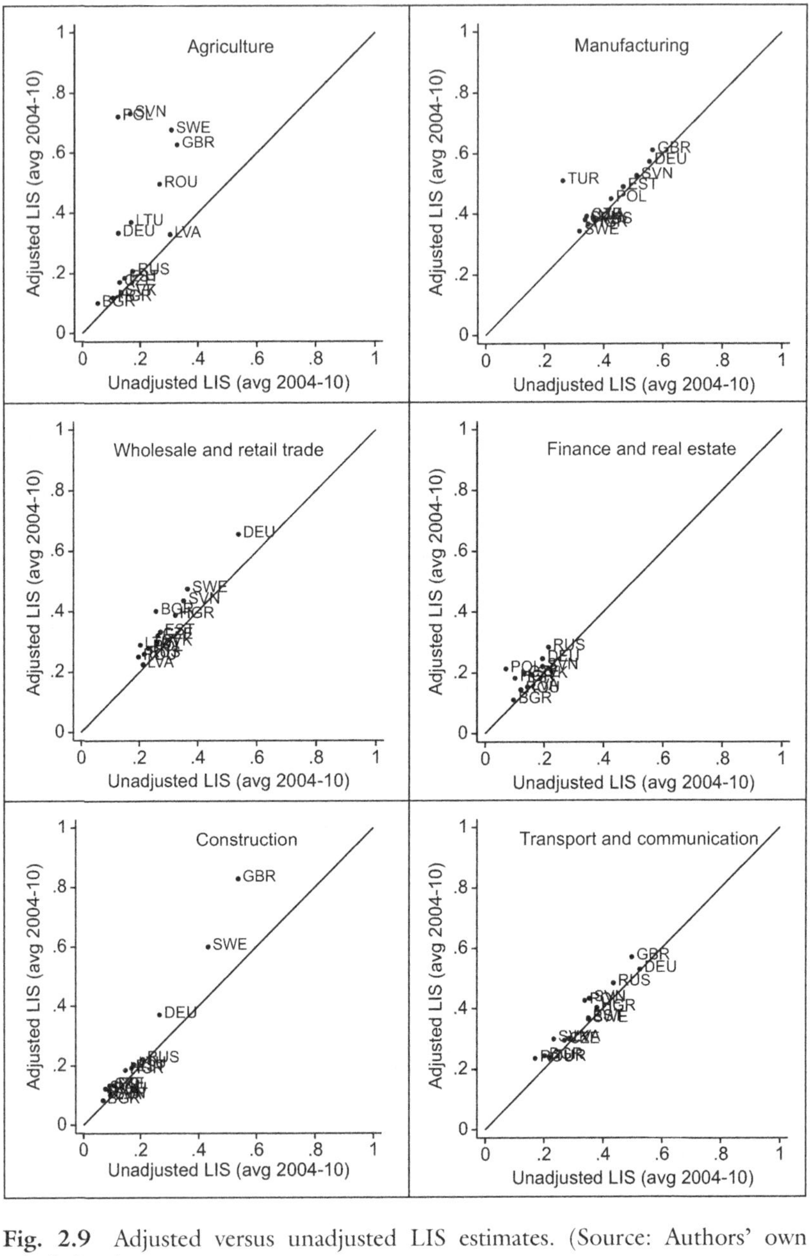

Fig. 2.9 Adjusted versus unadjusted LIS estimates. (Source: Authors' own calculations)

To conclude, the evidence from the LiTS data suggests that the agriculture sector is a greater source of the self-employment error. The agriculture sector also has the least correlation between the adjusted and unadjusted LIS figures at 0.54. The rest of the sectors all show a high correlation at over 0.95, aside from manufacturing at 0.70 and finance and real estate at 0.80.

References

Barkai, S. 2016. *Declining Labor and Capital Shares.* University of Chicago, November.

Bridgman, B. 2014. *Is Labor's Loss Capital's Gain?: Gross Versus Net Labor Shares.* BEA.

Eden, M., & Gaggl, P. 2015. *On the Welfare Implications of Automation.* The World Bank.

Gammarano, R. 2018. Paid employment vs vulnerable employment: a brief study of employment patterns by status in employment.

Gollin, D. 2002. Getting income shares right. *Journal of Political Economy, 110*(2), 458–474.

Gomme, P. and P. Rupert. 2004. *Measuring Labor's Share of Income. Policy Discussion Paper* 7. Federal Reserve Bank of Cleveland.

Gomme, P., & Greenwood, J. 1995. On the Cyclical Allocation of Risk. *Journal of Economic Dynamics and Control, 19*(1–2), 91–124.

ILO. 2018. *World Employment Social Outlook 2018.* Geneva: International Labour Organization.

ILO Department of Statistics Data and Protection Analysis Unit. 2019. *The Global Labour Income Share and Distribution.* International Labour Organization.

Kapsos, S., & Bourmpoula, E. 2013. *Employment and Economic Class in the Developing World.* Geneva: ILO.

Karabarbounis, Loukas, and Brent Neiman. 2014. "The Global Decline of the Labor Share." *Quarterly Journal of Economics* 129 (1): 61–103.

Kehrig, M., and N. Vincent. 2017. Growing Productivity Without Growing Wages: The Micro-Level Anatomy of the Aggregate Labor Share Decline. CESifo Working Paper Series 6454, CESifo Group Munich.

Koh, Dongya, Raul Santaeulalia-Llopis, and Yu Zhang. 2016. Labor Share Decline and Intellectual Property Products Capital," Working Papers 927, Barcelona Graduate School of Economics.

Life in Transition Survey. 2010. European Bank for Reconstruction and Development. <https://www.ebrd.com/what-we-do/economic-research-anddata/data/lits.html>

Lübker, M. 2007. "Labour Shares." *Technical Brief* No. 1. Geneva: ILO, P. I. Department.

Mućk, J., McAdam, P., & Growiec, J. 2018. Will the "True" Labor Share Stand Up? An Applied Survey on Labor Share Measures. *Journal of Economic Surveys, 32*(4), 961–984.

Paul, S. and H. Isaka 2019. Labor Income Share at the Firm Level: Global Trends, IZA Discussion Paper No. 12852. [December].

Rognlie, M. 2016. Deciphering the Fall and Rise in the Net Capital Share: Accumulation or Scarcity?. *Brookings Papers on Economic Activity, 2015*(1), 1–69.

Rognlie, Matthew. 2015. "Deciphering the Fall and Rise in the Net Capital Share: Accumulation or Scarcity?" *Brookings Papers on Economic Activity* 46 (1): 1–69.

Steven, 2004. Self-employment in the United States: An Update. *Monthly Labor Review* (July), 13–23.

Wakita, S. 2006. The Lost Decade in the Japanese Labor Market: Labor's share and Okun's Law. *Public Policy Review, 2*(1), 77.

Zhou, Minghai. 2016. *Labor's Share of Income: Another Key to Understand China's Income Inequality*. Singapore: Springer. https://www.springer.com/kr/book/9789811001727 (accessed 26 November 2018).

CHAPTER 3

Global Trends in Labor Income Share: Country Level

This chapter examines the correlates of the average labor income share (LIS) using data at the country level. We examine a range of variables, from the gross domestic product (GDP), informal sector, self-employment, trade, and agriculture. A range of literature can be used to explain the potential effects of the variables on the average labor income, including LaPorta and Shleifer (2014) on informality and development, Gollin et al. (2014) on the agricultural productivity gap, and Karabarbounis and Neiman (2014) on the global decline of the labor share. These categories are tested on both an aggregate and a specific level based on the country's income.

3.1 Data

In contrast to its simple definition of the labor income share, which is the share of labor income in national income, measuring it with available data is not so straightforward. While national income is easily found in national accounting statistics in the form of GDP, labor income equivalent is not as it involves both income earned by wage employees and income earned by the self-employed. National accounting statistics in many countries usually record the total wage bill of employees as "compensation of employees." However, these statistics often do not record self-employed income, and even if they do, it is generally difficult to isolate a labor income component

S. Paul, *Labor Income Share*,
https://doi.org/10.1007/978-981-15-6860-2_3

as self-employed income consists of compensation for both the labor and capital that self-employed workers own.

Several approaches have been proposed for estimating the labor income share using available data (Table 3.1). A conventional approach divides the total compensation of employees by GDP without taking self-employed income into consideration (denoted as LIS_{unadj}). This may be a reasonable approximation of the labor income share in developed countries where the share of the self-employed in the total number of employees is low, but this is likely to underestimate the labor income share in developing countries where self-employment in the informal sector is prevalent. To include self-employed income in the labor income, Gollin (2002) proposes three adjustment approaches, relying on three different assumptions. Two of Gollin's (2002) approaches use mixed income, which is the total income earned by self-employed workers, to extrapolate self-employed income: The first adds the entire amount of mixed income to the compensation of employees, assuming that self-employed workers do not possess capital (denoted as LIS_{G1}), while the second assumes that the labor income share of self-employed workers is the same as that of wage employees (denoted as LIS_{G2}). Instead of mixed income, Gollin's (2002) third approach uses the employment structure of a country to estimate the labor income share.

Table 3.1 Estimation approaches

$$LIS_{unadj} = \frac{CoE}{GDP}$$

$$LIS_{G1} = \frac{CoE + MI}{GDP}$$

$$LIS_{G2} = \frac{CoE}{GDP - MI}$$

$$LIS_{G3} = \frac{\frac{CoE}{E} \times TE}{GDP}$$

CoE: compensation of employees, *MI*: mixed income, *E*: the number of wage employees, *TE*: the number of total employees

It assumes that self-employed workers earn the same average wage as employees (denoted as LIS_{G3}).

All currently available data sets that cover low- and middle-income countries have estimated the labor income share using these approaches. van Treeck (2017) reviews labor income share data and compares them by dividing them into six groups in terms of their coverage, adjustment approaches, and data sources (Table 3.2). As each data set uses different adjustment approaches and data sources, estimated labor income shares differ from one another.

The first group of data sets primarily relies on data from the United Nations System of National Accounts (UN SNA) for estimating the labor income share. It records GDP for almost all countries around the world as well as data on compensation of employees for about two-thirds of low- and middle-income countries. The computed unadjusted labor share covers 93 low- and middle-income countries with an average time span of 15.3 years per country and 1421 observations (denoted as SNA unadj.). For countries with mixed income data available, mixed income adjusted labor income shares are computed (denoted as SNA G1 and SNA G2). As only about one third of developing countries reported mixed income, these adjustments result in a reduction in the number of countries to only 38. The adjusted labor share using the employment structure of a country is also calculated with ILO's data of Key Indicators of the Labour Market (KILM), which produces estimates for 73 countries (denoted as SNA G3). The second group of data sets extends the coverage of data from UN SNA and KILM by including additional national data sources. A group of researchers at ILO add data from OECD statistics and from the PRC's and Brazil's statistical offices, which produces estimates of the labor income share for 73 countries (denoted as ILO unadj./adj.).

The Penn World Tables (PWT) expands the coverage of self-employed income adjusted labor income shares by using proxy variables for countries whose mixed income data are not available. As most self-employed workers in low- and middle-income countries are active in agriculture, the PWT uses value added in agriculture recorded in the World Input-Output Database (WIOD) as a proxy for self-employed income. To construct a "best estimate" labor share, it utilizes the most plausible adjustment

Table 3.2 Overview of labor share measures for low- and middle-income countries since 1990

Data set	*Obs.*	*Years*	*Ctry*	*Mean*	*Median*	*Min*	*Max*	*SD*
SNA unadj.	1421	15.3	93	35.3	35.5	5.4	90.7	11.8
SNA G1	508	13.4	38	56.5	56.1	26.2	87	10.4
SNA G2	508	13.4	38	45.6	46	21	73.4	8.5
SNA G3	766	10.5	73	62	55.5	21.5	658.4	33.8
ILO unadj.	1044	14.3	73	39.6	39.9	3.4	93.8	14
ILO adj.	1044	14.3	73	56.9	56.2	3.4	231.7	25.1
PWT	2298	24.7	93	52	52.6	9	86.6	13.1
Trapp	1421	15.3	93	46.8	47	6	90.7	12.5
WIOD unadj.	258	16.1	16	42.3	44.5	22.2	61.8	8.5
WIOD adj.	258	16.1	16	53.2	53.4	31.5	104.5	11.3
UNIDO	1072	11.2	96	29.9	28.3	1.7	140.9	14

Data set	Adj. approach	Data sources	Authors
SNA unadj.	Unadj.	UN SNA	UN (2017)
SNA G1	G1	UN SNA	UN (2017)
SNA G2	G2	UN SNA	UN (2017)
SNA G3	G3	UN SNA, KILM	UN (2017), ILO (2017)
ILO unadj.	Unadj.	UN SNA, KILM, OECD, China NBS, SNA brazil	
ILO adj.	G3	UN SNA, KILM, OECD, China NBS, SNA Brazil	Charpe et al. (2014)
PWT	G2 (47%), G1[a] (47%), G3 (3%), unadj. (3%)	UN SNA, WIOD	Feenstra et al. (2015)
Trapp	G3[b] full (50%), G3[b] 2/3 (18%), G1 (4%), G2 (21%), unadj. (6%)	UN SNA, FAOSTAT, WB WDI	Trapp (2015)
WIOD unadj.	Unadj.	WIOD SEA	Timmer et al. (2015)
WIOD adj.	G3	WIOD SEA	Timmer et al. (2015)
UNIDO	Corp. manuf. sector	INDSTAT2	UNIDO (2015)

Source: van Treeck (2017)

[a]Agricultural value added used as proxy for mixed income

[b]Agricultural employment share used as proxy for self-employment share

approach for each country and year. When mixed income data are available, the PWT computes the LIS_{G2}-definition labor income share. For a few anomalous countries whose unadjusted labor share exceeds 0.7, the PWT directly uses the unadjusted labor share as it seems reasonable that this share already includes self-employed labor income. For the remaining countries where mixed income data are not available, the PWT calculates LIS_{G3}-definition labor income share and LIS_{G1}-definition labor income share where value added in agriculture is used in place of mixed income and adopts the lower one as the labor share of the country.[1] Trapp (2015) also uses proxy variables of agriculture to compute the labor income share. She obtains data of the share of agricultural employment in total employment from Food and Agricultural Organization of the United Nations Statistics (FAOSTAT) and the World Bank (WB) World Development Indicators (WDI) and uses this as proxy for the share of self-employment. Her data set is also a combination of different adjustment approaches comprising LIS_{G3} (68%), LIS_{G2} (21%), LIS_{unadj} (6%), and LIS_{G1} (4%).

The Socio-Economic Accounts (SEA) from the WIOD and Industrial Statistics Database of the United Nations (INDSTAT) databases from the UN's Industrial Development Organization (UNIDO) can be used to calculate the labor income share by sector and by other characteristics. The WIOD project gathers data on employment, labor compensation, and value added from several national statistics offices. The WIOD provides not only aggregated data but also disaggregated data by 35 sectors or skills (low-, medium-, and high-skilled). The UNIDO INDSTAT is a large industrial statistics database that covers only the corporate manufacturing sector. It provides both aggregated and disaggregated data from 23 industries. In the database, 96 low- and middle-income countries are covered from the 1970s.

In our analyses, we primarily rely on the PWT data set as it has a broad coverage in terms of both country and year. The data set is also preferable because it uses the most plausible adjustment approach for each country and year, not resorting to a one-size-fits-all approach. While the UNIDO data set has the largest coverage in terms of country, this data set is not preferable for our analysis as the database includes only the corporate manufacturing sector. As mentioned above, the PWT employs four adjustment methods to calculate labor income share.

[1]For a few cases where the chosen labor income share is less than 40% and the share of GDP going to fixed assets is larger than 50%, the PWT adopts the larger of the two.

3.2 Gross Domestic Product (GDP) and the Labor Income Share

The first study is a regression of the labor income share (average LIS of 2000s) on GDP values. We include the GDP average of 2000s in US dollars, GDP per capita in 2005, and the log GDP (USD) average of 2000s. Through this we find the relationship between the GDP on the labor income share.

In Fig. 3.1, an aggregate analysis of the impact of GDP on the labor income share shows that a unit increase in GDP correlates with a raise the labor income share, but this is close to zero. The cluster of countries provides difficulty to determine a clear relationship from these countries. Excluding the United States as an outlier provides a clearer positive coefficient and stronger goodness of fit.

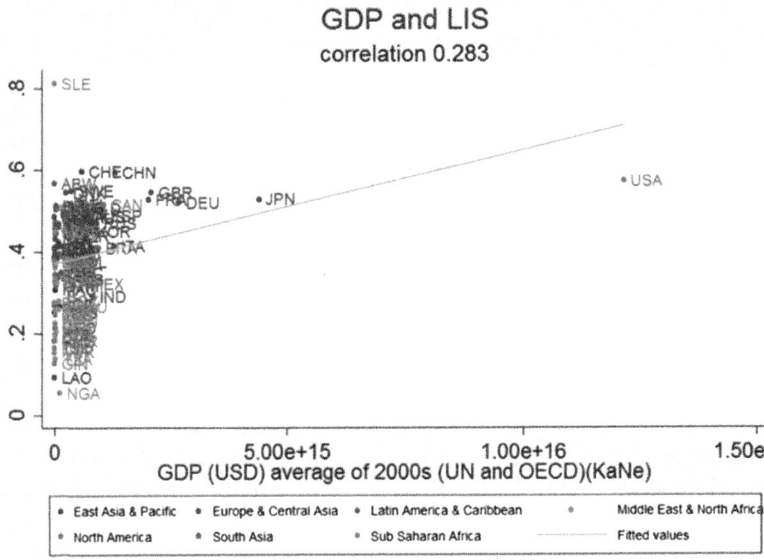

Fig. 3.1 The GDP and the labor income share: full sample of countries. (Source: The GDP and labor income share figures are taken from calculations by Karabarbounis and Neiman (2014) using UN and OECD data)

Data focused on high-income countries shows a smaller increase of labor income share by GDP and a slightly weaker goodness of fit of 8.6% (Fig. 3.2). The countries are clustered together in a similar fashion. Upper middle-income countries also show a minimal relationship of GDP with the labor income share, but with a considerably weaker goodness of fit of 0.3%. These countries are no longer clustered together but do not show noticeable patterns. The lower middle-income countries still show a positive but minimal change in labor income share from a rise of GDP, but with a stronger goodness of fit. These countries are also clustered, though this is more sporadic particularly due to China, Russia, Iran, and Papua New Guinea. Low-income countries show a significantly weaker relationship and goodness of fit. The cluster of countries continues to be seen and outliers can be identified in India and Sierra Leone. This cluster can

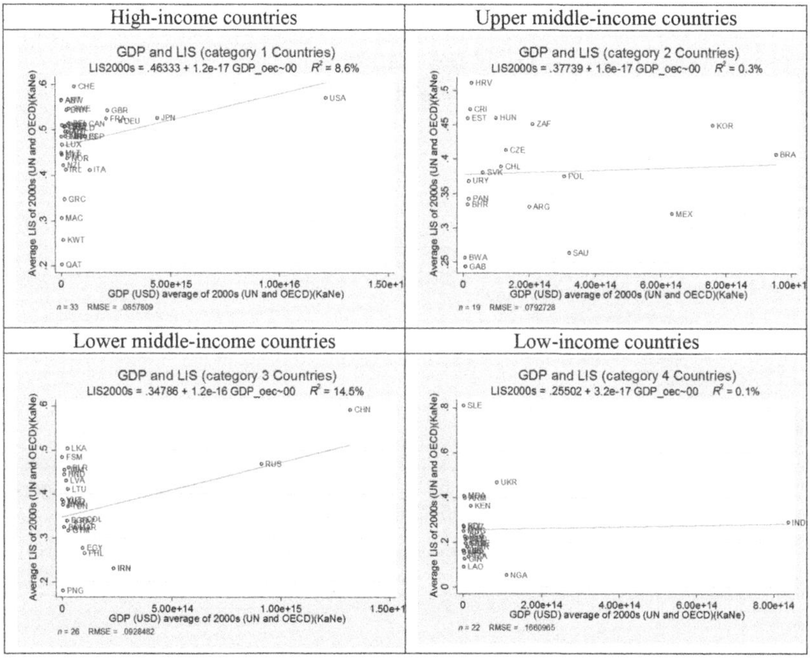

Fig. 3.2 The GDP and the labor income share, by income groups. (Source: The GDP and labor income share figures are taken from calculations by Karabarbounis and Neiman (2014) using UN and OECD data)

additionally be seen with low-income countries. In all categories, the analysis on labor income share and GDP shows a positive correlation between these two. However, there is a minimal impact, a weak goodness of fit of equation and a lack of noticeable regional patterns, so we conclude that these variables show a weak correlation.

On an aggregate level, we find that there is a positive correlation between the GDP per capita and the average labor income share (Fig. 3.3). A unit increase in the GDP per capita results on average to an increase in the labor income share with a high goodness of fit of equation.

For high-income countries, we observe a positive correlation between the two variables with an increase in the labor income share of close to zero for every unit increase in GDP per capita. The goodness of fit is 6.2% (Fig. 3.4). The upper middle-income countries share similarities with high-income countries in the relationship between GDP per capita and

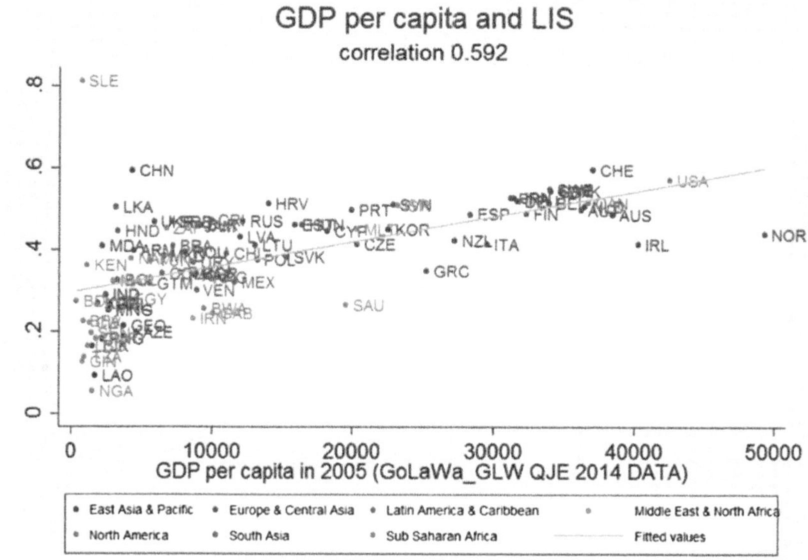

Fig. 3.3 The GDP per capita and the labor income share: full sample of countries. (Source: The GDP per capita figures are taken from calculations by Gollin et al. (2014). The labor income share figures are taken from calculations by Karabarbounis and Neiman (2014) using UN and OECD data)

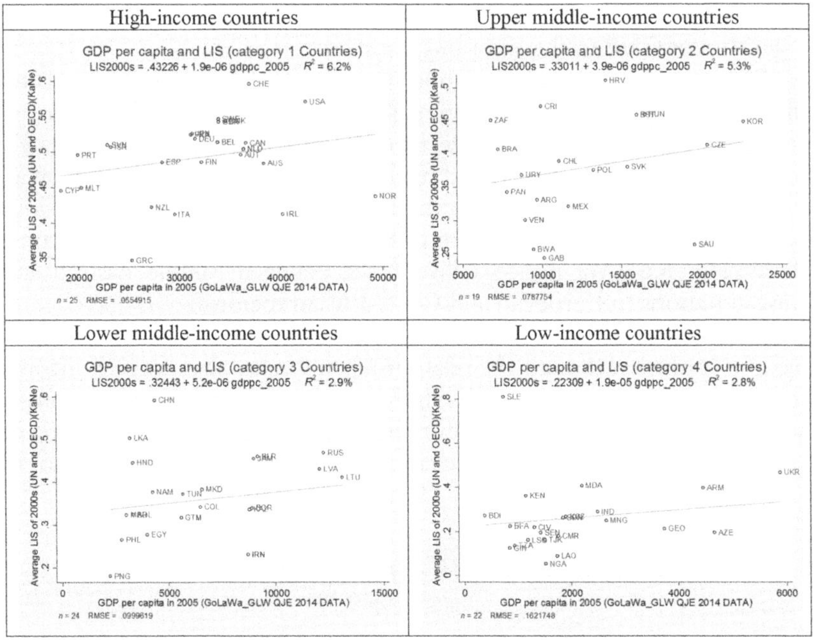

Fig. 3.4 The GDP per capita and the labor income share, by income groups. (Source: The GDP per capita figures are taken from calculations by Gollin et al. (2014). The labor income share figures are taken from calculations by Karabarbounis and Neiman (2014) using UN and OECD data)

labor income share alongside a similar goodness of fit. The lower middle-income countries also demonstrate a similarly positive relationship. However, the goodness of fit has dropped to a weak level. Finally, the least developed countries continue the positive relationship between the two variables and the weak goodness of fit. There is a notable regional pattern of sub-Saharan African countries at a lower point and European and Central Asian countries grouped at a higher point of GDP per capita, with Sierra Leone as an outlier due to high average labor income share and low GDP per capita. All categories of labor income share and GDP per capita additionally show a general positive trend. However, the negligible magnitude, a weak goodness of fit, and minimal regional patterns identified with the labor income share and GDP data continue demonstrating a weak relationship (Fig. 3.4). We then look at the relationship between the logarithm of GDP to the labor income share.

We observe a positive correlation between the labor income share and the log form of GDP for the aggregate level (Fig. 3.5). A 1% log increase correlates with a higher average labor income share by approximately 0.021%. More insight is provided by further testing the relationship on an individual category analysis. The high-income countries show a positive correlation between the log form of GDP and the average labor income share (Fig. 3.6). We notice a divergence between Middle Eastern and African regions to European and Central Asian regions.

The same pattern as mentioned above persists in the upper middle-income countries, though the relationship is weaker than in high-income countries and the goodness of fit is half the value. This relationship changes among lower middle-income countries, where a unit increase in the log of GDP shows a decrease in average labor income share. The goodness of fit

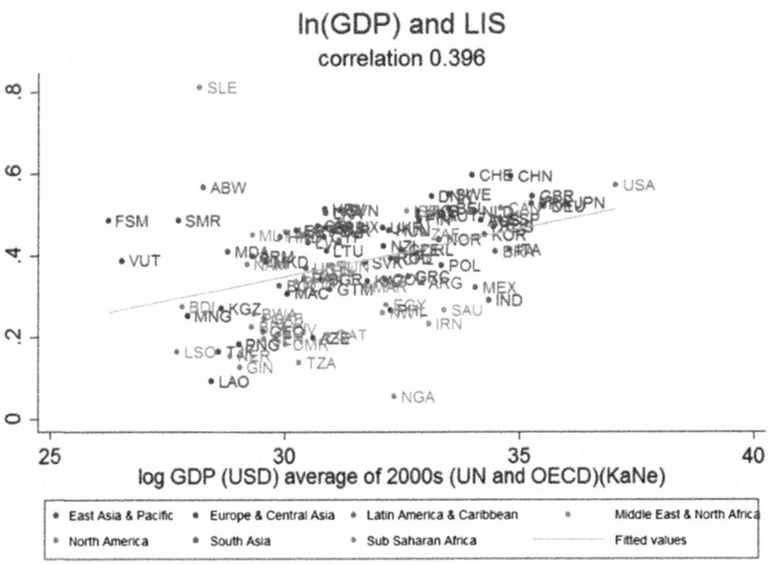

Fig. 3.5 The log GDP and the labor income share: full sample of countries. (Source: The log GDP and labor income share figures are taken from calculations by Karabarbounis and Neiman (2014) using UN and OECD data)

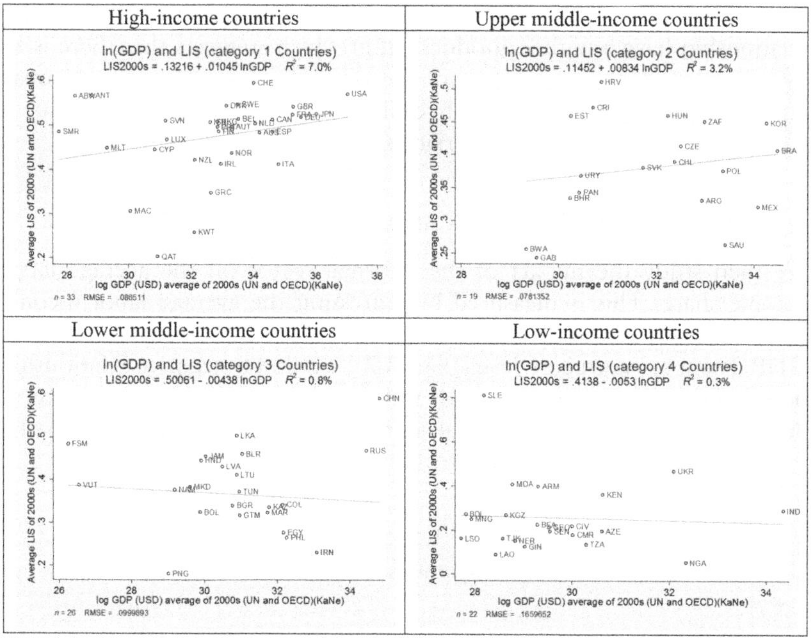

Fig. 3.6 The GDP per capita and the labor income share, by income groups. (Source: The log GDP and labor income share figures are taken from calculations by Karabarbounis and Neiman (2014) using UN and OECD data)

of equation appears to be further weakened. Finally, this negative relationship continues among low-income countries where an increase in the log of GDP shows a decrease in the labor income share, but to a much smaller degree. The goodness of fit continues to remain at substantially weak level.

Testing the relationship between labor income share and log GDP shows a varying relationship between positive and negative correlations in different categories. The goodness of fit values are even lower for this particular relationship and continue to decrease as the country incomes grow lower, which in addition to the lack of regional patterns show this relationship to be inconclusive. We suggest that more studies need to address this factor to evaluate whether such correlation is significant.

In conclusion, the tests all show similar trends. The GDP and GDP per capita both feature a weakly positive correlation, a weak goodness of fit, and no noticeable regional patterns. The tests with log GDP vary between a positive and negative relationship, though the categories with a positive relationship have a higher goodness of fit which suggests that there is an overall continuance of this trend. However, the minimal impact, weak goodness of fit, and lack of noticeable regional patterns demonstrate a weak correlation between the variables.

3.3 Informal Sector and the Labor Income Share

We then study the impact of the informal sector on the average labor income share. This is measured by regressing the average labor income share (average LIS of 2000s) against the informal sector percentage of GDP. From an aggregate level (Fig. 3.7), we find a negative relationship between the informal sector GDP and the average labor income share. A percent increase in the informal sector GDP shows a decrease in the

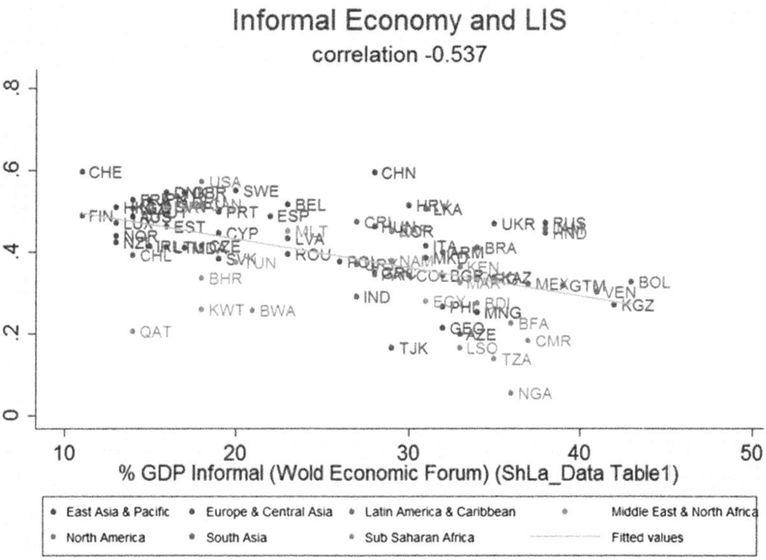

Fig. 3.7 The informal sector and the labor income share: full sample of countries. (Source: The informal sector GDP figures are taken from LaPorta and Shleifer (2014). The labor income share figures are taken from calculations by Karabarbounis and Neiman (2014) using UN and OECD data)

average labor income share by an average of approximately 0.007% with a 28.8% goodness of fit. The high-income countries also reveal a weak negative relationship between the informal sector and the average labor income share, where a percent increase in the informal sector correlates with a decrease in the labor income share by approximately half of the aggregate data (Fig. 3.8). The goodness of fit significantly weakens for these countries at 3.7%.

For upper middle-income countries, a unit increase in the informal sector is equivalent to a decrease in the labor income share, to a less extent than high-income countries. We continue to see a weakening goodness of fit at now only 1.8%. European and Central Asian countries have a higher average LIS and informal economy to GDP ratio relative to the Latin American and Caribbean countries. We also find a weak correlation among

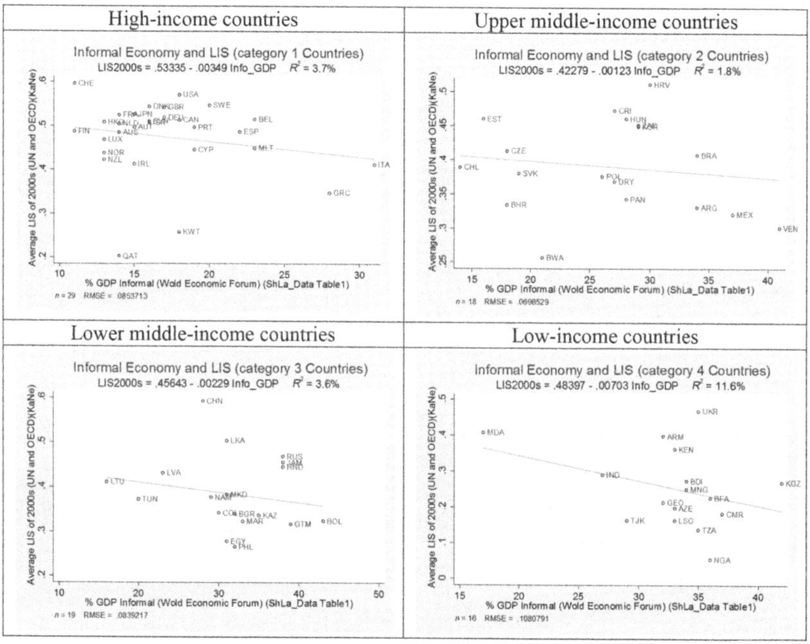

Fig. 3.8 The informal sector and the labor income share, by income groups. (Source: The informal sector GDP figures are taken from LaPorta and Shleifer (2014). The labor income share figures are taken from calculations by Karabarbounis and Neiman (2014) using UN and OECD data)

lower middle-income countries. A unit increase in the informal sector shows a decrease in the average labor income share by approximately 0.0023%. The goodness of fit is small at 3.6%. Finally, the correlation in low-income countries remains weak at 0.007% of labor income share rising with every unit increase in the informal sector GDP but contains a stronger goodness of fit of 11.6%.

We also analyze the impact of value added per worker in both the informal and formal sector on the labor income share (Fig. 3.9), where we find a positive relationship with an increase of approximately 0.12% in labor income share for every unit of value added per worker. The goodness of fit has greatly weakened at 1.6%.

Throughout the categories in informal economy to labor income share, we consistently find a weak negative trend between the informal sector GDP and average labor income share. The goodness of fit is very weak aside from low-income countries and there are minimal regional patterns, showing a weak and inconclusive relationship.

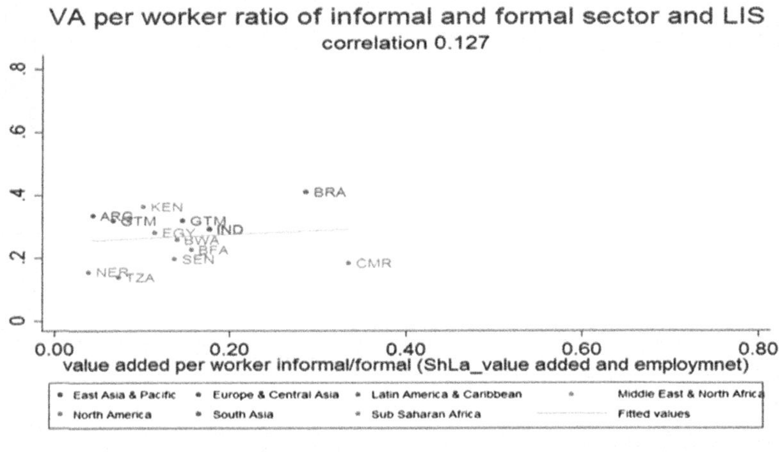

Fig. 3.9 VA per worker ratio between informal and formal sector and the labor income share. (Source: The value added per worker ratio of informal and formal sector figures is taken from LaPorta and Shleifer (2014). The labor income share figures are taken from calculations by Karabarbounis and Neiman (2014) using UN and OECD data)

3.4 Self-Employment and the Labor Income Share

We next test the relationship between finding the impact of the percent of the self-employment on the average labor income share (average LIS of 2000s). We observe that on an aggregate level, there is a clear negative correlation between the self-employment ratio and the average labor income share, with each percent increasing the share of self-employment decreasing the average labor income share on average by approximately 0.005% with a goodness of fit of 42.5% (Fig. 3.10).

In Fig. 3.11, the high-income countries show a slightly negative correlation between the percent of self-employment and the average labor income share, where a percent increase in self-employment shows a decrease in the labor income share by 0.0016%. There is also a much weaker goodness of fit at 1.2%. We also observe that many countries from

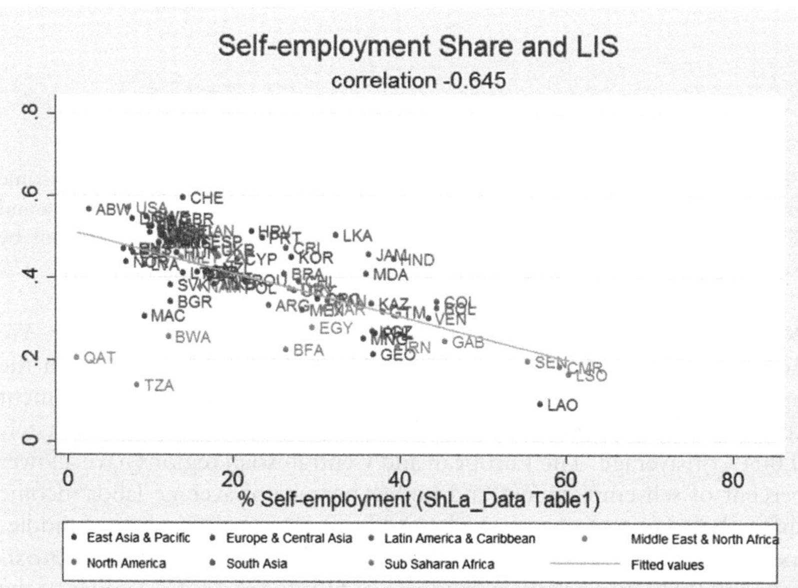

Fig. 3.10 The self-employment share and the labor income share: full sample of countries. (Source: The self-employment share figures are taken from LaPorta and Shleifer (2014). The labor income share figures are taken from calculations by Karabarbounis and Neiman (2014) using UN and OECD data)

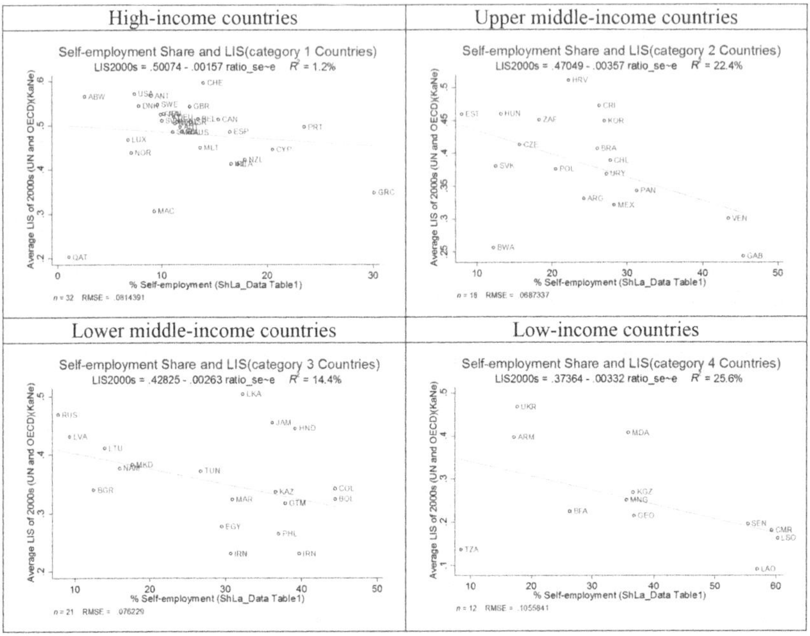

Fig. 3.11 The self-employment share and the labor income share, by income groups. (Source: The self-employment share figures are taken from LaPorta and Shleifer (2014). The labor income share figures are taken from calculations by Karabarbounis and Neiman (2014) using UN and OECD data)

North America, Europe, and Central Asia are clustered together. We notice a stronger negative correlation between the two variables in the upper middle-income countries, where an increase in self-employment correlates with a decrease in the labor income share by approximately 0.004% on average. The European and Central Asian regions have a lower percent of self-employment and higher percent of average labor income share than Latin American and Caribbean regions. The lower middle-income countries show a clear negative relationship at a rate of approximately 0.003% and a weaker goodness of fit value at 14.4%. Similar to the upper middle-income category, Europe and Central Asian countries have a relatively high labor income share and low self-employment, contrasting Latin America and The Caribbean.

Finally, we continue to observe a negative relationship between the self-employment and average labor income share in low-income countries. An increase in the self-employment correlates with a decrease in the labor income share by 0.003% on average, more so than for lower middle-income countries. Additionally, the goodness of fit is relatively high at 25.6%. Components of the regional pattern in other categories can be identified here. All categories show a negative correlation between self-employment and average labor income share with a generally strong goodness of fit and clear regional patterns among the upper and lower middle-income countries.

3.5 Trade and the Labor Income Share

We investigate the impact of trade on labor income share by first focusing on trade volume. This is accomplished by regressing the average labor income share (average LIS of 2000s) on the trade volume. On an aggregate level, we observe a positive correlation between trade openness and the average labor income share (Fig. 3.12). We also deduce that a unit increase in the trade volume leads to an increase in the average labor income share by approximately 0.78% on average. However, the goodness of fit is weak at 4.1% and there are no regional patterns, so a clear relationship is difficult to establish.

We observe in high-income countries a weak positive relationship of the change in trade volume on the average labor income share (Fig. 3.13). A unit increase in the trade volume shows an increase in average labor income share by approximately 0.2% and the fitness of equation is substantially weak at 0.7%. Countries in North Africa and the Middle East are majorly concentrated at the lower end of trade volume and labor income share. We find the pattern to be further reinforced in the upper middle-income countries. There is a stronger relationship between trade openness and average labor income share and the goodness of fit is 24.4%. We also observe stronger and clearer regional patterns where the Latin American and Caribbean countries experience the lowest trade volume and labor income share, but a greater trade volume and higher labor income share in European and Central Asian countries. This positive effect continues with lower middle-income countries where a unit increase in the trade volume is associated with an increase in the labor income share by 1.16%. However, we see a weaker goodness of fit at 10.9%.

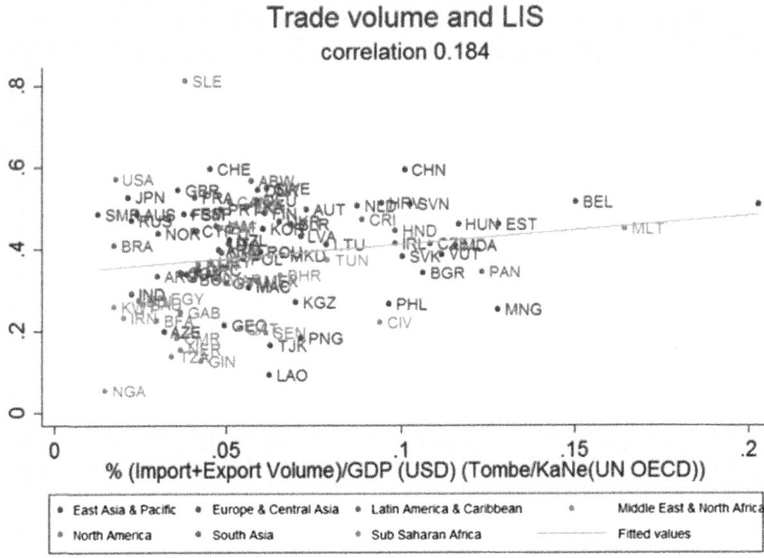

Fig. 3.12 Trade volume and the labor income share: full sample of countries. (Source: The figures on trade volume are taken from Tombe (2015). The figures on GDP and labor income share are calculations taken from Karabarbounis and Neiman (2014) using UN and OECD data)

The low-income countries follow the same trend (Fig. 3.13), where a unit increase in the trade volume is associated with an increase the average labor income share by approximately 0.7%, but with a weak goodness of fit of 1.5%. In parallel to the upper middle-income category, sub-Saharan countries diverge from European and Central Asian countries by sharing a lower trade volume and labor income share. A clear positive correlation between the trade volume and the labor income share can be noticed in each category and there are some regional patterns to substantiate the data. However, the significantly weak goodness of fit persists aside from upper middle-income countries. Consequently, this data gives some suggestion that countries with increased trade openness and open economies also have a higher trade volume and labor income share.

We next examine the impact of the percent of both import and export over GDP on the average labor income share (average LIS of 2000s). We

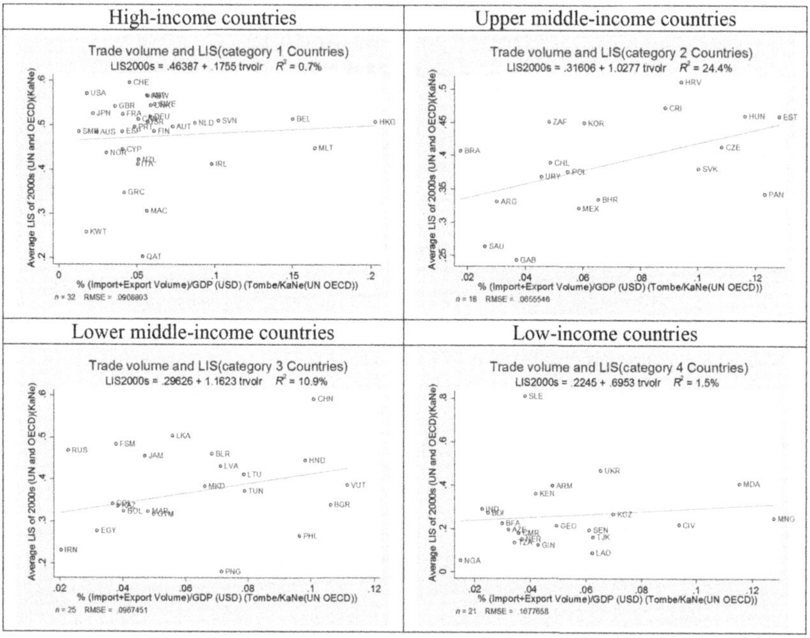

Fig. 3.13 Trade volume and the labor income share: by income groups. (Source: The figures on trade volume are taken from Tombe (2015). The figures on GDP and labor income share are calculations taken from Karabarbounis and Neiman (2014) using UN and OECD data)

first study the impact of import volume over the average labor income share. On an aggregate level, these share a positive relationship (Fig. 3.14). A unit increase in the import volume shows an increase in the average labor income share by approximately 0.77% on average. The goodness of fit is weak at 1.6%. Hong Kong is a heavy outlier due to a high import volume.

High-income countries have a weak positive correlation between the variables, where a percent increase in the import volume is associated with an increase in labor income share on average by approximately 0.12% (Fig. 3.15). This is also demonstrated through the weak goodness of fit at 0.2%. We continue to observe a stronger relationship in upper middle-income countries where an increase in the import volume ratio shows an increase in the average labor income share by 0.85% with a goodness of fit

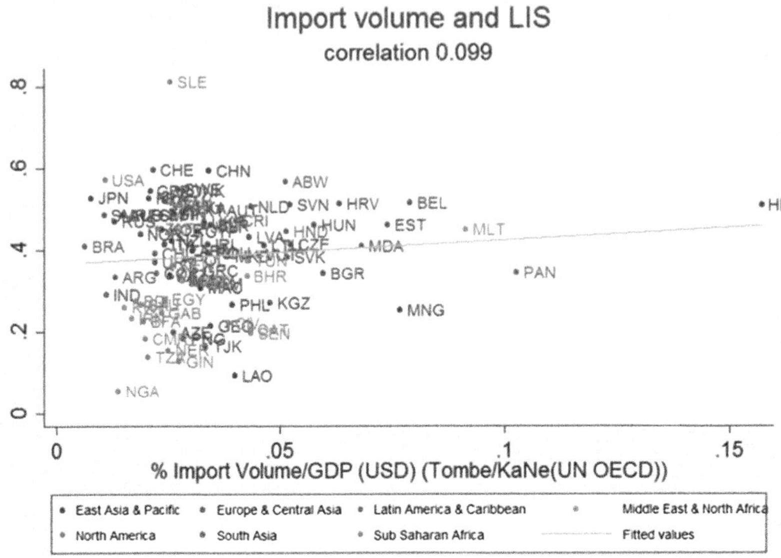

Fig. 3.14 Import volume and the labor income share: full sample of countries. (Source: The figures on import volume are taken from Tombe (2015). The figures on GDP and labor income share are calculations taken from Karabarbounis and Neiman (2014) using UN and OECD data)

at 8.1%. There is a divergence between Latin American and Caribbean countries with a lower labor income share and import volume relative to the European and Central Asian countries. This pattern continues to persist in lower middle-income countries where an increase in the import volume ratio is associated with an increase in the average labor income on average by approximately 2.15% with a goodness of fit of 6.4%. Finally, we observe a positive relationship among low-income countries, where a percent increase in the import volume is correlated with an increase in the average labor income share by 1.06%. However, the goodness of fit falls to 1.1%. We also observe a weak vertical increase from the sub-Saharan region to the European and Central Asian region. Each category shows a slight positive relationship between the import trade volume and the average labor income share. However, the weak goodness of fit shared between all categories means no strong conclusions can be found.

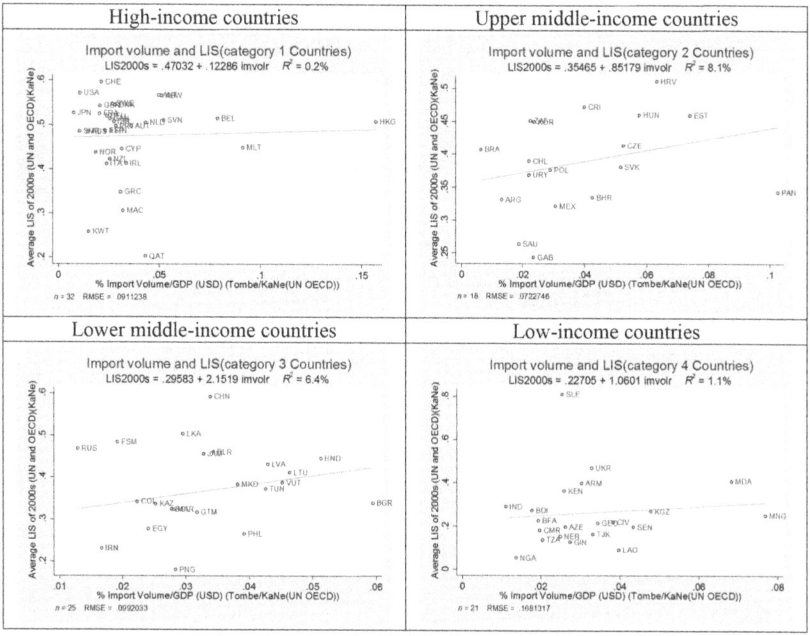

Fig. 3.15 Import volume and the labor income share, by income groups. (Source: The figures on import volume are taken from Tombe (2015). The figures on GDP and labor income share are calculations taken from Karabarbounis and Neiman (2014) using UN and OECD data)

We then move on to testing the export side and its impact on the labor income share. The aggregate level shows a slight positive correlation between the export volume and the average labor income share by 1.88% (Fig. 3.16). However, the small goodness of fit at 6.1% limits the significance. There is a positive correlation among high-income countries of approximately 0.59% in labor income share for every percent increase in the export volume of GDP, and a small goodness of fit at 1.6%. Upper middle-income countries show strong results with the inputs positively associated at 2.96% with a goodness of fit of 42.1% (Fig. 3.17). There is a substantial divergence shifting from Latin American and Caribbean countries to countries in Europe and Central Asia.

We continue to observe this pattern among lower income countries, where the magnitude of the effect is at approximately 1.82% in the labor

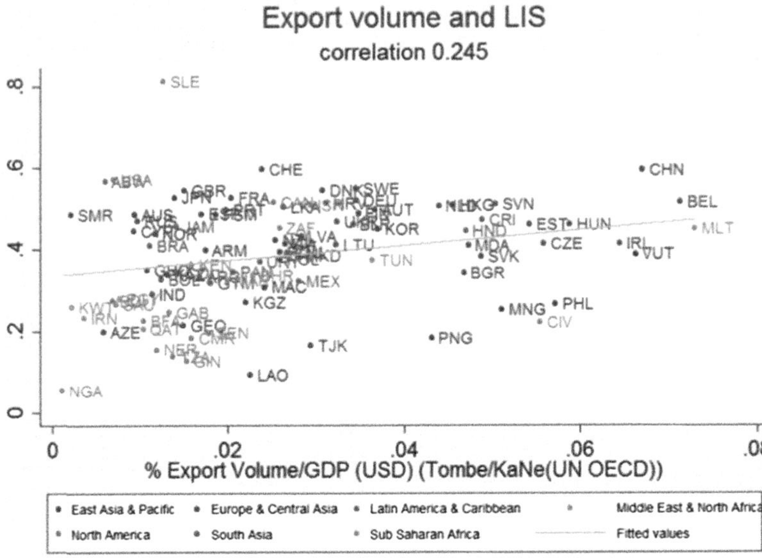

Fig. 3.16 Export volume and the labor income share: full sample of countries. (Source: The figures on export volume are taken from Tombe (2015). The figures on GDP and labor income share are calculations taken from Karabarbounis and Neiman (2014) using UN and OECD data)

income for every unit increase in the ratio of export volume. However, we observe a weaker goodness of fit without regional patterns. Finally, we find this trend to continue with low-income countries showing an increase of approximately 1.47% in average labor income share with every increase in the export volume ratio. While acknowledging the low goodness of fit of 1.7%, we note a clear shift from the sub-Saharan region with a low ratio of export to GDP to higher value in European and Central Asian countries. Sierra Leone is an exception with a low export-GDP ratio and a high value of labor income share.

Considering the trade relationship on the exports side, we also find a consistent positive relationship with a labor income share. There is a small goodness of fit aside from the upper middle-income category. We find a consistent positive correlation evident through the tests on all the measures of trade. Throughout these tests, the upper middle-income

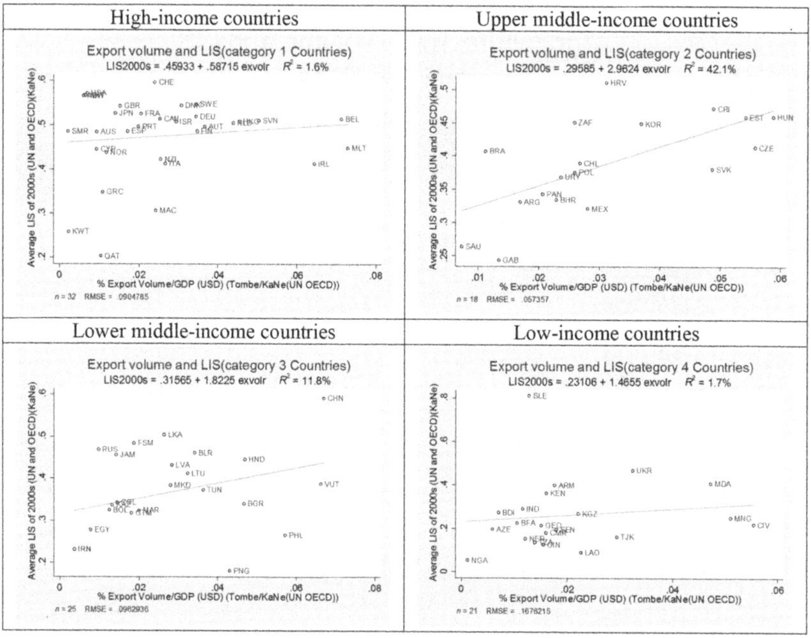

Fig. 3.17 Export volume and the labor income share, by income groups. (Source: The figures on export volume are taken from Tombe (2015). The figures on GDP and labor income share are calculations taken from Karabarbounis and Neiman (2014) using UN and OECD data)

categories constantly show a much greater goodness of fit relative to other categories. However, the relatively low goodness of fit in all other tests still leaves the overall relationship to be inconclusive.

3.5.1 *Agricultural Trade and the Labor Income Share*

We then analyze the potential impact of the overall agricultural trade volume on the labor income share. We test this by regressing the average labor income share (average LIS of 2000s) against the ratio of percent of agricultural trade volume percentage of GDP. An aggregate test shows a negative correlation between the agricultural trade volume and the labor income share (Fig. 3.18). A 1% increase in agricultural trade volume sees an average labor income share decrease by approximately 2.34%. This has

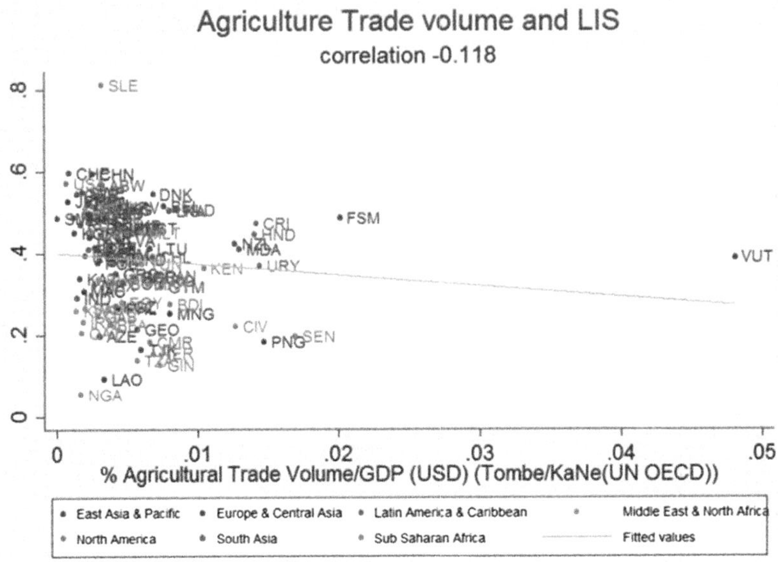

Fig. 3.18 Agricultural trade and the labor income share: full sample of countries. (Source: The agriculture trade volume figures come from Tombe (2015). The GDP and labor income share figures are taken from calculations by Karabarbounis and Neiman (2014) using UN and OECD data)

limited utility due to the cluster of countries together and Vanuatu as an outlier.

Among high-income countries, the data shows no relationship between the two variables and no goodness of fit (Fig. 3.19). Among the upper middle-income countries, we observe a positive correlation between the two variables of a unit increase of the agricultural trade volume to GDP ratio and approximately a 3.16% increase in labor income share, though the goodness of fit remains weak at 2.7%. This weak positive correlation between the two variables continues in lower middle-income countries, where a unit increase in the agricultural trade volume shows an increase in the labor income share by 1.09%. The goodness of fit remains weak at 1.1%.

We finally observe a weak negative correlation between the agricultural trade volume and the labor income share for low-income countries, where

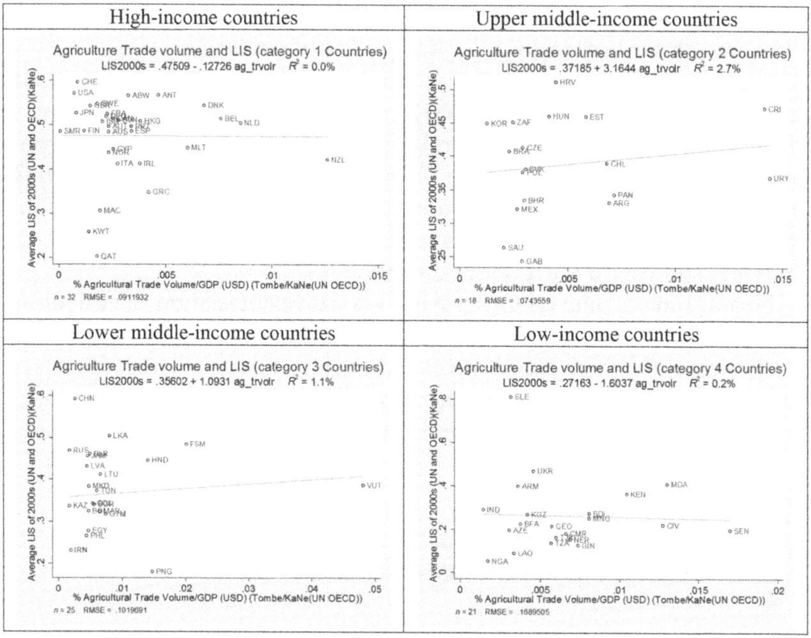

Fig. 3.19 Agricultural trade and the labor income share, by income groups. (Source: The agriculture trade volume figures come from Tombe (2015). The GDP and labor income share figures are taken from calculations by Karabarbounis and Neiman (2014) using UN and OECD data)

a unit increase in the agricultural trade volume decreases the labor income share by 1.6%. Sierra Leone is an outlier with high percent of average labor income share. We do not observe any strong correlation between the agricultural trade volume and labor income share. The relationship varies between positive and negative, the goodness of fit is consistently weak at under 3%, and there are no clear regional patterns at the aggregate and categorical levels. Therefore, no strong conclusions can be drawn from this relationship.

We then test the correlation between the agricultural imports and exports percentage of GDP with the labor income share (average LIS of 2000s). An aggregate level shows a negative correlation between the agriculture import and average labor income share, where a percent increase in the agriculture import volume to GDP ratio shows a decrease in the average labor income share by an average of approximately 21% (Fig. 3.20). However, this is limited by a goodness of fit of only 6.3%.

High-income countries have no relationship between average LIS and agricultural import volume of GDP, confirmed by no goodness of fit (Fig. 3.21). We observe a similar relationship among upper middle-income countries and a goodness of fit at only 0.3%. Lower middle-income countries also contain a positive relationship at a 9.6% increase in labor income share for each percent increase in the agricultural import volume to GDP ratio and still have a low goodness of fit at 0.7%.

Finally, low-income countries have a negative correlation of agriculture import and labor income share of 3.28%, in contrast with the previous categories where there is a positive relationship. The goodness of fit is very weak at 0.2%. The data shows there is either none or a weak correlation between agricultural imports and the labor income share with small

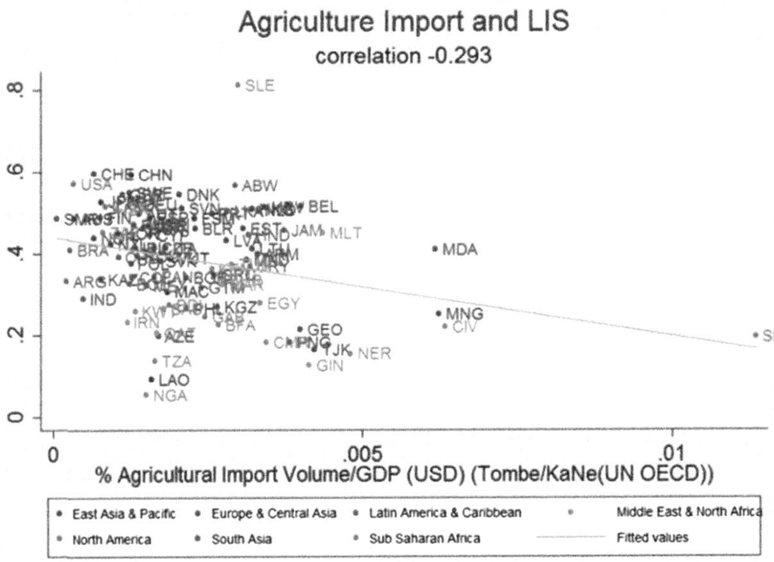

Fig. 3.20 Agricultural import and the labor income share: full sample of countries. (Source: The agriculture import volume figures come from Tombe (2015). The GDP and labor income share figures are taken from calculations by Karabarbounis and Neiman (2014) using UN and OECD data)

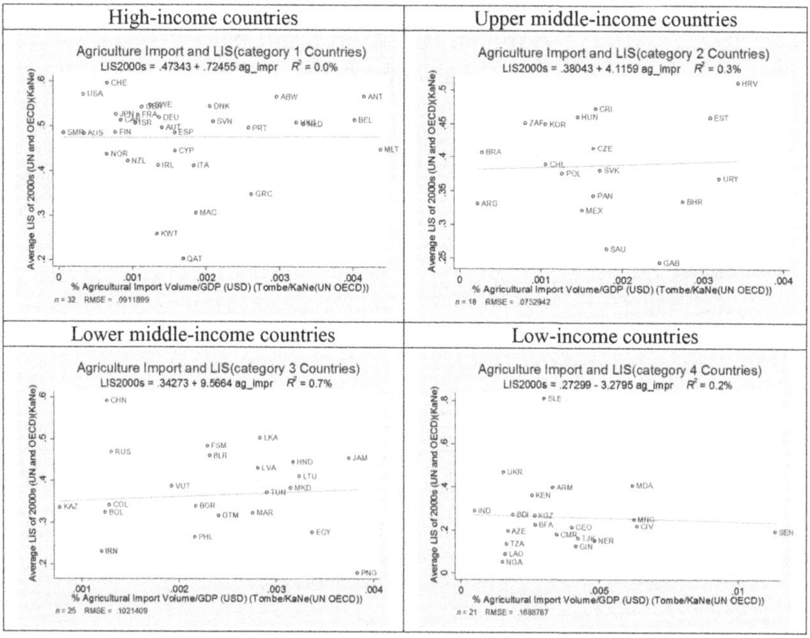

Fig. 3.21 Agricultural import and the labor income share, by income groups. (Source: The agriculture import volume figures come from Tombe (2015). The GDP and labor income share figures are taken from calculations by Karabarbounis and Neiman (2014) using UN and OECD data)

coefficients and goodness of fit values less than 1%. We also deduce no regional patterns among all the categories of countries. Consequently, we cannot conclude any substantial relationship between agricultural imports and the average labor income share.

The aggregate level shows a very weak negative correlation between the agriculture export volume and labor income share (Fig. 3.22). Each increase in the percent of agriculture export to GDP shows a decrease in the labor income share on average to by 0.87%. However, the goodness of fit is at only 0.1%. The cluster of countries here shares similarities to the aggregate tests where there is a cluster of countries with an outstanding outlier. High-income countries show no relationship between these two variables, demonstrated by the goodness of fit of 0% (Fig. 3.23). For upper middle-income countries, we find a slight positive correlation of 3.13%.

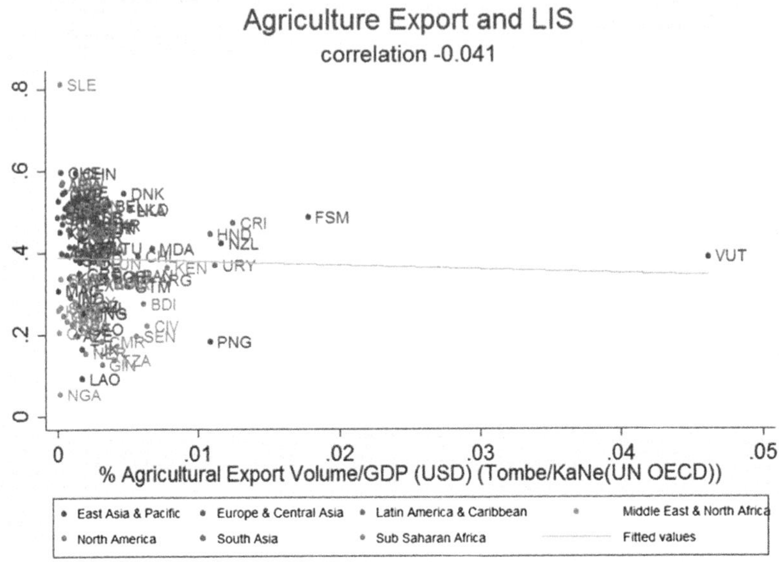

Fig. 3.22 Agricultural export and the labor income share: full sample of countries. (Source: The agriculture export volume figures come from Tombe (2015). The GDP and labor income share figures are taken from calculations by Karabarbounis and Neiman (2014) using UN and OECD data)

There is also a weak goodness of fit of 2.5%. Low middle-income countries show a positive relationship but both this relationship and goodness of fit is weaker than upper middle-income countries. Finally, low-income countries resemble the pattern of high-income countries with a 0% goodness of fit. The data on agricultural export percentage of GDP reflects the data of agricultural import percentage of GDP, where there is either none or a weak variation of labor income share is explained by the variation in agricultural exports. Most of the goodness of fit values are below 1%, aside from upper middle-income countries, and no clear regional patterns can be found. Consequently, no strong conclusions can be found from testing this relationship.

For all the tests on agricultural trade volume, agricultural exports, and agricultural imports as a percentage of GDP on the labor income share, we find no significant conclusions. The goodness of fit continuously is at a

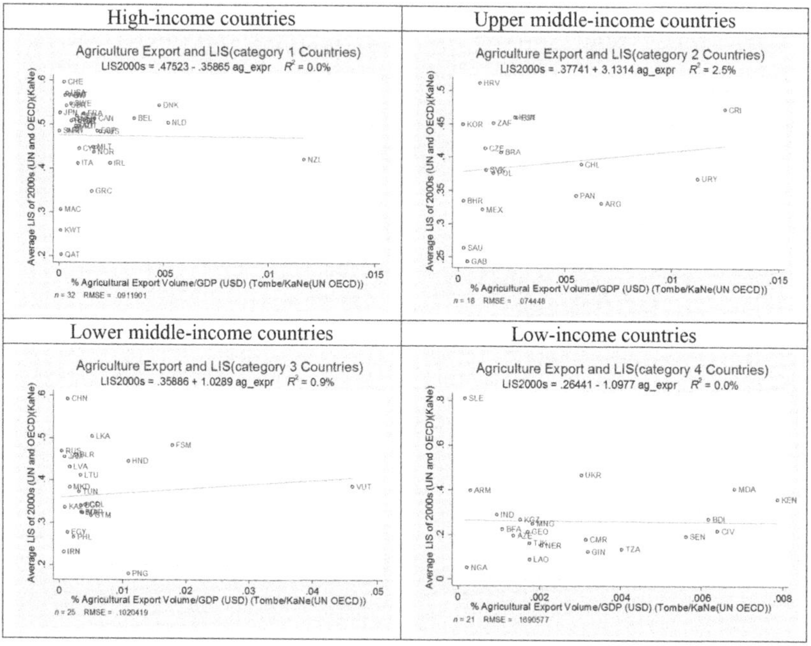

Fig. 3.23 Agricultural export and the labor income share, by income groups. (Source: The agriculture export volume figures come from Tombe (2015). The GDP and labor income share figures are taken from calculations by Karabarbounis and Neiman (2014) using UN and OECD data)

weak level through each of these variables and the relationship varies from positive to negative, so no solid relationship can be traced.

3.5.2 *Non-agricultural Trade and the Labor Income Share*

We next evaluate the impact of non-agricultural trade volume on the labor income share. This is tested by regressing the average labor income share (average LIS of 2000s) against the non-agricultural trade volume percentage of GDP (Fig. 3.24).

Looking at it from an aggregate level, we deduce a positive correlation between the non-agricultural trade volume and the average labor income share. A percent increase in the non-agricultural trade volume is associated with a raise in the average labor income share on average by 0.9%. However,

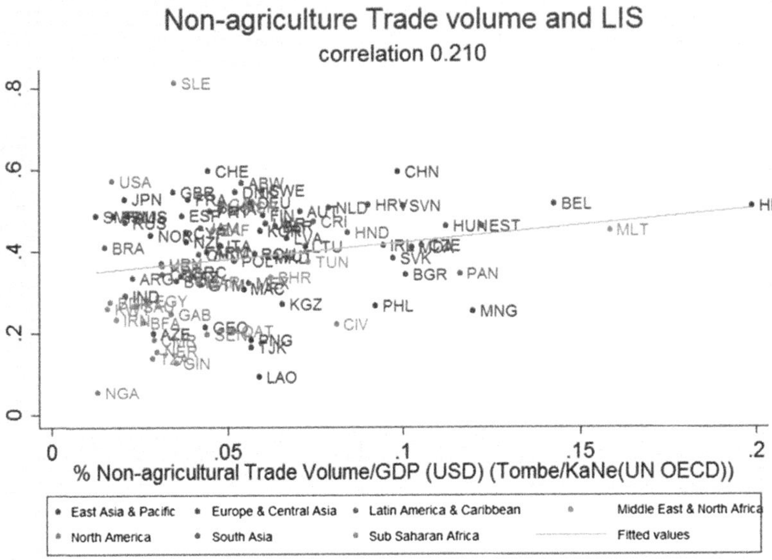

Fig. 3.24 Non-agricultural trade and the labor income share: full sample of countries. (Source: The non-agriculture trade volume figures come from Tombe (2015). The GDP and labor income share figures are taken from calculations by Karabarbounis and Neiman (2014) using UN and OECD data)

the goodness of fit is only 5.2% and there are no distinctive regional patterns. The high-income countries show a weak positive correlation between the two variables, where there is an increase in the labor income share by approximately 0.18% to each unit increase in the non-agricultural trade volume (Fig. 3.25). The goodness of fit is very low at 0.7%. The upper middle-income countries also show that a unit increase in the non-agricultural trade volume shows an increase in the labor income share, by approximately 1%. This is supported by a much stronger goodness of fit at 23%. There are clear regional patterns of a growing average LIS and non-agricultural trade volume from the Latin American and Caribbean regions to the European and Central Asian regions.

We continue to observe this positive correlation between the variables among the lower middle-income countries, where a unit increase in the non-agricultural trade volume increases the labor income share by

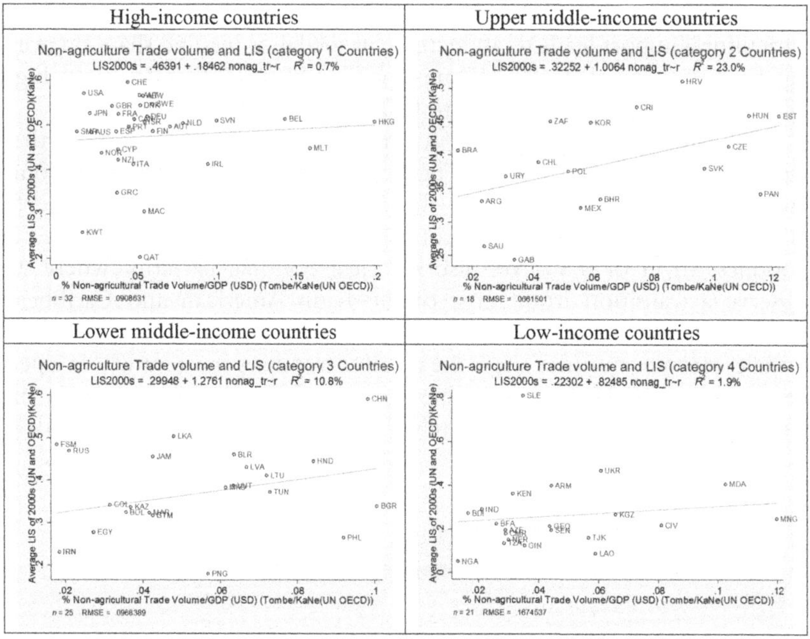

Fig. 3.25 Non-agricultural trade and the labor income share, by income groups. (Source: The non-agriculture trade volume figures come from Tombe (2015). The GDP and labor income share figures are taken from calculations by Karabarbounis and Neiman (2014) using UN and OECD data)

approximately 1.28% and the goodness of fit has reduced to 10.8%. The positive relationship between the two variables continues in low-income countries by approximately 0.825% for every unit increase in the non-agricultural trade volume. But this has a weaker goodness of fit at only 1.7%. All categories show a positive correlation between the non-agricultural trade volume percentage of GDP and the average labor income share. Aside from upper middle-income countries, this relationship is minimal with a weak goodness of fit with a lack of strong regional patterns.

We then investigate the effect of non-agricultural import and exports on the average labor income share. We test this relationship by regressing the average labor income share (average LIS of 2000s) against the ratio of percentage of non-agricultural import and export volume percentage of GDP. We start by evaluating the impact of non-agricultural import on the average labor income share, where we find that an increase in the non-agricultural import leads to an increase in the labor income share on average by approximately 0.94%. Hong Kong is a heavy outlier due to its high non-agricultural import volume to GDP (Fig. 3.26).

High-income countries show a minimal positive relationship with a weak goodness of fit of 0.2% (Fig. 3.27). Within upper middle-income countries, a percent increase in the non-agriculture import volume to GDP ratio increases the labor income share by 0.874%. There is a greater goodness of fit of 8.3%. We also see clear regional patterns, where we observe a transition from most of the Latin American and Caribbean region to most of the European and Central Asian region. The lower middle-income countries show the positive trend is persistent where a percent increase in the non-agricultural import leads to an increase in the labor income share by approximately 2.24%. The goodness of fit is at 6.4%.

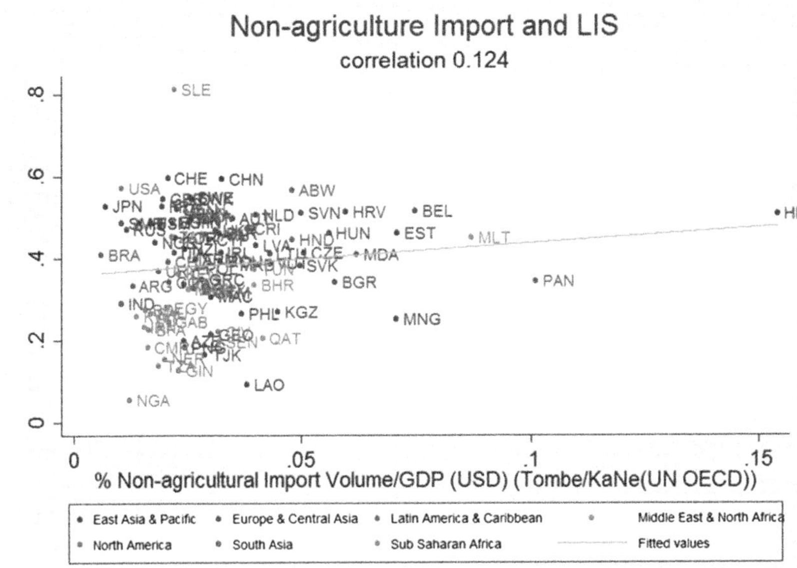

Fig. 3.26 Non-agricultural import and the labor income share: full sample of countries. (Source: The non-agriculture import volume figures come from Tombe (2015). The GDP and labor income share figures are taken from calculations by Karabarbounis and Neiman (2014) using UN and OECD data)

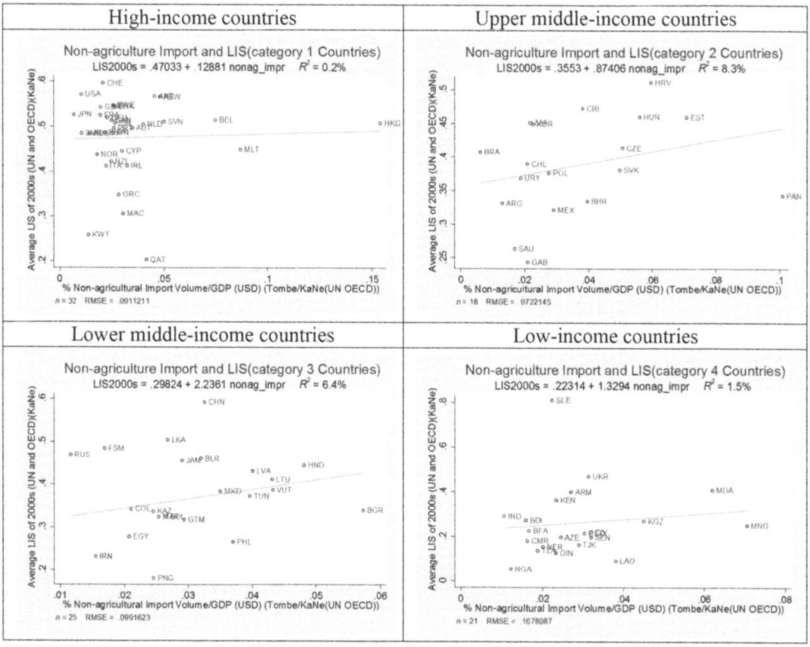

Fig. 3.27 Non-agricultural import and the labor income share, by income groups. (Source: The non-agriculture import volume figures come from Tombe (2015). The GDP and labor income share figures are taken from calculations by Karabarbounis and Neiman (2014) using UN and OECD data)

Finally, low-income countries maintain the positive relationship at a rate of 1.33%. The goodness of fit is 1.5%. Sierra Leone is an outlier due to a high average labor income share. In the non-agricultural import volume percentage to GDP and average labor income share, we can also find a consistent positive relationship but a weak goodness of fit and no clear regional patterns. We then test the correlation between the non-agricultural export and the labor income share.

An aggregate analysis finds a positive relationship between the non-agricultural export and the labor income share, where an increase in the non-agricultural export correlates with a rise in the labor income share by 2.16% (Fig. 3.28). The goodness of fit is 7.4%. Within the high-income category, we see a positive relationship with each unit increase in the non-agricultural export associated with a 0.62% increase in the average labor

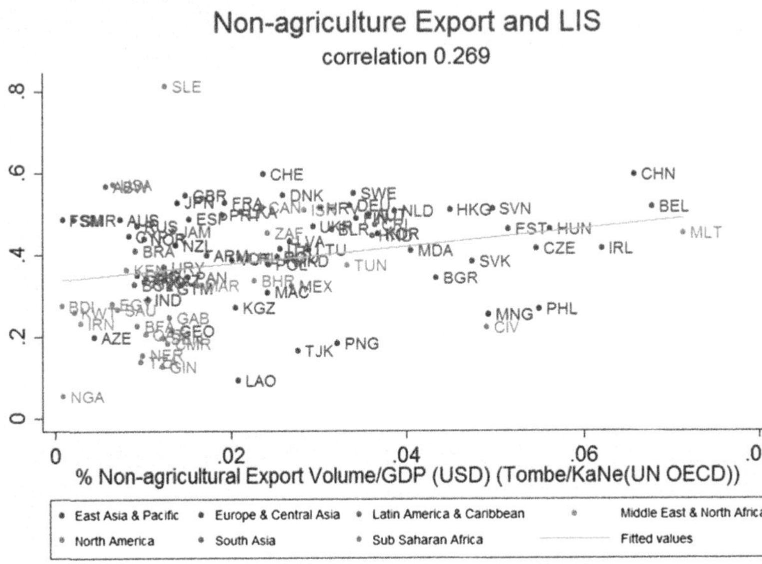

Fig. 3.28 Non-agricultural export and the labor income share: full sample of countries. (Source: The non-agriculture export volume figures come from Tombe (2015). The GDP and labor income share figures are taken from calculations by Karabarbounis and Neiman (2014) using UN and OECD data)

income (Fig. 3.29). The goodness of fit is weak at 1.7%. There is a clear positive correlation in higher middle-income countries where a unit increase in the non-agricultural export shows an increase in the labor income share by approximately 2.76%, with a strong goodness of fit at 37%. Clear regional patterns can be found with a transition from the Latin American and Caribbean region to the European and Central Asian region.

We continue to find a positive relationship between the two variables among the lower middle-income countries where an increase in non-agricultural exports is attributed to an increase in the labor income share by 2.02%. The goodness of fit has dropped to 11.2%. The positive correlation between both the variables continues in low-income countries, where increasing the non-agricultural export measure by one unit finds an increase in the labor income share by 1.64%. However, the goodness of fit falls even further to 2%.

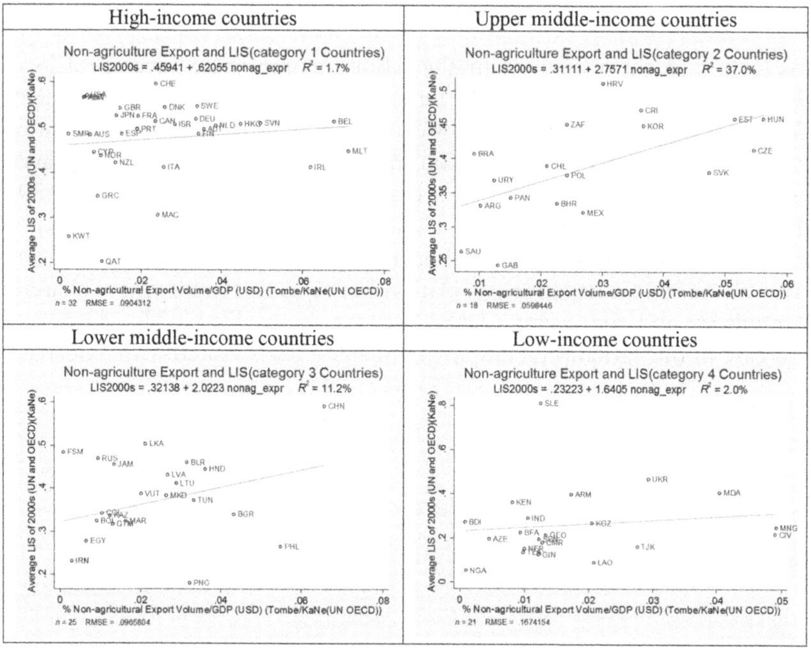

Fig. 3.29 Non-agricultural export and the labor income share, by income groups. (Source: The non-agriculture export volume figures come from Tombe (2015). The GDP and labor income share figures are taken from calculations by Karabarbounis and Neiman (2014) using UN and OECD data)

Through all categories, we find a consistent positive correlation between the non-agricultural export volume and the average labor income share. While upper middle-income countries show a strong goodness of fit and notable regional patterns, all other categories show a weak relationship between the variables and a weak goodness of fit. Therefore, we conclude that there is some evidence that non-agricultural export is correlated positively with the labor income share. All variables concerning non-agricultural trade show a positive relationship with the labor income share. While strong relationships can be found in some cases, the results mostly consist of a weak goodness of fit and a lack of regional patterns that give difficulty for any substantial relationship to be found.

3.6 Agriculture and the Labor Income Share

We first find the variations in the labor income share (average LIS of 2000s) from the variations in the percent of the employment share in agriculture. On an aggregate level, we observe a clear negative correlation where a unit increase in the agricultural employment share shows an average decrease of 0.0033% in the average labor income share (Fig. 3.30). The goodness of fit is high at 36.1%, and there is an outlier again in Sierra Leone due to its high average labor income share. In high-income countries we observe a negative correlation between the employment share in agriculture and the average labor income share (Fig. 3.31). A percent increase in the agricultural employment share is associated with a decrease

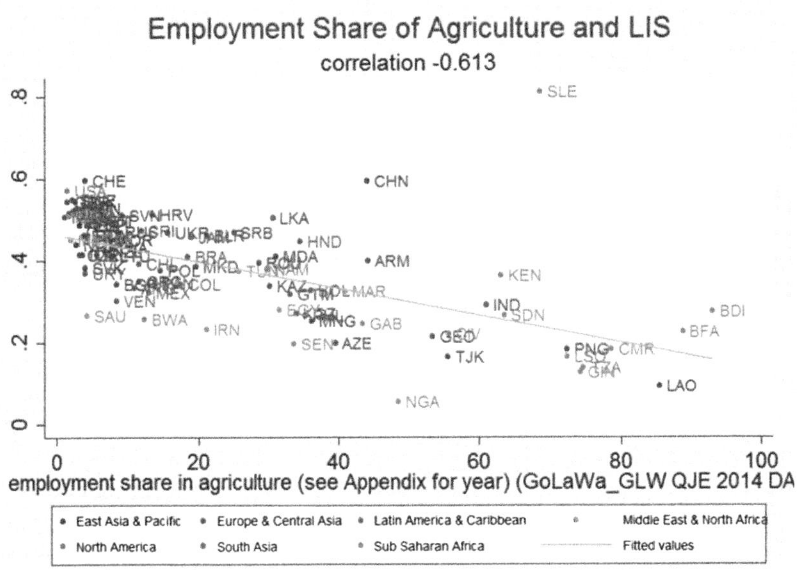

Fig. 3.30 Employment share of agriculture and the labor income share: full sample of countries. (Source: The employment share in agriculture figures come from Gollin et al. (2014). The labor income share figures are taken from calculations by Karabarbounis and Neiman (2014) using UN and OECD data)

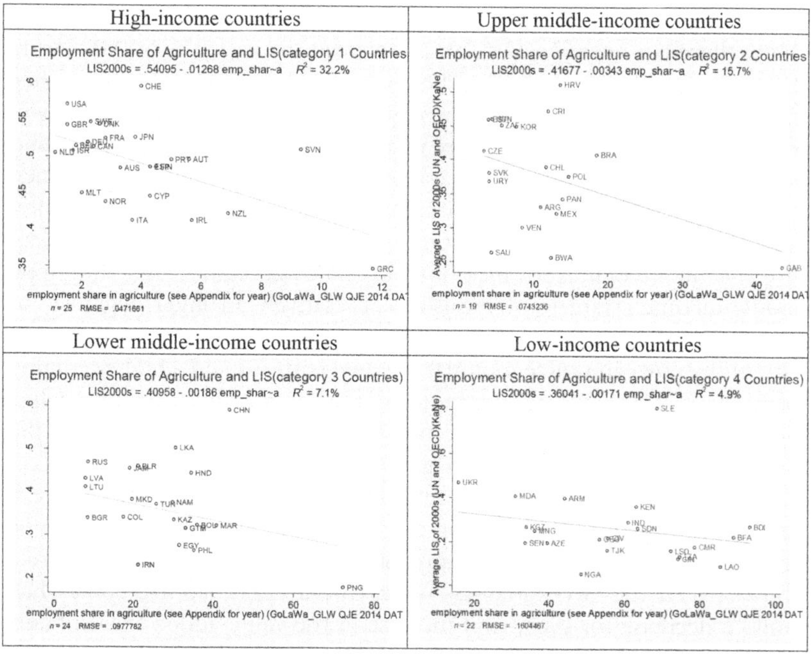

Fig. 3.31 Employment share agriculture and the labor income share, by income groups. (Source: The employment share in agriculture figures come from Gollin et al. (2014). The labor income share figures are taken from calculations by Karabarbounis and Neiman (2014) using UN and OECD data)

in the labor income share on average by approximately 0.013%. The goodness of fit is strong at 32.2%.

A similar pattern is reflected for upper middle-income countries, where we continue to observe a negative correlation between the employment share in agriculture and the average labor income share. However, this relationship weakens where a unit increase in the employment share decreases the labor income share by approximately only 0.003% with a smaller goodness of fit at 15.7%. For lower middle-income countries, the negative correlation continues where an increase in the employment share shows a decrease in the labor income share by 0.002%, and the goodness of fit continues to halve at 7.1%. The countries in this category also are further away from a cluster form.

This relationship is the weakest among the low-income countries, where there is a negative correlation between the variables of 0.002% and a goodness of fit at only 4.9%. The countries continue to disperse. There is a minimal regional trend of European and Central Asian countries with relatively lower employment share in agriculture and higher average labor income share, while the sub-Saharan region occupies higher employment share in agriculture and lower average labor income share. All categories demonstrate a negative correlation between the average share in agriculture and the average labor income share. The aggregate, high, and upper middle-income countries demonstrate a relatively stronger negative correlation and goodness of fit, providing the test between these variables with utility. We can notice minimal regional patterns and a higher employment share in agriculture in countries at a lower level of income, which could indicate the different structures of the low-income economies that tend to have a higher share of an agriculture sector.

We then investigate the potential effect of the value-added share in agriculture on the average labor income share (average LIS of 2000s) through a regression test. The aggregate analysis shows a negative correlation between the two variables, where the average labor income share shows a decrease for every unit increase in the value-added share of agriculture by 0.005% on average (Fig. 3.32). The goodness of fit is 20%. Sierra Leone continues to be an outlier with a high valued-added share in agriculture and high average labor income share. Within the high-income countries, a percent increase in the value-added share of agriculture shows a decrease in average labor income share on average by 0.029% (Fig. 3.33). The goodness of fit continues to be strong at 26.2%.

For upper middle-income countries, there is a weakly positive relationship where an increase in the value-added share in agriculture shows an increase in the average labor income share by approximately 0.004%. However, the goodness of fit has significantly reduced to 0.5%. Across the lower middle-income countries, a percent increase in the value-added share in agriculture correlates to a negative change in the labor income share on average by 0.005%. The goodness of fit is at 10.5%. Finally, the low-income countries show a similar pattern to high-income countries where every percent increase in the value-added share in agriculture is attributed to approximately 0.002% increase in the average labor income share.

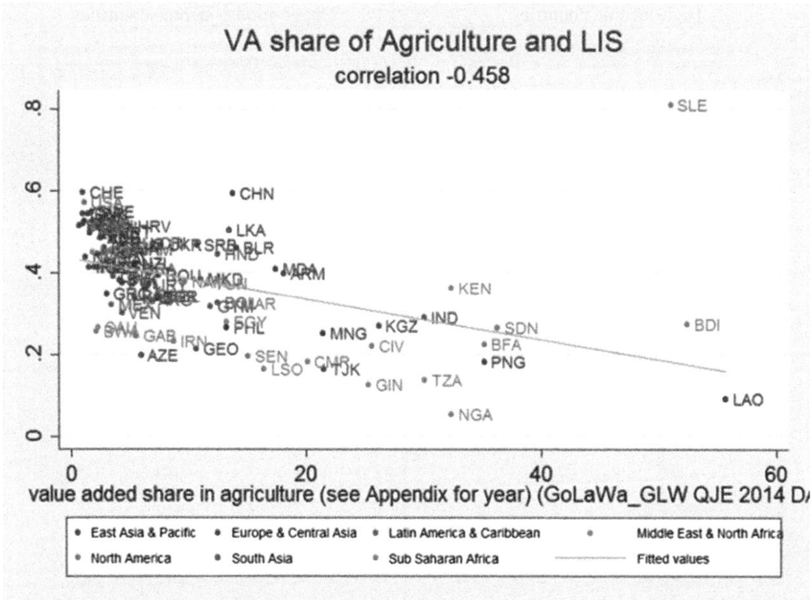

Fig. 3.32 Value-added share of agriculture and the labor income share: full sample of countries. (Source: The value-added share in agriculture figures Lagakos and Waugh (2013). The labor income share figures are taken from calculations by Karabarbounis and Neiman (2014) using UN and OECD data)

Through these categories we can find an overall negative correlation between the average value-added share in agriculture and the average labor income share. While the relationship varies from positive to negative between the average value-added share in agriculture and the average labor income share in different country categories, the goodness of fit is much stronger in the categories in which a negative relationship can be found, showing an overall negative correlation. We also find that the value share of agriculture increases in countries with lower incomes. Both the tests on value-added and employment share of agriculture demonstrate a weak negative relationship with the average labor income share, with generally high goodness of fit levels, providing the test with legitimacy.

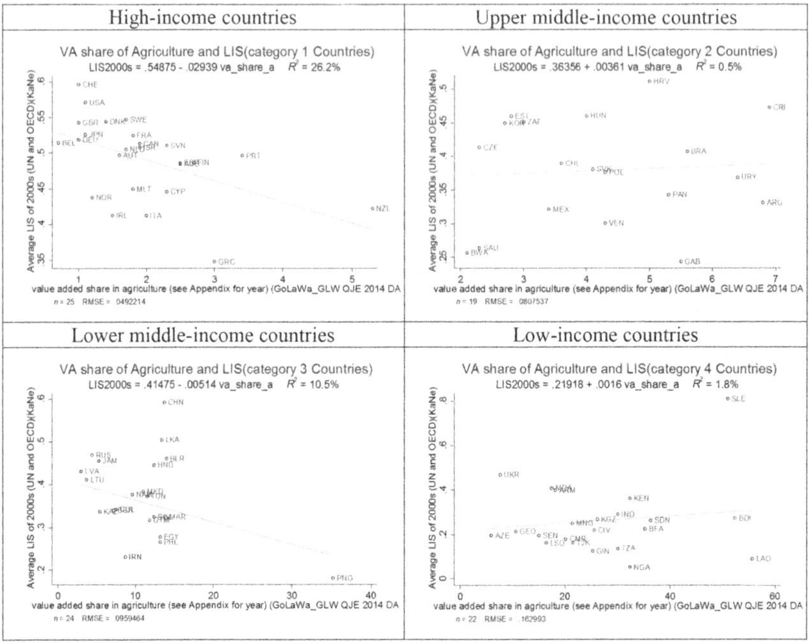

Fig. 3.33 Value-added share of agriculture and the labor income share, by income groups (Source: The value-added share in agriculture figures Lagakos and Waugh (2013). The labor income share figures are taken from calculations by Karabarbounis and Neiman (2014) using UN and OECD data)

References

Charpe, M., S. Lee, D. Arias, and S. Bridji. 2014. Does income distribution matter for development? Trends in labour share of income and their economic impacts in developing countries. World of Work Report: ILO, Chap. 8.

Feenstra, R. C., R. Inklaar, and M. P. Timmer. 2015. The Next Generation of the Penn World Table. *American Economic Review* 105(10): 3150–3182.

Gollin, D. 2002. Getting income shares right. *Journal of Political Economy, 110*(2), 458–474.

Gollin, D., D. Lagakos, and M. E. Waugh. 2014. The agricultural productivity gap. *The Quarterly Journal of Economics*, 129(2): 939–993.

ILO. (2017). Key Indicators of the Labour Market (KILM). Available: http://www.ilo.org/ilostat/faces/ilostat-home/home?_adf.ctrl-state=1b2e7htvgk_4&_afrLoop= 286517921545847

Karabarbounis, Loukas, and Brent Neiman. 2014. "The Global Decline of the Labor Share." *Quarterly Journal of Economics* 129 (1): 61–103.

Lagakos, and Waugh. 2013. Selection, Agriculture, and Cross-Country Productivity Differences. *American Economic Review*, 103(2): 948–980.

LaPorta, Rafael and Andrei Shleifer. 2014. Informality and Development. *Journal of Economic Perspectives*, 28(3): 109–126.

Timmer, M. P., E. Dietzenbacher, B. Los, R. Stehrer, and G. de Vries. 2015. An Illustrated User Guide to the World Input Output Database: The Case of Global Automotive Production. *Review of International Economics* 23(3): 575–605.

Tombe, Trevor. 2015. The Missing Food Problem: Trade, Agriculture, and International Productivity Differences. *American Economic Journal: Macroeconomics 7* (3): 226–258.

Trapp, K. 2015. Measuring the Labour Income Share of Developing Countries: Learning from Social Accounting Matrices. UNU-WIDER Working Paper 41.

UN. 2017. United Nations System of National Accounts. Available: http://data.un.org/Explorer.aspx?d=SNA

UNIDO. 2015. Industrial Statistics Database – 2015 edition. Available: http://www.unido.org/resources/statistics/statistical-databases/indstat2-2015-edition.html.

van Treeck, K. 2017. The Labor Income Share of Developing Countries: Data Review and Analysis of International Panel Data. Paper presented at the 5th Conference of the Regulating for Decent Work Network at the International Labour Office Geneva. Switzerland.

CHAPTER 4

Global Trends in Labor Income Share: Sector Level

Despite steady growth of the literature on labor income share (LIS), empirical studies are mostly limited to country-level analyses. At the sectoral level, data on labor income share are available only for advanced countries. This chapter overcomes this constraint and provides some preliminary outcomes from a novel dataset (Oishi and Paul 2018) at the sectoral level (10 sectors) for 53 countries, including 20 developing countries.

4.1 Data

4.1.1 Data Sources and Country Coverage

We use three data sources, the Groningen Growth and Development Centre (GGDC) 10-Sector Database, the Socio-Economic Account (SEA), and ILOSTAT. The Groningen Growth and Development Centre publishes the GGDC 10-Sector Database.[1] It provides comparable long-run macroeconomic statistics on the sectoral level for 42 countries[2] for 1950–2013. The World Input-Output Database (WIOD) provides the Socio-Economic Account (SEA).[3] This dataset provides macroeconomic statistics such as industrial output, capital investment and stocks, and

[1] https://www.rug.nl/ggdc/productivity/10-sector/.
[2] Including West Germany.
[3] http://www.wiod.org/database/seas13.

S. Paul, *Labor Income Share*,
https://doi.org/10.1007/978-981-15-6860-2_4

employment by skill type. It covers 40 countries for the period from 1995 to 2009. It estimates the data mainly based on EU KLEMS (EU-level analysis of capital (K), labor (L), energy (E), materials (M), and service (S) inputs), EUROSTAT, and the OECD's Structural Analysis database (STAN). ILOSTAT[4] is a data source that the International Labour Organization (ILO) compiles, and it stores broad statistics on labor and consumer, population, and socio-economic issues. In general, the labor and earnings survey is based on definitions and concepts that the ILO generates; therefore, it provides comparability to a certain extent. However, as governmental or regional bodies or international organizations collect each dataset independently, the comparison among countries should receive appropriate attention when applying nonstandard classifications or concepts. In case special attention is necessary, the ILO provides notes. In addition, it offers information on the data source, its characteristics, any change in methodologies, and indications of unreliability for each value. Appendices 2 and 3 summarize this information over time and among countries.

Table 4.1 shows the availability of data for 53 countries across 5 regions based on the most recent World Bank classification of countries (9 from East Asia and the Pacific, 27 from Europe and Central Asia, 8 from Latin America and the Caribbean, 2 from the Middle East and North Africa, 2 from North America, and 5 from sub-Saharan Africa). Countries enter this list when we have data for at least 1 year in at least 1 sector. Out of 53 countries, 20 are developing countries (based on the World Bank classification), of which 5 are from the East Asia and the Pacific region and 5 are from sub-Saharan Africa. We have data for only 1 year for 3 countries (Italy, Colombia, and Peru), and for 45 countries data are available for at least 5 years. As is evident from Table 4.1, data in most of the country cases are available from the mid-1990s. The People's Republic of China has sectoral labor income share data available for the longest period (23 years), followed by Denmark (16 years) and Sweden (15 years). The earliest year for which data are available is 1969 (agriculture, the United States), and 2011 is the most recent year for which data are available in most of the countries.

[4] https://www.ilo.org/ilostat/faces/wcnav_defaultSelection?_adf.ctrl-state=6ghjloohd_110&_afrLoop=316028130615831&_afrWindowMode=0&_afrWindowId=6ghjloohd_107#!%40%40%3F_afrWindowId%3D6ghjloohd_107%26_afrLoop%3D316028130615831%26_afrWindowMode%3D0%26_adf.ctrl-state%3Dbl8xscafv_9.

Table 4.1 Data coverage by region, country, and year

Region	*Country*	*Starting year*	*Ending year*	*# Years (N)*
East Asia and Pacific	Australia	1995	2006	9
	People's Republic of China	1986	2008	23
	Indonesia	2000	2010	11
	Korea, Rep. of	1993	2008	14
	Malaysia	2000	2001	2
	Philippines	1996	2008	9
	Singapore	1998	2008	11
	Taipei, China	1983	2008	8
	Thailand	2010	2010	1
Europe and Central Asia	Austria	1995	2007	13
	Belgium	1995	2007	13
	Bulgaria	1996	2008	13
	Cyprus	1998	2006	9
	Czech Republic	1996	2007	12
	Denmark	1995	2011	16
	Estonia	1995	2008	14
	Finland	1995	2008	14
	France	1997	2006	8
	Germany	1996	2008	13
	Greece	2000	2006	3
	Hungary	1995	2008	14
	Ireland	1996	2006	11
	Italy	1995	1995	1
	Latvia	1995	2008	14
	Lithuania	1995	2008	14
	Luxembourg	1995	2008	14
	Netherlands	1994	2005	12
	Poland	1995	2006	12
	Portugal	1998	2008	11
	Russian Federation	1995	2009	9
	Slovak Republic	1995	2008	14
	Slovenia	1995	2008	14
	Spain	1999	2008	10
	Sweden	1993	2007	15
	Turkey	1995	2005	11
	United Kingdom	1995	2008	14

(*continued*)

Table 4.1 (continued)

Region	*Country*	*Starting year*	*Ending year*	*# Years (N)*
Latin America and Caribbean	Argentina	2004	2010	6
	Bolivia	2005	2009	5
	Brazil	1994	2011	17
	Chile	2006	2011	4
	Colombia	2002	2011	8
	Costa Rica	1998	2008	7
	Mexico	1991	2004	12
	Peru	2002	2011	10
Middle East and North Africa	Egypt, Arab Rep.	1996	2007	12
	Malta	2000	2008	9
North America	Canada	1995	2008	14
	United States	1969	2008	10
Sub-Saharan Africa	Botswana	1997	2010	14
	Ethiopia (excludes Eritrea)	2005	2005	1
	Ghana	2006	2006	1
	Mauritius	1999	2010	12
	Tanzania	2006	2006	1

Source: Authors' own calculations

Table 4.2 shows the country-level labor income share data coverage for 10 sectors.[5] Country–year data are mostly unavailable for OTH (available only for 16 out of 53 countries). Data for AGR and GOV are unavailable for 19 and 18 countries, respectively. On the other hand, the data coverage significantly improves for sectors like MIN, MAN, PU, and TRA. In each of these sectors, we manage to calculate the labor income share for around 50 countries. Among the developing country sample, we find a representative time series (data available for at least 10 years in certain sectors) for the People's Republic of China, Indonesia, Peru, Mauritius, Mexico, Egypt, and Botswana. For the People's Republic of China, data are available for 7 sectors (MIN, MAN, PU, WRT, TRA, FIRE, and GOV) for the period from 1986 to 2008, for the Philippines for 8 sectors (AGR, MIN, MAN, PU, CON, WRT, TRA, and FIRE) for the period from 1996

[5] We follow the Groningen Growth Data Center (GGDC) classification of 10 sectors (AGR, MIN, MAN, PU, CON, WRT, TRA, FIRE, GOV, and OTH).

Table 4.2 Data coverage by region, country, and 10 sectors

Region	*Country*	*Years*	*AGR*	*MIN*	*MAN*	*PU*	*CON*	*WRT*	*TRA*	*FIRE*	*GOV*	*OTH*
East Asia and Pacific	Australia	9	5	6	6	6	6	6	6	6	6	0
	People's Republic of China	23	0	23	23	23	0	21	23	23	23	0
	Indonesia	11	11	11	11	11	11	11	11	11	11	11
	Korea, Rep. of	14	0	14	14	14	14	0	13	0	0	0
	Malaysia	2	0	0	2	0	0	0	0	0	0	0
	Philippines	9	9	9	9	9	9	9	9	9	0	0
	Singapore	11	0	0	11	0	11	11	10	10	0	0
	Taipei, China	8	0	8	8	8	0	5	8	8	8	0
	Thailand	1	1	1	1	1	1	1	1	1	1	1

(*continued*)

Table 4.2 (continued)

Region	*Country*	*Years*	*AGR*	*MIN*	*MAN*	*PU*	*CON*	*WRT*	*TRA*	*FIRE*	*GOV*	*OTH*
Europe and Central Asia	Austria	13	0	0	13	13	13	9	9	9	9	9
	Belgium	13	0	9	13	9	13	9	9	9	1	0
	Bulgaria	13	13	13	13	13	13	13	13	13	13	0
	Cyprus	9	6	9	9	9	9	9	9	9	9	0
	Czech Republic	12	12	12	12	12	12	12	12	12	12	0
	Denmark	16	0	16	0	16	0	0	16	0	0	0
	Estonia	14	14	14	14	14	14	14	14	14	14	0
	Finland	14	0	14	14	14	14	14	14	14	14	0
	France	8	0	4	4	4	4	4	4	4	4	4
	Germany	13	11	13	13	13	13	2	2	2	0	0
	Greece	3	0	3	3	3	3	1	3	3	0	0
	Hungary	14	14	14	14	14	14	14	14	14	14	0
	Ireland	11	0	11	11	11	0	0	0	0	0	0
	Italy	1	0	1	1	1	1	1	1	0	0	0
	Latvia	14	14	14	14	14	13	14	14	14	14	0
	Lithuania	14	14	14	12	14	14	14	14	14	14	0
	Luxembourg	14	0	14	14	14	14	14	1	1	0	0
	Netherlands	12	5	12	12	12	12	12	12	12	12	0
	Poland	12	12	12	12	12	12	12	12	12	12	0
	Portugal	11	0	0	0	11	11	11	0	11	1	0
	Russian Federation	9	9	9	9	9	9	9	9	9	9	0
	Slovak Republic	14	14	14	14	14	14	14	14	14	14	0
	Slovenia	14	14	14	14	14	14	14	14	14	14	0
	Spain	10	0	10	10	10	10	10	10	0	0	0
	Sweden	15	15	15	15	15	15	15	15	0	8	0
	Turkey	11	6	11	11	11	5	4	4	0	0	0
	United Kingdom	14	14	14	14	0	14	0	14	0	0	0

Latin America and Caribbean	Argentina	6	6	6	6	6	6	6	6	6	6	6
	Bolivia	5	0	5	5	5	0	0	5	5	0	5
	Brazil	17	0	9	9	9	9	9	8	9	9	0
	Chile	4	1	4	4	4	4	4	4	4	0	1
	Colombia	8	8	8	8	8	8	2	8	8	0	2
	Costa Rica	7	7	6	6	5	6	6	6	6	1	3
	Mexico	12	12	12	12	12	12	12	12	12	12	12
	Peru	10	7	9	8	9	9	8	8	9	0	8
Middle East and North Africa	Egypt, Arab Rep.	12	11	12	12	11	0	11	12	12	2	2
	Malta	9	6	8	9	9	9	9	9	9	9	0
North America	Canada	14	14	14	14	14	14	14	14	14	14	14
	United States	10	10	0	0	0	0	0	0	0	0	0
Sub-Saharan Africa	Botswana	14	8	14	14	11	14	14	14	11	2	0
	Ethiopia (excludes Eritrea)	1	1	1	1	1	1	1	1	1	1	1
	Ghana	1	1	1	1	1	1	1	1	1	1	1
	Mauritius	12	12	12	12	12	12	12	12	12	12	2
	Tanzania	1	0	1	1	1	1	1	1	1	1	0

Source: Authors' own calculations

Note: Each column under disaggregated sector headings represents the number of years for which labor income share data are available for a country. The column "# of years" shows the total number of years for which data are available for a country in at least one sector to 2008, for Brazil for 8 sectors (MIN, MAN, PU, CON, WRT, TRA, FIRE, and GOV) for the period from 1994 to 2002, for Mexico for all 10 sectors for the period from 1991 to 2004, and, finally, for both Egypt (1996–2007) and Botswana (1997–2010), data are available for 8 sectors (AGR, MIN, MAN, PU, CON, WRT, TRA, and FIRE). We discuss these country cases in greater detail in Sect. 3. In certain countries, data are available for only 1 sector. For example, the labor income share in manufacturing in Malaysia is available for 2000 and 2001. In the United States, the labor income share in agriculture is available only for 10 time points between 1969 and 2011.

4.1.2 *Methodology*

When studies use labor as one of the factors to produce national income, they define the labor income share as a ratio showing "how much of national income accrues to labor" (Lübker 2007). Therefore, the definition of the labor income share at the spectral level is as follows for year *t* and sector *k*:

$$LIS \equiv \frac{Labor\ income_{tk}}{\text{National income}_{tk}}$$

However, it is not straightforward in its computation. Various issues stem from the accounting method of national income, treatment of intangible inputs, measurement of non-private sectors and informal sectors, and attribution of mixed income (i.e., the income for non-wage workers, as researchers regard non-wage workers as not only contributing to labor factors, so their income includes revenue from other contributions). Among them, huge debates and substantial literature exist on the treatment of proprietors' income and indirect taxes less subsidies, as ambiguity is always present when attempting to measure the actual economic activities. One approach to tackling this issue is to impute the figures following Cooley and Prescott (1995); however, in this paper, we employ an alternative approach that Gomme and Rupert (2004) inspire and calculate the sectoral labor income share as follows:

$$LIS = \frac{Compensation\ of\ employees_{tk}}{\text{Value added}_{tk}}$$

This computation is plausible if we assume that the portion of "ambiguous" income is the same as that of the remainder of the sectors. According to Gomme and Rupert (2004), the literature supports this assumption,[6] and this method enables us to compute the labor income share using obtainable statistics.

$$\frac{Compensation\ of\ employees_{tk}}{\text{Value added}_{tk}} = \frac{Average\ monthly\ earning_{tk} \times 12 \times Number\ of\ employees_{tk}}{\text{Value added}_{tk}}$$

We evaluate both earnings and value added in the current value in the local currencies. We adjust the currency unit for countries that experienced redenomination or the introduction of a new currency in their sample periods. Appendix 5 lists each adjustment of that currency unit. For the classification of economic activity, we follow the GGDC 10-sector classification based on International Standard Industrial Classification of All Economic Activities (ISIC) Rev. 3. An accurate reconstruction of ISIC Rev. 4 to Rev. 3 is not possible without detailed data according to the four-digit-level ISIC. Therefore, though some countries collect data according to ISIC Rev. 4, especially in recent years, we limit the data to those available with ISIC Rev. 3.

We obtain the denominator, estimated value added, from the GGDC and SEA. Among them, the 30 countries and regions that the GGDC[7] and SEA cover complement the rest.[8] The SEA released in 2012 provides value added for 35 economic activities based on ISIC Rev. 3. For the countries that the SEA covers, we obtain the value added for 10 sectors by simple aggregation of the 35 sectors. In the numerator, we obtain the mean nominal monthly earnings of employees and the number of employees from ILOSTAT. Data are available for 18 sectors. These 18 sectors are

[6]See Appendix 3 for the concept of ambiguous and unambiguous elements of national income.

[7]Brazil, the People's Republic of China, Denmark, France, India, Indonesia, Italy, Japan, the Republic of Korea, Mexico, the Netherlands, Spain, Sweden, Taipei, China, the United Kingdom, and the United States.

[8]Australia, Austria, Belgium, Bulgaria, Canada, Cyprus, the Czech Republic, Estonia, Finland, Germany, Greece, Hungary, Ireland, Latvia, Lithuania, Luxembourg, Malta, Poland, Portugal, the Russian Federation, the Slovak Republic, Slovenia, and Turkey.

aggregated into 10 sector levels after calculating the total labor income for each of the 18 categories. Among the 10 sectors, WRT, FIRE, CON, and OTH are a combination of the 18 sector categories. Taking a close look at the data, we find significant differences in the size of employment and the average earnings at the 18-sector level even within the same category at the 10-sector level. Therefore, if any of the 18-sector-level values are missing, we do not impute the labor income for their 10-sector level. We relax this conservative computation for AGR and the countries without 18-sector-level employment data. Regarding AGR, many countries do not have separate earnings data for the 18-sector-level "fishery" from the "agriculture" sector. In those cases, we assume that the employees in the agriculture sector and in the fishery sector have the same level of earnings on average.[9] For the countries and regions for which detailed employment data are not available,[10] we use the GGDC employment data and multiply them by the simple average of the available 18-sector earnings data within each of the 10-sector categories. Appendix 4 summarizes the aggregation scheme.

Regarding the earnings data, weekly or hourly earnings are only available for some countries.[11] We multiply the hourly working hour data by the weekly working hour data obtained from ILOSTAT. Multiplying weekly earnings by 4.33 turns them into monthly figures. As for the hourly working hours and the number of employees, we interpolate and extrapolate the missing values by assuming monotonic time trends. If possible, we estimate the time trend for the 2000s and the 1990s separately.[12]

We calculate the broader sector labor income share based on the ten-sector-level economic activities. They are the average of the labor income share in ten sectors weighted by the number of employees at the 10-sector level. Note that we compute two labor income shares for the tertiary

[9] The impact of using the agriculture sector earnings as a proxy for the fishery sector earnings on the calculation of the labor income share in AGR should be small, as the size of the fishery sector is small relative to that of agriculture.

[10] The People's Republic of China, Taipei China, and the United States.

[11] Weekly earnings are available for the dataset for Australia, Egypt, Great Britain, United States, Canada, and Ireland. Hourly wages are available in some of the datasets for Denmark, Spain, Sweden, Australia, Austria, Germany, and Malta.

[12] One exception is Canada, where only the data for 2016 are available. We extrapolate the data to every year.

sector, one including PU, WRT, TRA, FIRE, GOV, and OTH and the other excluding GOV and OTH. We exclude these two sectors because they require careful attention. Studies often exclude GOV from the computation of the labor income share to avoid complications in the interpretation of the government sector regarding taxes and subsidies (Gomme and Rupert 2004). Moreover, its comparability is limited, as countries differ in accounting for the government output. For example, while some countries measure the output using solely wages, others impute capital compensation.[13] With regard to OTH, we exclude it from the alternative computation since it includes a sub-sector for which the labor income share is one. The included sub-sector is "activities of private households as employers and undifferentiated production activities of private households"; as this sector's output solely consists of labor compensation, the labor income share of this sector should be one.[14]

With the conservative aggregation and limited imputation method at the cost of a smaller number of observations, we still have unreliable values that exceed 1. Of 4221 calculated labor income shares, 275 are above 1 throughout the 10 sectors. We eliminate them from our sample individually, for the entire sector for the specific country, or for whole datasets. First, if we observe that hikes in either employment or earnings cause the unreliable values, for example in Peru in the year 2002, we eliminate those observations. Secondly, if we observe multiple unreliable values in a specific sector, we eliminate all the values for the sector, for example AGR and OTH for Brazil. In this case, we suspect that the unreliable values could be due to the sector-specific characteristics. For example, in the construction sector, the number of employees could be the accumulation of the headcount of short-time workers, while the earnings are for full-time workers. As another example, the degree of inclusion of the informal sector may vary among value added, earnings, and employment. In those cases, we cannot obtain a meaningful labor income share with the available dataset, so we eliminate those sectors. Thirdly, for the countries that have multiple data sources for

[13] For a further discussion on growth accounting for the government sector, see for example Mas (2005).

[14] For a further discussion on this sector, see for example the EU KLEMS Consortium's "EU KLEMS Growth and Productivity Accounts Version 1" (2007). http://www.euklems.net/data/EUKLEMS_Growth_and_Productivity_Accounts_Part_II_Sources.pdf.

computing the labor income, if some of them include unreliable values in addition to having unignorable differences from other sources, we drop all the calculated values from the same dataset, for example for Brazil after the year 2003, as this might cause a problem when we analyze the change over time. After these eliminations, 3868 observations remain in total.

4.2 Descriptive Evidence

We categorize the 10 GGDC disaggregated sectors into the following 3 broad categories: (1) the primary sector, consisting of AGR and MIN; (2) the secondary sector, consisting of MAN and CON; and (3) the tertiary sector, consisting of the remaining six sectors (PU, WRT, TRA, FIRE, GOV, and OTH). Table 4.3 shows the average (unweighted) figures (across all countries) for these broad sectors and the 10 disaggregated sectors. On average, employees in both the secondary and the tertiary sector enjoy about 35% of the total income, whereas in the primary sector the labor income share averages around 25%. In some countries, the labor income share in the primary sector reaches 87%. At the disaggregated level, GOV accounts for the largest share of the labor income (46%), followed by TRA, MAN, WRT, and TRA, each with an average of 40%. On the other hand, PU (16%) and MIN (22%) are the sectors with the

Table 4.3 Summary statistics of the sectoral labor income share (unweighted)

	Observations	*Mean*	*Standard deviation*	*Min*	*Max*
Primary	495	0.28	0.18	0.01	0.87
Secondary	506	0.35	0.14	0.08	0.73
Tertiary	516	0.36	0.15	0.05	0.92
AGR	317	0.40	0.25	0.01	0.97
MIN	480	0.20	0.14	0.00	0.82
MAN	492	0.40	0.14	0.07	0.97
PU	486	0.16	0.11	0.03	0.74
CON	438	0.32	0.22	0.03	1.00
WRT	419	0.40	0.16	0.04	0.97
TRA	455	0.40	0.16	0.09	0.97
FIRE	392	0.28	0.19	0.03	0.99
GOV	307	0.46	0.15	0.14	0.93
OTH	82	0.33	0.18	0.10	0.99

Source: Authors' own calculations

Note: Agriculture, hunting, forestry, and fishing (AGR); Mining and quarrying (MIN); Manufacturing (MAN); Electricity, gas, and water supply (PU); Construction (CON); Wholesale and retail trade, hotels, and restaurants (WRT); Transport, storage, and communication (TRA); Finance, insurance, real estate, and business services (FIRE); Government services (GOV); Community, social, and personal services (OTH) smallest share of the labor income. At the disaggregated level, except in PU and MIN, the maximum labor income share for the rest of the sectors crosses the 90% threshold.

4.2.1 Cross-Country Comparison by Sectors

In Fig. 4.1, we compare the unweighted regional averages of the labor income share across three broad categories. On average, labor receives the smallest share of income in the primary sectors in all the regions except the Middle East and North Africa (MENA) and sub-Saharan Africa (SSA). In East Asia and the Pacific (EAP) and North America, the labor income share is the largest in the tertiary sector, whereas in the Europe and Central Asia region, the secondary sector shows the most favorable returns to labor. Another point to note is that the average sectoral labor income share across sectors is of a similar magnitude in the Middle East and North Africa and the sub-Saharan Africa region. However, in other regions, such as North America and East Asia and the Pacific, the labor income share in the primary sectors is significantly smaller than that in the other sectors.

We next compare the broad sectoral outcomes at the country level. We find considerable variation in the labor income share estimates within each

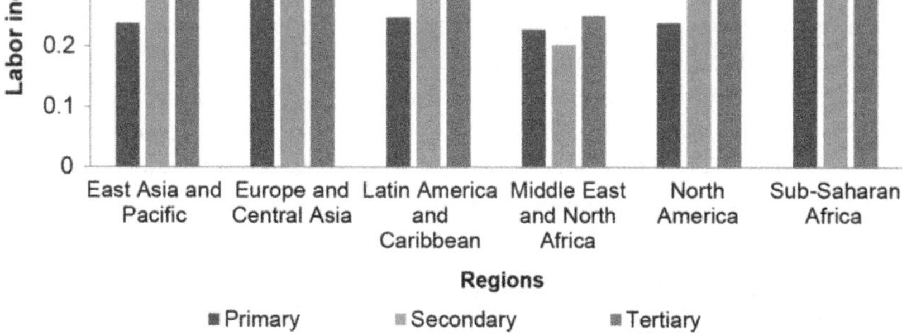

Fig. 4.1 Labor income share (broad sectors) across regions. (Source: Authors' own calculations)

region and within each broad category of sectors. In the East Asia and the Pacific region, the Republic of Korea and Taipei, China show the highest average labor income share across sectors, while in the Philippines it is as little as 2% in the primary sector. In the same region, laborers in Republic of Korea and Taipei, China enjoy a larger income share in the secondary sector. On the other hand, Spain is the only country in our sample to have an average labor income share over 50% in all sectors. In the Latin America and Caribbean region, Costa Rica accounts for the largest labor income share in both the primary sector and the tertiary sector, whereas Brazil tops the list in the secondary sector.

Overall, we find no discernable trends or similarities in the estimates of the labor income share within a country across sectors or within a sector across countries within a region. On average, the labor income share in developing countries is slightly smaller than that in developed countries (Table 4.4).

4.2.2 Country Case Studies

In this section, we provide an in-depth analysis for four developing countries: the People's Republic of China (East Asia and the Pacific), Brazil (Latin America and the Caribbean), Egypt (the Middle East and North Africa), and Botswana (sub-Saharan Africa). For the People's Republic of China, data are available for 7 sectors (MIN, MAN, PU, WRT, TRA, FIRE, and GOV) for the period from 1986 to 2007. Figure 4.2 plots the time series of the estimates of the labor income share for 7 sectors. We find a steady downward trend in GOV and MIN since the early 1990s, whereas WRT and FIRE show an upward trend. One possible reason for the declining labor income share in MIN could be that MIN has become more capital intensive over time. The labor income share is the smallest in PU, followed by MIN and manufacturing.

For Brazil, we estimate the labor income shares for 8 sectors (MIN, MAN, PU, CON, WRT, TRA, FIRE, and GOV) for the period from 1994 to 2002. The labor income shares in TRA and MAN show a downward trend and the same applies to CON since the late 1990s. The income share for laborers is small in PU, TRA, and MIN. For both the People's Republic of China and Brazil, we find a relatively smaller level of the labor income share in MIN, especially since the late 1990s. This could be due to the more capital-intensive technologies that MIN has introduced in both countries. At the same time, the smaller income share in PU could be due

Table 4.4 Labor income share (broad sectors) across countries

Region	*Country*	*Primary*	*Secondary*	*Tertiary (1)*	*Tertiary (2)*
East Asia and Pacific	Australia	0.137	0.343	0.359	0.404
	People's Republic of China	0.287	0.290	0.375	0.409
	Indonesia	0.363	0.160	0.322	0.354
	Korea, Rep. of	0.264	0.637	0.513	0.513
	Malaysia		0.363		
	Philippines	0.018	0.115	0.121	0.121
	Singapore		0.291	0.328	0.328
	Taipei, China	0.260	0.563	0.382	0.417
	Thailand	0.097	0.075	0.145	0.151
Europe and Central Asia	Austria		0.466	0.263	0.262
	Belgium	0.287	0.380	0.267	0.273
	Bulgaria	0.090	0.249	0.175	0.216
	Cyprus	0.190	0.368	0.236	0.272
	Czech Republic	0.170	0.273	0.214	0.248
	Denmark	0.094		0.702	0.702
	Estonia	0.185	0.323	0.254	0.283
	Finland	0.124	0.337	0.379	0.416
	France	0.380	0.371	0.432	0.411
	Germany	0.346	0.515	0.166	0.166
	Greece	0.323	0.340	0.278	0.278
	Hungary	0.124	0.301	0.240	0.268
	Ireland	0.191	0.269	0.203	0.203
	Italy	0.286	0.446	0.353	0.353
	Latvia	0.345	0.251	0.206	0.238
	Lithuania	0.353	0.261	0.208	0.251
	Luxembourg	0.299	0.286	0.274	0.274
	Netherlands	0.151	0.545	0.674	0.756
	Poland	0.541	0.307	0.244	0.296
	Portugal		0.302	0.630	0.632
	Russian Federation	0.119	0.293	0.245	0.270
	Slovak Republic	0.171	0.272	0.192	0.230
	Slovenia	0.633	0.346	0.319	0.363
	Spain	0.644	0.581	0.511	0.511
	Sweden	0.571	0.439	0.418	0.459
	Turkey	0.439	0.434	0.174	0.174
	United Kingdom	0.290	0.661	0.553	0.553

(*continued*)

Table 4.4 (continued)

Region	*Country*	*Primary*	*Secondary*	*Tertiary (1)*	*Tertiary (2)*
Latin America and Caribbean	Argentina	0.030	0.168	0.294	0.325
	Bolivia	0.155	0.613	0.520	0.374
	Brazil	0.239	0.586	0.453	0.487
	Chile	0.102	0.286	0.355	0.337
	Colombia	0.293	0.284	0.320	0.295
	Costa Rica	0.438	0.422	0.535	0.547
	Mexico	0.245	0.213	0.220	0.268
	Peru	0.334	0.325	0.403	0.340
Middle East and North Africa	Egypt, Arab Rep.	0.269	0.216	0.310	0.324
	Malta	0.174	0.184	0.128	0.154
North America	Canada	0.182	0.424	0.500	0.489
	United States	0.320			
Sub-Saharan Africa	Botswana	0.092	0.266	0.294	0.314
	Ethiopia (excludes Eritrea)	0.768	0.622	0.313	0.363
	Ghana	0.855	0.520	0.389	0.420
	Mauritius	0.589	0.390	0.352	0.406
	Tanzania	0.160	0.286	0.516	0.531

Source: Authors' own calculations

Note: The primary sector is composed of AGR and MIN; the secondary sector consists of MAN and CON. We use two definitions of the tertiary sector: the tertiary (1) sector consists of PU, WRT, TRA, and FIRE; the tertiary (2) sector consists of PU, WRT, TRA, FIRE, GOV, and OTH

to increasing use of computers, arguably reducing the number of employees (Fig. 4.3).

We present in Fig. 4.4 the sectoral labor income share trends for Egypt (1996–2007) and in Fig. 4.5 the same for Botswana (1997–2002). Data for both countries are available for 8 sectors (AGR, MIN, MAN, PU, CON, WRT, TRA, and FIRE). In Egypt, the labor income shares in AGR and PU show an upward trend since the early 2000s. The labor income share in MIN is by far the smallest. There is not much oscillation in the sectoral labor income share trends for other sectors. Botswana is the only country from sub-Saharan Africa for which we can estimate sectoral time series for a decent period of ten years. In Botswana, the labor income shares in both AGR and TRA increase over time. However, like the People's Republic of China, Egypt, and Brazil, MIN is the sector with the smallest share of the labor income. Overall, we find some robust evidence

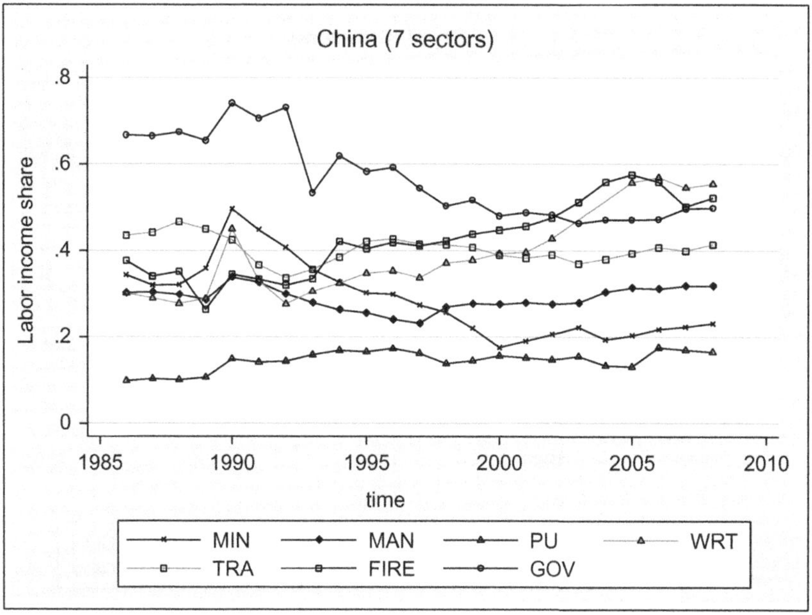

Fig. 4.2 Sectoral labor income share: The People's Republic of China. (Source: Authors' own calculations)

that PU and MIN have predominantly become sectors with a smaller share of the labor income.

4.3 Manufacturing Versus Services

In this section, we compare the labor income share trends between two broad sectors, manufacturing and services. If the elasticity of substitution between factor inputs is different from one and varies across sectors (e.g., manufacturing versus services), then the sectoral labor income share trends could follow different trajectories. In a recent study on the United States, Alvarez-Cuadrado et al. (2015) show that the larger decline in the labor income share in manufacturing relative to that in services is partly due to larger elasticity of substitution (in other words higher elasticity of substitution between capital and labor) in manufacturing associated with much faster labor-augmenting productivity growth relative to services. Alvarez-Cuadrado et al. (2015) use Jorgenson's 35-sector KLEM database for 16

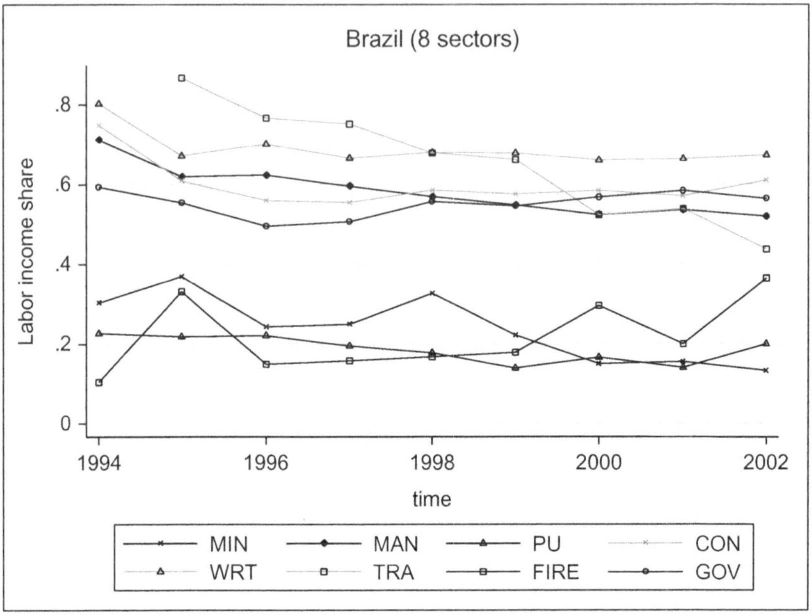

Fig. 4.3 Sectoral labor income share: Brazil. (Source: Authors' own calculations)

developed economies. They calculate the labor income share for 2 broad sectors, manufacturing and services, which they compute as the compensation of employees over the value added. In Fig. 4.6, we compare the average labor income share between the manufacturing and the service sector across 16 developed economies for the period from 1970 to 2007.

On average, the labor income share in the manufacturing sectors is larger than that in the service sectors. In countries like Hungary, Japan, and Spain, the sectoral gap in the labor income share between manufacturing and services is less than 3 percentage points, whereas, in countries like Greece, Denmark, and Portugal, the gap is more than 15 percentage points. As the next step, we investigate how changes in the sectoral labor income share are related to the observed global decline in the aggregate labor income share. This also helps us to understand better the role of structural transformation in the decline of the labor income share. Figure 4.7 shows a scatterplot of 16 countries between changes in the labor income shares in manufacturing and changes in the labor income

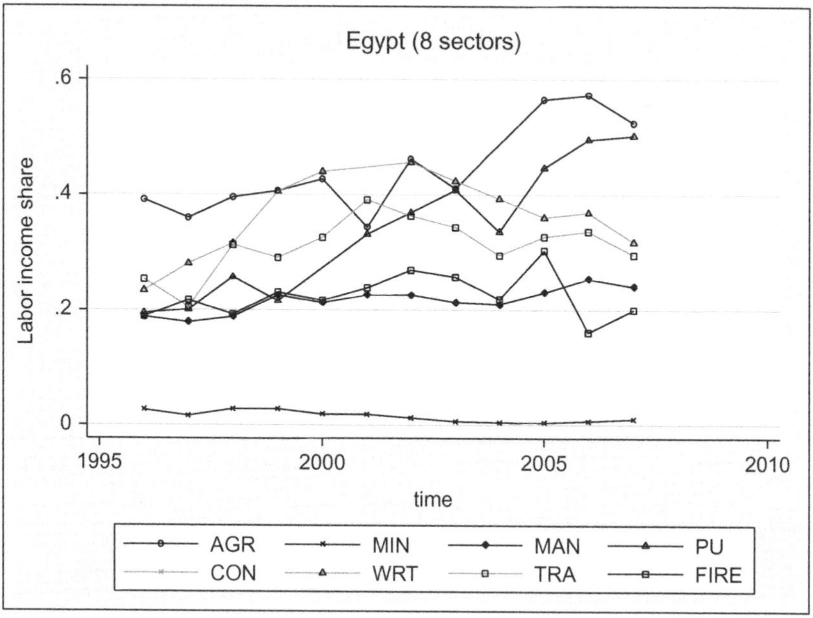

Fig. 4.4 Sectoral labor income share: Egypt. (Source: Authors' own calculations)

share in services. We find 4 categories of countries. Belgium is the only country that shows an increase in the labor income share in both sectors. The next category consists of Greece, Hungary, Denmark, and Portugal, where the labor income share declines only in the manufacturing sector.

Spain, France, and the UK make up the next group of countries, which experience a drop in the labor income share only in services. Finally, the largest group of countries (Australia, Austria, Finland, Japan, Italy, Germany, Sweden, and the Netherlands) shows a declining labor income share in both sectors. These four groups of countries demonstrate heterogeneous relationships between structural transformation and movements in the labor income share. We find the largest decline in the labor income share (in terms of percentage point differences) in services and manufacturing in Japan and Portugal, respectively.

We next derive similar statistics using our newly constructed dataset on 53 countries. Table 4.5 shows the unweighted regional average of changes in the labor income share for the primary, secondary, and tertiary sectors.

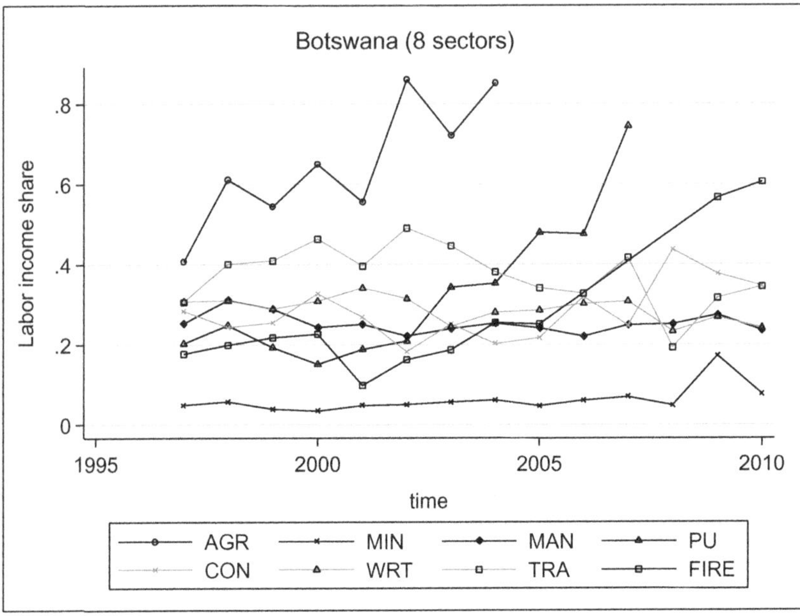

Fig. 4.5 Sectoral labor income share: Botswana. (Source: Authors' own calculations)

The outcomes for the primary sector are mixed; however, in almost all the regions (except the Middle East and North Africa), there is a decline in the labor income share in the secondary sector. It is necessary to note that, since the period of coverage in our data varies considerably across countries, we have no choice but to take the unweighted average changes based on the starting year and the ending year for each country. Overall, the average periodic change in the labor income share in the secondary sector and the primary sector shows a downturn; however, in the tertiary sector, we find exactly the opposite trend. Regional diversity is predominant. For example, in the East Asia and the Pacific region, the labor income share declines in all the sectors, whereas, in the Middle East and North Africa (MEAN) and the Latin America and Caribbean (LAC) region, all the sectors show an increase in the average labor income share.

As the final step, we plot the changes in the labor income share in the secondary sector against the change in the labor income share in the tertiary sector. In the left-hand panel of Fig. 4.8, the scatter plot shows this

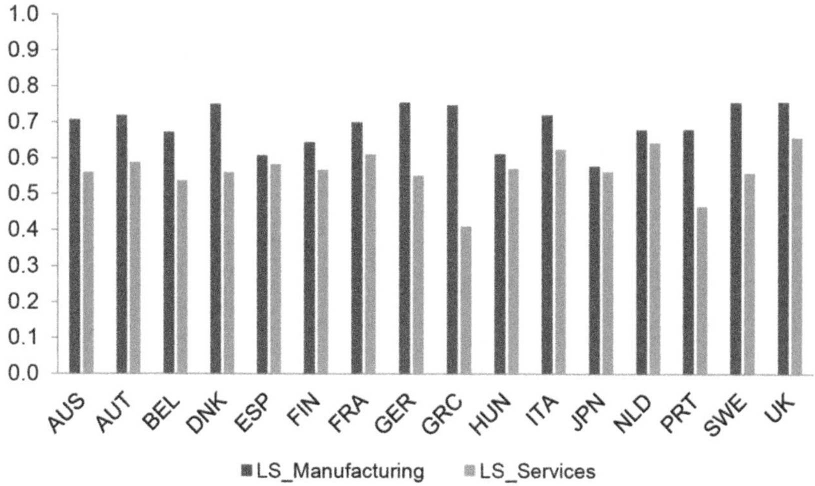

Fig. 4.6 Average sectoral labor income share for 16 developed countries, 1970–2007. (Source: Authors' elaboration based on Alvarez-Cuadrado et al. (2015); original data source: http://www.euklems.net)

relation for 27 European and Central Asian countries. It emerges that the average figures in Table 4.5 are not particularly informative regarding the simultaneous movement in the labor income share in the tertiary and the secondary sector. A glance at the graph suggests a positive correlation between the changes in the 2 sectors across the 27 European and Central Asian countries. Since our data cover a relatively shorter period, we cannot directly compare Fig. 4.8 with Fig. 4.7, even though there are some countries common in both graphs (e.g., AUT and HUN). The average periodic change in the labor income share in the tertiary sector favors laborers the most in Germany and the least in Luxembourg. Similarly, the change in the labor income share in the secondary sector is most favorable in Greece and Lithuania and least favorable in Austria.

The right-hand panel of Fig. 4.8 shows a scatter plot of the periodic change in the labor income share in the secondary sector against the same in the tertiary sector for countries from other regions, mostly comprising developing countries. Among the developing countries, the change in the labor income share in the tertiary sector is the largest in Costa Rica and the smallest in Peru. At the same time, the change in the labor income share in the secondary sector is the largest in Costa Rica and the smallest

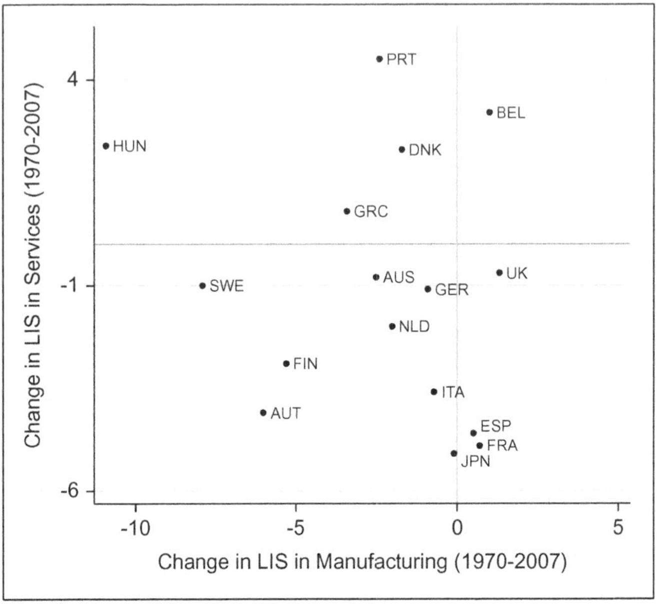

Fig. 4.7 Changes in labor income shares: manufacturing versus services, 1970–2007. (Source: Authors' elaboration based on Alvarez-Cuadrado et al. (2015); original data source: http://www.euklems.net)

Table 4.5 Changes in labor income shares (broad sectors)

	Growth of the labor income share		
	Primary	*Secondary*	*Tertiary*
East Asia and the Pacific	−0.163	−0.031	−0.012
Europe and Central Asia	0.001	−0.034	0.001
Latin America and Caribbean	0.000	0.066	0.076
Middle East and North Africa	0.020	0.114	0.068
North America	0.058	−0.147	−0.205
Sub-Saharan Africa	−0.094	−0.072	0.090
All countries	−0.024	−0.015	0.014

Source: Authors' own calculations

Note: In our sample, the data coverage varies considerably across countries; as a result, the average changes are based on the starting year and the ending year for each country

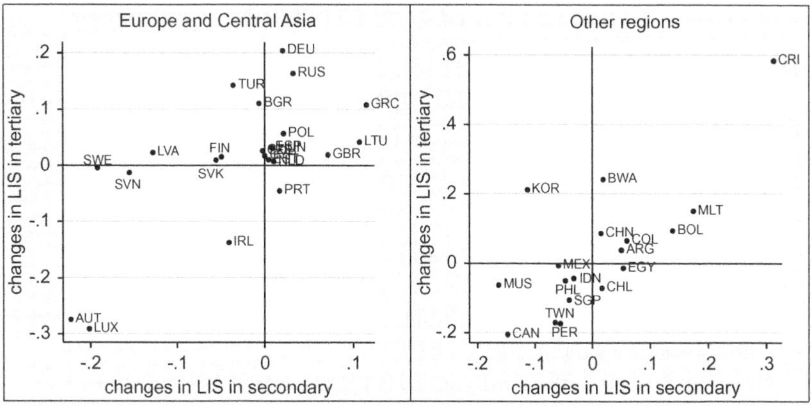

Fig. 4.8 Changes in labor income shares: manufacturing versus services (newly constructed data). (Source: Authors' own calculations. Note: In our sample, the data coverage varies considerably across countries; as a result, the average changes are based on the starting year and the ending year for each country)

in Mauritius. Like the case for countries from the Europe and Central Asia region, we find a correlation between changes in the labor income share between tertiary and secondary sectors for countries from other regions. However, such findings should be interpreted with caution, mainly due to the unbalanced nature of our panel data. We have missing observations for many sectors, and data are available only for a few years for many countries.

Appendix 1. Employment by Sex and Economic Activity (Thousands)

The employed comprise all persons of working age who, during a specified brief period, were in the following categories: (a) paid employment (whether at work or with a job but not at work); or (b) self-employment (whether at work or with an enterprise but not at work). The data are disaggregated by economic activity according to the latest version of the International Standard Industrial Classification of All Economic Activities (ISIC) available for that year. Economic activity refers to the main activity of the establishment in which a person worked during the reference period and depends not on the specific duties or functions of the person's job but on the characteristics of the economic unit in which this person worked.

Part 1: Countries Covered by the GGDC 10-sector Database

Argentina

Source: Permanent Household Survey (Urban) [Encuesta Permanente de Hogares (Urban)]

Period: 1991–2010

Notes .

- Methodology revised every year from 1991 to 2002.
- Break in series in 2003.
- Data reference period: annual or annual average in 1991–1995; incomplete years in 1996–2010.
- Age coverage—minimum age: 10 years from 1996 to 2003.
- Notes on total in 2007: "Nonstandard age group: including 10–14."
- The survey covers only metropolitan areas and main cities.
- Warning on the use of statistical series: researchers should use statistical series published after January 2007 and before December 2015 with caution. The Instituto Nacional de Estadicitica y Censos (INDEC), based on the statement in decrees 181/15 and 55/16, is undertaking the investigations required to ensure the regularity of data collection and processing.

Bolivia

Source: Household Survey [Encuesta de Hogares]

Period: 1999 and 2005–2009

Notes

- Methodology revised in 2005.
- The data reference period of 1999 is November.
- B in 2008 and 2009 is unreliable according to the ILO's note.
- Q in 2009 is unreliable according to the ILO's note.

Botswana (1/2)

Source: Labor Force Survey

Period: 1996, 1998, 2000, 2003, and 2006

Notes

- Data reference period: annual or annual average for the years 1996, 1998, 2000, 2003, and 2006.

- Population coverage: including armed forces and/or conscripts in 1996, 1998, 2000, 2003, and 2006.
- Age coverage—minimum age: 12 years in 1996, 1998, 2000, 2003, and 2006.
- Note on A for 1996, 1998, 2000, 2003, and 2006: "Nonstandard economic activity: excluding B."

Botswana (2/2)
Source: Botswana Core Welfare Indicators (Poverty) Survey
Period: 2009

- Q in 2009 is unreliable according to the ILO's note.

Brazil (1/2)
Source: Annual Labor Force Survey [Pesquisa Nacional por Amostra de Domicílios]
Period: 1995–1999, 2001–2009, and 2011
Note:

- Q in 1996, 1999, 2002, 2006–2009, and 2011 is unreliable according to the ILO's notes.

c.f. Another source, the "Monthly Employment Survey" [Pesquisa Mensal de Emprego], is available for the years 2004–2013. This covers only metropolitan areas and main cities.
Chile (1/3)
Source: Population census [Censos de población]
Period: 2002
Note:

- The reference period is April.

Chile (2/3)
Source: National Survey on Socio-Economic Conditions [Encuesta de Caracterización Socioeconómica Nacional]
Period: 2011 (2013 is available)
Chile (3/3)
Source: National Employment Survey [Encuesta Nacional de Empleo]
Period: 2009 and 2010 (2011–2013 are also available)

Note:

- B-I in 2009 is quite different from that in 2010.

The People's Republic of China
Source: Employment and wage statistics based on enterprises' reports
Period: 1986–2008
Notes

- The reference period is annual or the annual average in 1995, 1996, and 1998–2008.
- The definition of "working time" is "hours actually worked" in 1995, 1996, and 1998–2008.
- Note on A for 1986–2008: "Nonstandard economic activity: including B."
- Note on C for 1986–2008: "Nonstandard economic activity: mining only."
- Note on G for 1986–2002 and 2005–2008: "Nonstandard economic activity: including H."
- Note on I for 2003: "Nonstandard economic activity: excluding communication."
- Note on L for 1986–2008: "Nonstandard economic activity: state organs, social organizations."
- Note on L for 1986–2002: "Nonstandard economic activity: including sporting activities and activities of membership organizations not elsewhere classified."

Colombia
Source: Integrated Household Survey [Gran Encuesta Integrada de Hogares]
Period: 2002–2011 (2012 and 2013 are available)
Notes

- Methodology revised in 2010.
- Age coverage—minimum age: 10 years in rural areas and 12 years in urban areas in 2004, 2008, and 2009.
- Data reference period: annual or annual average in 2009.
- Population coverage: excluding both institutional population and armed forces and/or conscripts in 2009.

- Note on A for 2004 and 2008: "Nonstandard economic activity: including B."
- Note on G for 2004 and 2008: "Nonstandard economic activity: including H."
- Note on L for 2004 and 2008: "Nonstandard economic activity: including M-O."

Costa Rica
Source: National Household Survey [Encuesta Nacional de Hogares]
Period: 1996–2008 (the ILO's metadata description is available from 1997)
Notes

- The reference period is July in 1997–2008.
- Age coverage—minimum age: 12 years in 1997–2008.
- Note on L for 1996–2000: "Nonstandard economic activity: including O."

Denmark
Source: EU Labour Force Survey
Period: 1992–2007
Notes

- Methodology revised in 2005.
- Data reference period: annual or annual average.
- B in 1996–2007 is unreliable according to the ILO's notes.
- C in 1992–2004 is unreliable according to the ILO's notes.
- P in 1995 and 1997–2006 is unreliable according to the ILO's notes.
- Q in 1993, 1999, 2000, 2003, 2006, and 2007 is unreliable according to the ILO's notes.
- X in 1995, 1996, 1998, 2001–2005, 2006, and 2007 is unreliable according to the ILO's notes.

Egypt (1/2)
Source: Population Census
Period: 1996
Note:

- The reference period is November.

- Note on A for 1996: "Nonstandard economic activity: including B."
- Note on J for 1996: "Nonstandard economic activity: including K."
- Note on O for 1996: "Nonstandard economic activity: including P-Q."

Egypt (2/2)
Source: Labour Force Sample Survey
Period: 1997–2008
Notes

- Data reference periods: incomplete year.
- Population coverage: excluding armed forces and/or conscripts.
- Age coverage—maximum age: 64 years.
- Q in 2008 is unreliable according to the ILO's note.

Ethiopia
Source: National Labor Force Survey
Period: 1999 and 2005
France
Source: EU Labour Force Survey
Period: 1992–2007
Notes

- The methodology changed in 2003 and 2005.
- Data reference period: annual or annual average.
- B in 2004 and 2007 is unreliable according to the ILO's note.
- C in 2004 is unreliable according to the ILO's note.
- Q in 1992–2002, 2004, 2006, and 2007 is unreliable according to the ILO's note.
- X in 1994–2002 is unreliable according to the ILO's note.

Ghana
Source: Living Standards Survey [Déclaration annuelle de Données Sociales]
Period: 2006
India
Source: National Sample Survey
Period: 2000, 2005, and 2010
Notes

- Data reference period: non-calendar year.
- Q in 2000 and 2005 is unreliable according to the ILO's note.

c.f. Another resource, the "Employment–Unemployment Survey," is available for 2005 and 2010. The values are larger than those of the National Sample Survey, especially for activity A-E.

Indonesia

Source: National Labour Force Survey

Period: 2000–2010

Notes

- Methodology revised in 2000.
- Q in 2003, 2005, and 2010 is unreliable according to the ILO's note.

Italy

Source: EU Labour Force Survey

Period: 1992–2007

Note:

- The methodology changed in 1992 and 2005.
- Unemployment definition: two criteria (not in employment and seeking).
- Data reference period: annual or annual average.

Japan

Source: Labour Force Survey

Period: 2003, 2004, and 2007

Note:

- Data reference period: annual or annual average in 2003 and 2004.

Kenya

c.f. A labor force survey is available in 1999.

Republic of Korea

Source: Economically Active Population Survey

Period: 1992–2008

Note:

- Break in series in 1999.

c.f. Another source, "Population Census," is available for the year 2000. Its reference period is November.

Malaysia
Source: Labor Force Survey
Period: 2001–2009
Notes

- Data reference period: annual or annual average.
- Population coverage: excluding armed forces and/or conscripts.

Mauritius (1/2)
Source: Continuous Multi-Purpose Household Survey
Period: 1995 and 2001–2010
Notes

- The methodology changed in 2001 and 2003.
- Data reference period: annual or annual average in 1995.
- Population coverage: excluding armed forces and/or conscripts in 1995.
- Age coverage—minimum age: 12 years in 1995 and 16 years after 2001.
- Note on A for 1995: "Nonstandard economic activity: including B."
- Note on J for 1995: "Nonstandard economic activity: including K."
- Note on M for 1995: "Nonstandard economic activity: including N."
- Note on O for 1995: "Nonstandard economic activity: including P-Q."
- C in 2002, 2004, 2005, and 2010 is unreliable according to the ILO's note.
- Q in 2004–2010 is unreliable according to the ILO's note.
- X in 2002 is unreliable according to the ILO's note.

Mauritius (2/2)
Source: Population Census
Period: 2000
Notes

- Data reference period: July.
- Age coverage—minimum age: 12 years.

c.f. Another source, "Official Estimation," is available for the years 2000–2008. Its data reference period is annual or annual average.

Mexico

Source: National Occupation and Employment Survey [Encuesta Nacional de Ocupación y Empleo]

Period: 1991, 1993, and 1995–2004

Note:

- The methodology changed in 1991, 1993, and 2004.

c.f. Another source, the Population Census [Censos de población], is available for 2000. Its data reference period is February and its lowest age coverage is 12 years.

Morocco

c.f. The National Employment Survey [Enquête nationale sur l'emploi] is available for the years 2000, 2002–2008, and 2011–2013.

The Netherlands

Source: EU Labour Force Survey

Period: 1992–2007

Notes

- Methodology revised in 2005.
- B in 1992–1996 and 1998–2007 is unreliable according to the ILO's note.
- P in 2000–2002 and 2004 is unreliable according to the ILO's note.
- Q in 1992, 1994–1999, 2002–2004, and 2005–2007 is unreliable according to the ILO's note.

Nigeria

c.f. Official estimates are available for the years 2005–2009.

Peru

Source: National Household Survey [Encuesta Nacional de Hogares]

Period: 2002–2011 (2012 and 2013 are also available)

c.f. An alternative source, the Permanent Employment Survey (Urban) [Encuesta permanente de Empleo (Urban)], is available for the period 1996–2009, though it covers only main cities or metropolitan areas.

The Philippines (1/2)

Source: Employment, Hours, and Earnings Survey

Period: 1996–1999, 2001, 2003, 2005, 2006, and 2008

Notes

- Break in series: unspecified type of break in 1999.
- Establishment size coverage: all establishments with at least 10 employees
  in 1996–1998 and at least 20 employees in 1999, 2001, 2003, 2005, 2006, and 2008.
- Data reference period: annual or annual average in 1996–1999, 2001, 2003, 2005, 2006, and 2008.
- Note on M for 1996–1999, 2001, 2003, 2005, 2006, and 2008: "Nonstandard economic activity: private education only."
- Note on N for 1996–1999, 2001, 2003, 2005, 2006, and 2008: "Nonstandard economic activity: excluding public medical, dental and other health services."

The Philippines (2/2)
Source: Labour Force Survey
Period: 2002
Notes

- Data reference period: annual or annual average.
- Population coverage: excluding armed forces and/or conscripts.
- The values are quite different (sometimes values are more than 10 times bigger than those of source (1/2))

Senegal
c.f. The Survey to Monitor Poverty in Senegal [Enquête de Suivi de la Pauvreté au Sénégal] is available for the year 2006.
Singapore
Source: Comprehensive Labour Force Survey
Period: 1985–1989, 1991–1999, and 2001–2005
Notes

- Methodology revised in 2001.
- Data reference period: June for 1994–2005.
- Population coverage: nationals and residents for 1994–2005.
- Notes on A for 1985–1989 and 1991–1996: "Nonstandard economic activity: including B"; 1997–1999 and 2001–2005: "Including B-C, E, X."

- Note on G for 1997: "Nonstandard economic activity: including H."
- Note on J for 1997: "Nonstandard economic activity: including K."
- Notes on L for 1997: "Nonstandard economic activity: including M-Q"; for 1998, 1999, and 2001–2005: "Including M."
- Note on M for 1985–1989 and 1991–1996: "Nonstandard economic activity: including N."

c.f. An alternative source, "Population Census," is available in 2000.

South Africa

c.f. The Quarterly Labour Force Survey is available from 2000 to 2013

Spain

Source: EU Labor Force Survey

Period: 1992–2007

Notes

- Methodology revised in 1993, 2001, and 2005.
- Data reference period: annual or annual average.
- Q in 1992, 1994–1996, 1998–2000, 2003, and 2007 is unreliable according to the ILO's note.

Sweden

Source: EU Labour Force Survey

Period: 1995–2007

Notes

- Methodology revised in 2005.
- Data reference period: annual or annual average.
- B is unreliable in 1995–2004, 2006, and 2007 according to the ILO's note.
- C is unreliable in 1995, 1996, and 1999 according to the ILO's note.
- P is unreliable in 1998, 1999, 2001, and 2005–2007 according to the ILO's note.
- Q is unreliable in 2001–2002, 2004, and 2006–2007.
- X is unreliable in 1996–2000, 2004, and 2005.

c.f. The Labour Force Survey is available in 1987–1989.

Tanzania

Source: Labour Force Survey

Period: 2006

Note:

- Methodology revised in 2006.

Thailand
Source: Labour Force Survey
Period: 2002–2010
Notes

- Methodology revised in 2010.
- Data reference period: third quarter in the years 2002 and 2003.
- Population coverage: excluding armed forces and/or conscripts in 2002 and 2003.
- Nonstandard economic activity: including repair and installation services for all activities in 2004–2008.

United Kingdom
Source: EU Labour Force Survey
Period: 1992–2007
Notes

- Methodology revised in 2005.
- Data reference period: annual or annual average for the years 1992–2007.
- B in the years 1995–1997, 1999–2001, 2003, and 2004 is unreliable according to the ILO's note.
- Q in the years 1999, 2003, and 2004 is unreliable according to the ILO's note.

c.f. An alternative source, "Official Estimates," is available from 1996 to 2005.

Part 2: Countries Covered by the Socio-Economic Account

Australia
Source: Labour Force Survey
Period: 1990–2008
Note:

- Break in series in 1994 and 2006.

Austria
Source: EU Labour Force Survey
Period: 1995–2007
Notes

- Break in series in 2005.
- Data reference period: annual or annual average.
- B in 1998, 2000, and 2004–2007 is unreliable according to the ILO's note.
- Q in 1994–2004 is unreliable according to the ILO's note.

Belgium
Source: EU Labour Force Survey
Period: 1992–2007
Note:

- Break in series in 1999, 2001, and 2005.
- Data reference period: annual or annual average.
- B in 1992, 1994, 1996, 1997, 2006, and 2007 is unreliable according to the ILO's note.
- Q in 2002 and 2003 is unreliable according to the ILO's note.

c.f. Another source, "Official Estimates [Estimations officielles]," is available for 1994–1999.

Bulgaria
Source: EU Labour Force Survey
Period: 2000–2007
Notes

- Break in series in 2001, 2003, and 2005.
- Data reference period: annual or annual average.
- B in 1992, 1994, 1996, 1997, 2006, and 2007 is unreliable according to the ILO's note.
- P in 2000, 2002, 2004, 2006, and 2007 is unreliable according to the ILO's note.
- Q in 2004, 2006, and 2007 is unreliable according to the ILO's note.
- X in 2002 and 2004 is unreliable according to the ILO's note.

c.f. Another source, "Official Estimates," is available for 1996–2006. (The number of employees in the agriculture sector has the largest difference among all the sectors. The number reported here is almost double to triple to that of the EU LFS). In addition, the Population Census is available for 2001.

Canada
Source: Labour Force Survey
Period: 2016

Cyprus
Source: EU Labour Force Survey
Period: 2000–2007
Notes

- Break in series in 2005.
- B in 2001–2004 and 2006–2007 is unreliable according to the ILO's note.
- C in 2001–2004 and 2006–2007 is unreliable according to the ILO's note.

Czech Republic
Source: EU Labour Force Survey
Period: 1993–2007
Notes

- Break in series in 2005.
- Data reference period: annual or annual average.
- B in 1997 to 2004 is unreliable according to the ILO's note.
- P in 1997 to 2004 and 2007 is unreliable according to the ILO's note.
- Q in 1997 to 2004, 2006, and 2007 is unreliable according to the ILO's note.
- X in 1997 to 2001, 2004, 2006, and 2007 is unreliable according to the ILO's note.

Estonia (1/2)
Source: Labour Force Survey
Period: 1989–1996
Notes

- Data reference period: annual or annual average.

- Population coverage: including armed forces and/or conscripts.
- Age coverage—maximum age: 69 years.

Estonia (2/2)
Source: EU Labour Force Survey
Period: 1997–2007
Notes

- Break in series in 2001 and 2005.
- Data reference period: annual or annual average.
- B in 1997, 1999, 2000, 2002–2004, 2006, and 2007 is unreliable according to the ILO's note.
- C in 1997, 2000, and 2002–2004 is unreliable according to the ILO's note.
- J in 1997, 2000, and 2002–2004 is unreliable according to the ILO's note.
- P in 1997–1999 and 2004–2006 is unreliable according to the ILO's note.
- Q in 2007 is unreliable according to the ILO's note.
- X in 2005–2007 is unreliable according to the ILO's note.

Finland (1/2)
Source: Labour Force Survey
Period: 1989
Note:

- Data reference period: annual or annual average.

Finland (2/2)
Source: EU Labour Force Survey
Period: 1990–2007
Notes

- Break in series in 2000 and 2005.
- Data reference period: annual or annual average.
- B in 1995, 1996, 1998, 1999, 2001–2004, 2006, and 2007 is unreliable according to the ILO's note.
- C in 1997 and 2001 is unreliable according to the ILO's note.

- P in 1995, 1996, 2004, 2006, and 2007 is unreliable according to the ILO's note.
- X in 1995 is unreliable according to the ILO's note.

Germany
Source: EU Labour Force Survey
Period: 1992–2007
Notes

- Break in series in 2005.
- Data reference period: annual or annual average.
- B in 1997, 2003, and 2004 is unreliable according to the ILO's note.

Greece
Source: EU Labour Force Survey
Period: 1992–2007
Notes

- Methodology revised in 1998, 2001, 2004, and 2005.
- Q in 1992–1997, 1999, 2002, 2006, and 2007 is unreliable according to the ILO's note.

Hungary (1/2)
Source: Labour Force Survey
Period: 1992–1995
Note:

- Data reference period: annual or annual average.
- Population coverage: excluding armed forces and/or conscripts.
- Age coverage—maximum age: 74 years.
- Note on A for 1992–1995: "Nonstandard economic activity: including B."

Hungary (2/2)
Source: EU Labour Force Survey
Period: 1996–2007
Notes

- Methodology change in 2001 and 2005.

- Data reference period: annual or annual average.
- B in 1996–2000, 2002–2004, 2006, and 2007 is unreliable according to the ILO's note.
- P in 1996–2000, 2002–2004, 2006, and 2007 is unreliable according to the ILO's note.
- Q in 1996–2000, 2002–2004, 2006, and 2007 is unreliable according to the ILO's note.

Ireland
Source: EU Labour Force Survey
Period: 1992–2007
Notes

- Methodology change in 2005.
- Data reference period: annual or annual average.
- B in 1998–2004, 2006, and 2007 is unreliable according to the ILO's note.
- Q in 1992–1997, 2006, and 2007 is unreliable according to the ILO's note.
- X in 1992, 1993, 1997, and 2004 is unreliable according to the ILO's note.

Latvia (1/2)
Source: Labour Force Survey
Period: 1996 and 1997
Notes

- Data reference period: annual or annual average.
- Population coverage: excluding armed forces and/or conscripts.

Latvia (2/2)
Source: EU Labour Force Survey
Period: 1998–2007
Notes

- Methodology revised in 2002 and 2005.
- Data reference period: annual or annual average.
- B in 1998, 2000, 2001, 2003, 2004, and 2006 is unreliable according to the ILO's note.

- C in 1998–2001, 2003, and 2004 is unreliable according to the ILO's note.
- J in 2001 and 2003 is unreliable according to the ILO's note.
- Q in 1998–2001, 2003, and 2004 is unreliable according to the ILO's note.
- X in 2006 and 2007 is unreliable according to the ILO's note.

Lithuania (1/2)
Source: Labour Force Survey
Period: 1997
Notes

- Data reference period: annual or annual average.
- Population coverage: excluding armed forces and/or conscripts.
- Age coverage—minimum age: 14 years.
- Note on A for 1997: "Nonstandard economic activity: including B."

Lithuania (2/2)
Source: EU Labour Force Survey
Period: 1998–2007
Notes

- Methodology change in 2002 and 2005.
- Data reference period: annual or annual average.
- B in 1998–2001, 2003–2004, 2006, and 2007 is unreliable according to the ILO's note.
- C in 1998–2001, 2003–2004, 2006, and 2007 is unreliable according to the ILO's note.
- J in 2001 and 2003–2007 is unreliable according to the ILO's note.
- P in 1998–2001, 2003–2004, 2006, and 2007 is unreliable according to the ILO's note.

c.f. Another source, the "Population Census," is available in 2001.
Luxembourg
Source: EU Labour Force Survey
Period: 1992–2007
Notes

- Methodology revised in 2003, 2005, and 2007.

- Data reference period: annual or annual average.
- C in 1992–1999, 2004, and 2006 is unreliable according to the ILO's note.
- E in 1993–2002 and 2004 is unreliable according to the ILO's note.
- K in 1992 is unreliable according to the ILO's note.
- X in 1993–2002, 2004, and 2006 is unreliable according to the ILO's note.

c.f. Another resource, "Official Estimates [Estimations officielles]," is available for 1995–2008. The total employment is almost 30% higher than that of the EU Labour Force Survey. Note that its data reference period is annual or annual average. The geographical coverage is nonstandard. The population coverage includes armed forces and/or conscripts. The institutional sector coverage is nonstandard.

Malta
Source: EU Labour Force Survey
Period: 2000–2007
Notes

- Methodology revised in 2005.
- Data reference period: annual or annual average.
- A in 2000–2002 and 2004 is unreliable according to the ILO's note.
- B in 2000–2004, 2006, and 2007 is unreliable according to the ILO's note.
- E in 2000 and 2002 is unreliable according to the ILO's note.
- P in 2006 and 2007 is unreliable according to the ILO's note.
- Q in 2002, 2006, and 2007 is unreliable according to the ILO's note.

Poland (1/2)
Source: Labour Force Survey
Period: 1995–1996
Notes

- Data reference period: annual or annual average.
- Population coverage: excluding armed forces and/or conscripts.

Poland (2/2)
Source: EU Labour Force Survey
Period: 2000–2007

Notes

- Methodology revised in 2005.
- Data reference period: annual or annual average.
- B in 2000–2004, 2006, and 2007 is unreliable according to the ILO's note.
- P in 2000–2004 and 2006 is unreliable according to the ILO's note.
- X in 2006 and 2007 is unreliable according to the ILO's note.

c.f. Another source, "Population Census," is available for 2002. Its data reference period is May.

Portugal
Source: EU Labour Force Survey
Period: 1992–2007
Notes

- Methodology revised in 2005.
- Data reference period: annual or annual average.
- B is unreliable in 2000–2004, 2006, and 2007 according to the ILO's note.
- P is unreliable in 2000–2004 and 2006 according to the ILO's note.
- X in 2006 and 2007 is unreliable according to the ILO's note.

c.f. Another data source, Population censuses [Recensements de population], is available in 2001. Its reference period is March.

Romania (1/2)
Source: Household Labour Force Survey
Period: 1994–1996
Notes

- Data reference period: March.
- Age coverage—minimum age: 14 years.
- Note on O for 1994–1996: "Nonstandard economic activity: including P-Q."

Romania (2/2)
Source: EU Labour Force Survey
Period: 1997–2007
Notes

- Methodology revised in 2002, 2003, and 2005.
- Data reference period: annual or annual average.
- B in 1997–2001, 2004, 2006, and 2007 is unreliable according to the ILO's note.
- Q in 2004, 2006, and 2007 is unreliable according to the ILO's note.

Russian Federation (1/2)
Source: Official Estimates
Period: 1990–1997 (2005, 2012, and 2013 are also available)
Notes

- Data reference period: annual or annual average.
- Note on G for 1990–1996: "Nonstandard economic activity: including H."
- Note on J for 1990–1996: "Nonstandard economic activity: including K."
- Note on P for 1990–1996: "Nonstandard economic activity: including P and X."

Russian Federation (2/2)
Source: Population Survey on Employment Problems
Period: 1998–2016
Notes

- Methodology revised in 2010.
- Data reference period: annual or annual average in 1997–2009.
- Geographical coverage: total national, excluding some areas in 1997–2009.
- Population coverage: excluding institutional population in 1997–2009.
- Age coverage—maximum age: 72 years in 1997–2009.
- Q in 2011, 2013, and 2014 is unreliable according to the ILO's note.
- A, J, L, O, and P show a huge difference between (1/2) and (2/2).

Slovakia
Source: EU Labour Force Survey
Period: 1994–2007
Notes

- Methodology change in 2005.
- B in 2004, 2006, and 2007 is unreliable according to the ILO's note.
- P in 1998–2001 is unreliable according to the ILO's note.
- Q in 2003, 2006, and 2007 is unreliable according to the ILO's note.
- X in 2003, 2006, and 2007 is unreliable according to the ILO's note.

c.f. Another source, "Labour Costs," is available in 2001. Its data reference period is May.

Slovenia (1/2)
Source: Labour Force Survey
Period: 1993–1995
Note:

- Data reference period: May.

Slovenia (2/2)
Source: EU Labour Force Survey
Period: 1996–2007
Notes

- Methodology revised in 2005.
- Data reference period: annual or annual average.
- B in 1998, 1999, 2004, 2006, and 2007 is unreliable according to the ILO's note.
- C in 1996–2004 is unreliable according to the ILO's note.
- E in 1998–2000, 2003, and 2004 is unreliable according to the ILO's note.
- P in 1996–1999, 2001, 2002, 2004, 2006, and 2007 is unreliable according to the ILO's note.
- Q in 2007 is unreliable according to the ILO's note.
- X in 1996–2004 is unreliable according to the ILO's note.

Turkey
Source: EU Labour Force Survey
Period: 2006–2007
Note:

- Data reference period: annual or annual average.

Appendix 2. Notes on Earnings Data

Part 1: Countries Covered by the GGDC 10-sector Database

Argentina

Source: Permanent Household Survey (Urban) [Encuesta Permanente de Hogares (Urban)]
Period: 2004–2006 and 2008–2010
Notes

- The survey covers only metropolitan areas and main cities.
- Warning on the use of statistical series: researchers should use the statistical series published after January 2007 and before December 2015 with caution. The INDEC, based on the statement in decrees 181/15 and 55/16, is undertaking the investigations required to ensure the regularity of data collection and processing.

Bolivia

Source: Household Survey [Encuesta de Hogares]
Period: 2005–2009
Note:

- B in 2006 is unreliable according to the ILO's note.

Botswana

Source: Survey of Employment and Employees
Period: 1997–2011
Notes

- The reference period is March in 1998, 2003, and 2005; September in 1999–2002, 2004, and 2006–2008; and annual or annual average in 2009–2011.
- The population coverage in 1999–2005 is nationals and residents.
- The definition of the "working time" concept used in 1999–2011 is "hours actually worked."
- Note on A for 1997–2005: "Nonstandard economic activity: including B."
- Note on A for 2006–2008: "Nonstandard economic activity: excluding hunting and forestry."

- Note on E for 2006–2008: "Nonstandard economic activity: excluding gas."
- Note on total: "Nonstandard economic activity: public sector only."

Brazil

Source: Other administrative records and related sources [Otros registros administrativos y fuentes relacionadas]

Period: 1994–2002

Notes

- Break in series: new or revalued currency in 1995.
- Working time concept: hours actually worked in 1995 and 1998–2002.
- Data reference period: December for the years 1998–2002.
- Note on A for 1994–2002: "Nonstandard economic activity: including B."
- Note on I for 1994–2002: "Nonstandard economic activity: services."

c.f. The Annual Labour Force Survey [Pesquisa Nacional por Amostra de Domicílios] is available for 2003–2009 (and for 1995–1999, 2001–2009, and 2011). However, the data require careful handling, as the differences among sectors are substantial. For example, the values of B in 2005 and 2006 and X in 2005 are three digits, Q in 2004, 2005, 2007, and 2008 is four digits, while other values are 9–11 digits.

Chile (1/2)

Source: Index for Remuneration and Labour Cost [Índice de Remuneraciones y Costo de la Mano de Obra]

Period: 2006–2008

Notes

- The reference period is April.
- The definition of "working time" is "hours actually worked."
- Note on C for 2006–2008: "Nonstandard economic activity: including D-Q."

Chile (2/2)

Source: National Survey on Socio-Economic Conditions [Encuesta de Caracterización Socioeconómica Nacional]

Period: 2011 (2013 is available)

The People's Republic of China

Source: Employment and wage statistics based on enterprises' reports

Period: 1986–2008

Notes

- The reference period is annual or annual average in 1995, 1996, and 1998–2008.
- The definition of "working time" is "hours actually worked" in 1995, 1996, and 1998–2008.
- Note on A for 1986–2008: "Nonstandard economic activity: including B."
- Note on C for 1986–2008: "Nonstandard economic activity: mining only."
- Note on G for 1986–2002 and 2005–2008: "Nonstandard economic activity: including H."
- Note on I for 2003: "Nonstandard economic activity: excluding communication."
- Note on L for 1986–2008: "Nonstandard economic activity: state organs, social organizations."
- Note on L for 1986–2002: "Nonstandard economic activity: including sporting activities and activities of membership organizations not elsewhere classified."

Colombia

Source: Integrated Household Survey [Gran Encuesta Integrada de Hogares]

Period: 2002–2007, 2010, 2011 (2012 and 2013 are available)

Notes

- Methodology revised in 2010.
- The data reference period of 2002–2007 is the fourth quarter.
- Population coverage: excluding armed forces and/or conscripts.
- Age coverage—minimum age: 10 years.
- The definition of "working time" is "hours actually worked" in 2002–2007.
- Note on C for 2002–2007: "Nonstandard economic activity: including D-Q."

Costa Rica
Source: National Household Survey [Encuesta Nacional de Hogares]
Period: 1998–2001, 2004, 2005, and 2008
Notes

- Methodology revised in 2008.
- The reference period is July in 1998–2001, 2004, 2005, and 2008.
- Job coverage: the main job currently held in 1998–2001, 2004, 2005, and 2008.
- The definition of "working time" is "hours actually worked" in 1998–2001, 2004, 2005, and 2008.
- Note on A for 1998–2001, 2004, 2005, and 2008: "Nonstandard economic activity: including B."
- Note on C for 1998–2001, 2004, 2005, and 2008: "Nonstandard economic activity: including D-Q."

Denmark
Source: Monthly Survey of Industrial Employment and Labor Costs
Period: 1995–2007 and 2009–2011 (2012 and 2013 are available)
Notes

- Methodology revised in 2007.
- Time unit: per hour in 1995–2007 and 2009–2011.
- Data reference period: annual or annual average in 1995–2007 and 2009–2011.
- Institutional sector coverage: private sector only in 1995–2007 and 2009–2011.
- Age coverage—minimum age: nonstandard minimum age in 1996–2006.
- Working time concept: hours actually worked in 1995–2007 and 2009–2011.
- Note on C for 1995–2007: "Nonstandard economic activity: including D-Q."

Denmark—Weekly Working Hours
Source: EU Labour Force Survey
Period: 1992–2007
Notes

- Methodology revised in 2005.
- B in 1994–2004, 2006, and 2007 is unreliable according to the ILO's note.
- C in 1992–2004, 2006, and 2007 is unreliable according to the ILO's note.
- P in 1995, 1997–2004, and 2007 is unreliable according to the ILO's note.
- Q in 1993, 1999, 2000, 2003, 2004, and 2007 is unreliable according to the ILO's note.
- X in 1995, 1996, 1998, 2001–2004, 2006, and 2007 is unreliable according to the ILO's note.

Egypt (1/2)
Source: Employment, Wages, and Hours of Work Survey
Period: 1996–2007
Notes

- Time unit: per week.
- The definition of "working time" is "hours actually worked."
- The reference period is October.
- Reference group coverage: wage earners/blue collar/production workers
- Establishment size coverage: all establishments with at least 10 employees.
- Note on A for 1996–2007: "Nonstandard economic activity: including B."
- Note on C for 1996–2007: "Nonstandard economic activity: including D-Q."
- E and F in 2000 and A in 2004 have hikes.

Egypt (2/2)
Source: Labour Force Sample Survey
Period: 2008
Notes

- Q in 2008 is unreliable according to the ILO's note.
- The values are smaller than the weekly payment in source (1/2).

Ethiopia

Source: National Labor Force Survey
Period: 2005
Note:

- B in 2005 is unreliable according to the ILO's note.

France
Source: Employment Survey [Enquête Emploi]
Period: 1999–2002
Notes

- Data reference period: annual or annual average.
- Working time concept: hours actually worked.
- Note on C for 1999–2002: "Nonstandard economic activity: including D-Q."

cf. Alternatively, the Quarterly Survey on the Economic Activity and Working Conditions of the Labour Force [Enquête trimestrielle sur l'activité et les conditions d'emploi de la main-d'oeuvre (ACEMO)] is available for the years 1997–1998 and the Annual Statement of Social Data [Déclaration annuelle de Données Sociales] for the years 2005–2006. However, the value of the former source is almost 10 times and the latter is about 40–70% of that of the Employment Survey.

Ghana
Source: Living Standards Survey [Déclaration annuelle de Données Sociales]
Period: 2006
Note:

- Denomination in 2007: 1 new Ghana cedi=1/10000 cedi.

Indonesia
Source: National Labour Force Survey
Period: 2000–2010
Notes

- Methodology revised in 2000.
- Q in 2003, 2005, and 2010 is unreliable according to the ILO's note.
- X in 2004–2006 is unreliable according to the ILO's note.

Italy
Source: Labour-Related Establishment Survey
Period: 1995
Note:

- Data reference period: annual or annual average.

Republic of Korea
Source: Survey on Labor Conditions by Employment Type
Period: 1993–1996 and 1999–2008
Notes

- Data reference period: annual or annual average.
- Establishment size coverage in 1993–1996: all establishments with at least 10 employees.
- Establishment size coverage in 1999–2008: all establishments with at least 5 employees.
- Working time concept: hours actually worked in 1993–1996 and 1999–2008.

Malaysia
Source: Survey of Manufacturing Industries
Period: 2000–2001
Note:

- The survey covers only D.

Mauritius (1/2)
Source: Survey of Employment and Earnings
Period: 1999–2008
Notes

- Note on A for 1999–2008: "Nonstandard economic activity: including B."
- Note on C for 1999–2008: "Nonstandard economic activity: including D-Q."

Mauritius (2/2)
Source: Continuous Multi-Purpose Household Survey

Period: 2009–2010 (2001–2008 are also available)
Notes

- C in 2010 is unreliable according to the ILO's note.
- Q in 2009–2010 is unreliable according to the ILO's note.
- The ILO notes that most of the values in C and Q are unreliable.
- Break in series in 2001 and 2003.

Mexico
Source: National Occupation and Employment Survey [Encuesta Nacional de Ocupación y Empleo]
Period: 1991, 1993, and 1995–2004
Notes

- Methodology change in 1995.
- Data reference period: second quarter in 1991, 1993, and 1995–2004.
- Age coverage—minimum age: 14 years for 1995–2004.
- Working time concept: hours actually worked for 1991, 1993, and 1995–2004.
- Note on A for 1991, 1993, and 1995–2004: "Nonstandard economic activity: including B."
- Note on C for 1991, 1993, and 1995–2004: "Nonstandard economic activity: including D-Q."

The Netherlands
Source: Annual Earnings Survey
Period: 1994–2005
Notes

- Break in series: new or revalued currency in 2001.
- The reference period is October in 1994 and December in 1995–2005.
- Working time arrangement coverage: full-time workers in 1994–2005.
- Working time concept: hours actually worked in 1994–2005.
- Note on A for 2001–2005: "Nonstandard economic activity: including B."

- Note on C for 2001–2005: "Nonstandard economic activity: including D-Q."

Peru
Source: National Household Survey [Encuesta Nacional de Hogares]
Period: 2002–2011 (2012 and 2013 are also available)
Note:

- The values in 2002 and 2003 are very high, especially for C in 2003.

c.f. An alternative source, "Permanent Employment Survey (Urban) [Encuesta permanente de Empleo (Urban)]" is available from 2003 to 2009, though it covers only main cities or metropolitan areas.

The Philippines
Source: Employment, Hours, and Earnings Survey
Period: 1996–1999, 2001, 2003, 2005, 2006, and 2008
Notes

- Break in series: unspecified type of break in 1999.
- Establishment size coverage: all establishments with at least 10 employees in 1996–1998.
- Establishment size coverage: all establishments with at least 20 employees in 1999, 2001, 2003, 2005, 2006, and 2008.
- Working time concept: hours actually worked in 1996–1999, 2001, 2003, 2005, 2006, and 2008.
- Data reference period: annual or annual average in 1996–1999, 2001, 2003, 2005, 2006, and 2008.
- Note on A for 1996–1999, 2001, 2003, 2005, 2006, and 2008: "Nonstandard economic activity: including B."
- Note on C for 1996–1999, 2001, 2003, 2005, 2006, and 2008: "Nonstandard economic activity: including D-Q."

c.f. An alternative data source, the "Integrated Survey," is available for 1998–2000. It has a break in series in 2000.

Singapore
Source: Records of the Central Provident Fund
Period: 1998–2008
Notes

- Methodology revised in 2005.
- Working time concept: hours actually worked.
- Note on L for 1998–2008: "Nonstandard economic activity: including M-Q."

Spain

Source: Survey of Wages in Industry and the Services [Encuesta de Salarios en la Industria y los Servicios]

Period: 1999–2008

Notes

- Time unit: per hour.
- Working time concept: hours actually worked.
- Data reference period: annual or annual average.
- Note on C for 1999: "Nonstandard economic activity: including D-Q and excluding L-Q."
- Note on C for 2000–2008: "Nonstandard economic activity: including D-Q."

Spain—Weekly Working Hours

Source: EU Labour Force Survey

Period: 1992–2007

Notes

- Methodology revised in 1993, 2001, and 2005.
- Q in 1992, 1994, 1999, 2000, 2002, 2003, and 2007 is unreliable according to the ILO's note.

Sweden

Source: Survey of Wages and Employment in Mining, Quarrying, and Manufacturing

Period: 1993–2007

Notes

- Time unit: per hour in 1994–2007.
- Break in series in 1997: unspecified type of break.
- Data reference period: September for 1994–2007.
- Institutional sector coverage: private sector only in 1994–2007.
- Reference group coverage: adults in 1994–2007

- Reference group coverage: wage earners/blue collar/production workers in 1994–2007
- Notes on A for 1993–2007: "Nonstandard economic activity: including B."
- No notes exist on 1993 but most of the descriptions also apply to 1993.

Sweden—Weekly Working Hours
Source: EU Labour Force Survey
Period: 1995–2007
Notes

- Methodology revised in 2005.
- B in 1995–1999, 2001–2004, 2006, and 2007 is unreliable according to the ILO's note.
- C in 1995, 1996, and 1998–2000 is unreliable according to the ILO's note.
- P in 1997–2001, 2006, and 2007 is unreliable according to the ILO's note.

Taipei, China
Source: Labour-Related Establishment Survey
Period: 1983–1985 and 2004–2008
Notes

- Data reference period: annual or annual average for the years 2004–2008.
- Working time concept: hours actually worked for the years 2004–2008.
- Notes on C for 1983–1985 and 2004–2008: "Nonstandard economic activity: including D-Q."
- Notes on E for 1983–1985 and 2004–2008: "Nonstandard economic activity: excluding water supply."
- Notes on I for 1983–1985 and 2004–2008: "Nonstandard economic activity: excluding communications."
- Notes on K for 1983–1985 and 2004–2008: "Nonstandard economic activity: excluding business services."

Tanzania
Source: Labour Force Survey

Period: 2006
Note:

- Methodology revised in 2006.

Thailand
Source: Labour Force Survey
Period: 2010
Note:

- Methodology revised in 2010.

United Kingdom
Source: Labour Force Survey
Period: 1995–2008
Notes

- Time unit: per week.
- Working time arrangement coverage: full-time workers.
- Working time concept: hours actually worked.
- Data reference period: annual or annual average.
- Notes on A for 1995–2008: "Nonstandard economic activity: including B."
- Notes on C for 1995–2008: "Nonstandard economic activity: including E."
- Notes on G for 1995–2008: "Nonstandard economic activity: including H."
- Notes on J for 1995–2008: "Nonstandard economic activity: including K."
- Notes on L for 1995–2008: "Nonstandard economic activity: including M-N."
- Notes on O for 1995–2008: "Nonstandard economic activity: including P-Q."

c.f. An alternative source, Short-Term (Monthly and Quarterly) Employment Statistics, is available for 1998–2007. The unit of the term is weeks, converted into monthly figures through multiplication by 4.33. Its reference period is April. It covers full-time workers.

United States

Source: Current Population Survey
Period: 1969–1970, 2000–2003, and 2005–2008
Notes

- Time unit: per week.
- Central tendency measure: median.
- Working time concept: hours actually worked.
- Data reference period: annual or annual average.
- The values in 1969 and 1970 are very small (less than 1/90 of the ones after 2000).

Part 2: Countries Covered by the Socio-Economic Account

Australia (1/2)
Source: Labour Force Survey
Period: 1985–1995 and 1997–2000
Notes

- Time unit: per week for the years 1997–2000.
- Job coverage: main job currently held for the years 1997–2000.
- Working time concept: hours actually worked for the years 1997–2000.
- Data reference period: annual or annual average for the years 1997–2000.
- Note on A for 1985–2000: "Nonstandard economic activity: including D-Q."
- Note on A: "Nonstandard economic activity: including B."
- The first to fourth notes only apply to the years 1997–2000, but they seem to be applicable to the data for 1985–1995.

Australia (2/2)
Source: Survey of Employee Earnings and Hours
Period: 1996, 1998, 2000, 2002, 2004, and 2006
Notes

- Time unit: per hour.
- Working time arrangement coverage: full-time workers.
- Working time concept: hours actually worked.
- Data reference period: May.

- Reference group coverage: adults
- Age coverage—minimum age: adults.
- Note on C for 1996, 1998, 2000, 2002, 2004, and 2006: "Nonstandard economic activity: including D-Q."

Australia—Weekly Working Hours
Source: Labour Force Survey
Period: 1987–1990
Notes

- Note on A for 1987–1990: "Nonstandard economic activity: including B."
- Note on C for 1987–1990: "Nonstandard economic activity: including D-Q."
- The ILO provides no full data description.

Austria (1/2)
Source: Insurance Records
Period: 1995–2003

- New currency introduced in 2000.
- Working time concept: hours actually worked.
- Note on C for 2001–2003: "Nonstandard economic activity: including D-Q."

Austria (2/2)
Source: Industrial Production Statistics
Period: 2004–2007 (1996–1998 and 2001–2003 are also available)

- Time unit: per hour.
- New currency introduced in 2000.
- Working time concept: hours actually worked.
- Note on D for 2001–2003: "Nonstandard economic activity: including C."

Austria—Weekly Working Hours
Source: EU Labour Force Survey
Period: 1995–2007
Notes

- Methodology revised in 2005.
- Job coverage: main and second job currently held in 1995–2007.
- Data reference period: annual or annual average in 1995–2007.
- B in 2002 and 2003 is unreliable according to the ILO's note.
- C in 2003–2005 is unreliable according to the ILO's note.
- X in 2004 is unreliable according to the ILO's note.
- B in 1995–2001, 2004–2007 are missing.
- X in 1995–2003, 2005–2007 are missing.

Belgium
Source: Labour Cost Survey
Period: 1995–2007

- New currency introduced in 1999.
- Unspecified type of break of the series in 1998.
- Data reference period: October 1995–2007.
- Reference group coverage: salaried employed/white collar/office workers in 1995–1998

Bulgaria
Source: Employed Persons and Wage and Salary Census
Period: 1996–2008
Notes

- New currency introduced in 1999.
- Note on A for 1996–2008: "Nonstandard economic activity: including B."
- Note on C for 1996–2008: "Nonstandard economic activity: including D-Q."

Canada
Source: Survey of Employment, Payrolls, and Hours
Period:
Note:

- Time unit: per week 1994–2008.
- Methodology revised in 1991.
- Working time concept: hours actually worked from 1994 to 2008.
- Data reference period: annual or annual average.

- Note on A: “Nonstandard economic activity: excluding 11.”
- Note on C for 1999–2008: “Nonstandard economic activity: including D-Q.”
- According to the ILO’s note, the time unit is per week only for 1994–2008, but this also seems to be applicable to the prior years.

Cyprus
Source: Employment Survey
Period: 1998–2006
Notes

- Data reference period: October.
- Reference group coverage: adults
- Reference group coverage: salaried employed/white collar/ office workers
- Age coverage—minimum age: adults.
- Working time concept: hours actually worked.
- Note on A for 2001–2006: “Nonstandard economic activity: including B.”
- Note on C for 2001–2006: “Nonstandard economic activity: including D-Q.”

The Czech Republic
Source: Report on Employment and Wages
Period: 1996–2007
Notes

- Data reference period: annual or annual average.
- Working time concept: hours actually worked.
- Note on A for 1996–2007: “Nonstandard economic activity: including B.”
- Note on C for 1996–2007: “Nonstandard economic activity: including D-Q.”
- Note on D for 1996–2007: “Nonstandard economic activity: including C, E.”
- The values in the year 2007 are estimates.

Germany
Source: Establishment Survey

Period: 1996–2008
Notes

- Time unit: per hour.
- New currency introduced from 2001.
- Unspecified break in series in 2006.
- Working time concept: hours actually worked.
- Data reference period: annual or annual average.
- Reference group coverage: wage earners/blue collar/production workers in 1996–2006

Germany—Weekly Working Hours
Source: EU Labour Force Survey
Period: 1995–2007
Notes

- Change in methodologies in 2005.
- Data reference period: annual or annual average.
- B in 1997, 2001, 2003, 2004, and 2007 is unreliable according to the ILO's note.

Estonia
Source: Survey of Wages and Salaries
Period: 1992–2008
Notes

- New or revalued currency from 1992.
- Data reference period: annual or annual average.
- Working time concept: hours actually worked.
- Note on A for 1992–2005: "Nonstandard economic activity: including B."
- Note on C for 1992–2005: "Nonstandard economic activity: including D-Q."

Finland
Source: Survey on Wages of Industrial Workers and Salaries of Industrial Employees
Period: 1996–2008
Notes

- New currency in 2001.
- Data reference period: fourth quarter.
- Working time arrangement coverage: full-time workers.
- Working time concept: hours actually worked.
- Excluding overtime and/or irregular bonuses in 2002–2008.
- Working time concept: hours actually worked in 2002–2008.
- Note on C: "Nonstandard economic activity: including D-Q."

Greece
Source: Quarterly Payroll Survey in Selected Industries
Period: 2000, 2002, and 2006
Hungary
Source: Employment and Earnings Survey
Period: 1992–2008
Notes

- Unspecified break in series in 1999.
- Note on A for 1992–2008: "Nonstandard economic activity: including B."
- Note on C for 1992–2008: "Nonstandard economic activity: including D-Q."

Ireland
Source: Earnings Hours and Employment Costs Survey
Period: 1996–2006
Notes

- Time unit: per week.
- Working time concept: hours actually worked.
- Data reference period: annual or annual average.
- Establishment size coverage: all establishments with at least 10 employees.

Latvia
Source: Survey of Economically Active Commercial Companies, Individual Merchants, Peasant or Fishermen Farms, Budgetary Institutions, Foundations, Associations, or Funds, as well as Administrative Data
Period: 1990–2008
Notes

- Data reference period: first quarter.
- Working time concept: hours actually worked.
- Note on A, C, D, E, G, H, I, J, K, L, N, O, and total in 1990 and 1991: "Nonstandard economic activity: private sector only."
- Note on A in 1995–2008: "Nonstandard economic activity: including B."
- Note on C in 1995–2008: "Nonstandard economic activity: including D-Q."
- Significant differences exist between 1991 and 1992.

Lithuania
Source: Monthly Earnings Survey
Period: 1993–2008
Notes

- Working time arrangement coverage: full-time workers in 1993–1996.
- Working time concept: hours actually worked in 1993–2008.
- Data reference period: annual or annual average in 1993 and 1997–2008; July in 1994 and 1995; and April in 1996.
- Establishment size coverage: all establishments with at least two employees in 1993.
- Note on A: "Nonstandard economic activity: including B" in 1993–2008.
- Notes on C: "Nonstandard economic activity: including D-Q" in 1993–2008; "Nonstandard economic activity: excluding mining and quarrying" in 1993–1996.

Luxembourg
Source: Semi-annual survey of earnings and average hours of work offered [Enquête semestrielle sur les gains et la durée moyenne du travail offerte]
Period: 1995–2008
Notes

- Break in series: new or revalued currency in 1999.
- Data reference period: October 1995–2008.
- Reference group coverage: salaried employed/white collar/office workers in 1997–2008

- Working time concept: hours actually worked in 1995–2008.

Malta
Source: Labour Force Survey
Period: 2000–2008
Notes

- Time unit: per hour in 2000–2008.
- Break in series: new or revalued currency in 2008.
- Working time concept: hours actually worked.
- Data reference period: annual or annual average.
- Note on A: "Nonstandard economic activity: including B" in 2000 and 2004–2008.
- Note on C: "Nonstandard economic activity: including D-Q" in 2000–2006 and 2008.

Malta—Weekly Working Hours
Source: EU Labour Force Survey
Period: 1995–2007
Notes

- Methodologies are revised in 2005.
- Data reference period: annual or annual average.
- Job coverage: main and second job currently held.
- A in 2000–2002 and 2004 is unreliable according to the ILO's note.
- B in 2000–2004 is unreliable according to the ILO's note.
- C in 2000–2003, 2006, and 2007 is unreliable according to the ILO's note.
- E in 2000 and 2002 is unreliable according to the ILO's note.

Poland
Source: Establishment Statistical Surveys
Period: 1993–2006
Notes

- Revalued currency in 1993.
- Data reference period: annual or annual average in 1993–2006.
- Working time concept: hours actually worked in 1993–2006.
- Note on A for 1993–2004: "Nonstandard economic activity: including B."

- Note on C for 1993–2006: “Nonstandard economic activity: including D-Q.”

Portugal
Source: [Enquête sur les Gains et la Durée du Travail]
Period: 1998–2008
Notes

- New currency introduced in 2002.
- Data reference period: annual or annual average in 1998–2008.
- Working time concept: hours actually worked in 1998–2008.
- Note on C: “Nonstandard economic activity: including D-Q.”

Romania
Source: [Enquête sur le Coût de la Main-d’oeuvre]
Period: 1992–2007
Notes

- Revaluation of the currency in 2005.
- Data reference period: annual or annual average in 1992–2007.
- Working time concept: hours actually worked in 1992–2007.
- Note on A: “Nonstandard economic activity: including B.”
- Note on C: “Nonstandard economic activity: including D-Q.”

Russian Federation
Source: Establishment Sample Survey on Employees’ Wages by Occupation
Period: 1995–1998 and 2005–2016
Notes

- Break in series: new or revalued currency in 1997.
- Data reference period: annual or annual average in 1997–1998.
- Data reference period: October in 2005–2016.
- Geographical coverage: total national, excluding some areas in 2005–2016.
- Working time concept: hours actually worked in 1997, 1998, and 2005–2016.
- Central tendency measure: weighted mean in 2005–2016.
- Job coverage: main job currently held in 2005–2016.

- Working time arrangement coverage: full-time workers in 2005–2016.
- Note on A for 1995–1998, 2005, and 2006: "Nonstandard economic activity: including B."
- Note on C for 1995–1998, 2005, and 2006: "Nonstandard economic activity: including D-Q."

Slovakia
Source: Labour-Related Establishment Survey
Period: 1991–2008
Notes

- Break in series: other or unspecified type of break in 1997.
- Data reference period: annual or annual average.
- Establishment size coverage: all establishments with at least 25 employees in 1991–1996 and 20 employees in 1997–2008.
- Working time concept: hours actually worked.
- Note on A for 1991–2008: "Nonstandard economic activity: including B."

Slovenia
Source: Monthly Reporting on Earnings and Persons in Paid Employment in Enterprises, Companies, and Organizations
Period: 1985–2008
Notes

- New currency introduced in 2007.
- Methodology revised in 2005.
- Data reference period: annual or annual average in 1994–2008.
- Working time concept: hours actually worked in 1994–2008.
- Components of earnings/wages: nonstandard components of earnings or wages in 2005–2008.

Turkey
Source: Annual Survey of Manufacturing Industry
Period: 1983–1989 and 1993–2005
Notes

- Unspecified break in series in 1989.
- Introduction of new currency in 2005.

- Data reference period: first semester in 1983–2001; annual or annual average in 2002–2005.
- Establishment size coverage: nonstandard establishment size coverage from 1983–1988; and all establishments with at least 10 employees in 1989 and 1993–2001.
- Working time concept: hours actually worked in 1983–1989 and 1993–2005.
- Note on C for 2002–2005: "Nonstandard economic activity: including D-Q."

Description of Weekly Working Hours

Indicator:	*Mean weekly hours worked per employed person by sex and economic activity*
Description:	We present data on hours of work, whenever possible, on the basis of the mean number of hours of work per week and with reference to hours worked in all jobs of employed persons and in all types of working time arrangements (e.g., full time and part time). Hours actually worked include (a) direct hours or the time spent carrying out the tasks and duties of a job; (b) related hours or the time spent maintaining, facilitating, or enhancing productive activities; (c) down time or time when a person in a job cannot work due to machinery or process breakdown, accident, lack of supplies, or power or Internet access; and (d) resting time or time spent in short periods of rest, relief, or refreshment, including tea, coffee, or prayer breaks, generally practiced by custom or contract according to established norms and/or national circumstances. Hours actually worked exclude time not worked during activities such as: (a) annual leave, public holidays, sick leave, parental leave or maternity/paternity leave, and other leave for personal or family reasons or civic duty; (b) commuting time between work and home when no productive activity for the job is performed; for paid employment, even when paid by the employer; (c) time spent on certain educational activities; for paid employment, even when authorized, paid, or provided by the employer; and (d) longer breaks distinguished from short resting time when no productive activity is performed (such as meal breaks or natural repose during long trips); for paid employment, even when paid by the employer. The employed comprise all persons of working age who, during a specified brief period, were in the following categories: (a) paid employment (whether at work or with a job but not at work); or (b) self-employment (whether at work or with an enterprise but not at work). Data are disaggregated by economic activity according to the latest version of the International Standard Industrial Classification of All Economic Activities (ISIC) available for that year. Economic activity refers to the main activity of the establishment in which a person worked during the reference period and depends not on the specific duties or functions of the person's job but on the characteristics of the economic unit in which this person works.

Appendix 3. Ambiguous and Unambiguous Labor Income Share

Assume that *"ambiguous" income* (Y^a), which consists of proprietors' income and indirect taxes less subsidies, is allocated to capital and labor in the same ratio as that of the rest of the sector; then, we decompose *total labor income* (Y^l) as follows:

$$Y^l = Y^{ul} + \text{LIS} \times Y^a$$

where

Y^{ul}: Unambiguous labor income (compensation of employees).

LIS: Labor income share.

We express the above equation using ***national income*** (Y):

$$Y^l = \text{LIS} \times Y = \text{LIS} \times \left(Y^{ul} + Y^{uk} + Y^a\right)$$

where

Y^{uk}: Unambiguous capital income (corporate profits, rental income, net interest income, and depreciation).

The above two equations enable us to express LIS using unambiguous elements:

$$\text{LIS} = \frac{Y^{ul}}{Y^{ul} + Y^{uk}}$$

Appendix 4. Aggregation Scheme

Broad sector	*GGDC 10-Sector*	*ILO STAT*	*SEA[a] 35-Sector code*	*ASD[b] sector name*	*ISIC Rev. 3.1 description for the GGDC 10 classification*
Primary	AGR	AtB	AtB	Agriculture	Agriculture, hunting and forestry, fishing
Primary	MIN	C	C	Mining	Mining and quarrying
Secondary	MAN	D	15 t16, 17 t18, 19, 20, 21 t22, 23, 24, 25, 26, 27 t28, 29, 30 t33, 34 t35, 36 t37	Manufacturing	Manufacturing
Tertiary	PU	E	E	Utilities	Electricity, gas, and water supply
Secondary	CON	F	F	Construction	Construction
Tertiary	WRT	G, H	50,51,52, H	Trade services	Wholesale and retail trade; repair of motor vehicles, motorcycles, and personal and household goods; hotels and restaurants
Tertiary	TRA	I	60, 61, 62, 63, 64	Transport services	Transport, storage, and communications
Tertiary	FIRE	J, K	J, 70, 71 t74	Business services	Financial intermediation, renting, and business activities (excluding owner-occupied rents)
(Tertiary[c])	GOV	L, M, N	L, M, N	Government services	Public administration and defense, education, health, and social work
(Tertiary[d])	OTH	O, P	O, P	Personal services	Other community, social, and personal service activities and activities of private households

[a]Socio-Economic Account

[b]Africa Sector Database

[c]Excluded in the alternative definition

[d]Excluded in the alternative definition

Appendix 5. Currency Adjustment for Revaluation and Introduction of New Currency

County	*Old currency*		*New currency*		*Year*	*Rate*
Austria	Austrian schilling	(ATS)	Euro	(EUR)	1999	13.7603 ATS/1EUR
Belgium	Belgian franc	(BEF)	Euro	(EUR)	1999	40.3399 BEF/1EUR
Brazil	Cruzeiro	(BRE)	Cruzeiro real	(BRR)	1993	1000 BRE/1BRR
Brazil	Cruzeiro real	(BRR)	Brazilian real	(BRL)	1994	2750 BRR/1BRL
Bulgaria	(Third) Bulgarian lev	(BGL)	(Fourth) Bulgarian lev	(BGN)	1999	1000 BGL/1BGN
Estonia	Estonian kroon	(EEK)	Euro	(EUR)	2011	15.6466 EEK/1EUR
Finland	Finnish markka	(FIM)	Euro	(EUR)	1999	5.94573 FIM/1EUR
France	French franc	(FRF)	Euro	(EUR)	1999	6.55957 FRF/1EUR
Germany	German mark	(DEM)	Euro	(EUR)	1999	1.95583 DEM/1EUR
Ghana	(Second) Ghanaian cedi	(GHC)	(Third) Ghanaian cedi	(GHS)	2007	10,000 GHC/1GHS
Italy	Italian lira	(ITL)	Euro	(EUR)	1999	1936.27 ITL/1EUR
Luxembourg	Luxembourgian franc	(LUF)	Euro	(EUR)	1999	40.3399 LUF/1EUR
Malta	Maltese lira	(MTL)	Euro	(EUR)	2008	0.4293 MTL/1EUR
Netherlands	Dutch guilder	(NLG)	Euro	(EUR)	1999	2.20371 NLG/1EUR
Portugal	Portuguese escudo	(PTE)	Euro	(EUR)	1999	200.482 PTE/1EUR
Romania	(Third) Romanian leu	(ROL)	(Fourth) Romanian leu	(RON)	2005	10,000 ROL/1RON
Russian Federation	(First) Russian ruble	(RUR)	(Second) Russian ruble	(RUB)	1998	1000 RUR/1RUB
Slovakia	Slovak koruna	(SKK)	Euro	(EUR)	2009	30.126 SKK/1EUR
Slovenia	Slovenian tolar	(SIT)	Euro	(EUR)	2007	239.64 SIT/1EUR
Turkey	(First) Turkish lira	(TRL)	(Third) Turkish lira	(TRY)	2005	1000,000 TRL/1TRY

References

Alvarez-Cuadrado, F., N. V. Long, and M. Poschke. 2015. *Capital–Labor Substitution, Structural Change and the Labor Income Share*. IZA Discussion Paper No. 8941.

Cooley, T. F. and E. C. Prescott. 1995. "Economic Growth and Business Cycles," in *Frontiers of Business Cycle Research*, pp. 1–38, ed. Princeton: Princeton University Press.

Gomme, P. and P. Rupert. 2004. *Measuring Labor's Share of Income. Policy Discussion Paper* 7. Federal Reserve Bank of Cleveland.

Lübker, M. 2007. "Labour Shares." *Technical Brief* No. 1. Geneva: ILO, P. I. Department.

Mas, M. 2005. "Public Capital, Internal Rate of Return and Growth Accounting." EU KLEMS Note. https://mpra.ub.uni-muenchen.de/15821/. (accessed 1 March 2018).

Oishi, Y. and S. Paul. 2018. "Sectoral Labor Income Share Dynamics: Cross-Country Evidence from a Novel Dataset." ADBI Working Paper 875. Tokyo: Asian Development Bank Institute. https://www.adb.org/publications/sectoral-labor-income-share-dynamics.

CHAPTER 5

Global Trends in Labor Income Share: Firm Level

Micro-level studies provide insightful knowledge on the drivers of the labor income share (LIS). This chapter uses a novel firm-level dataset (Paul and Isaka 2019) on the labor income share. Using the World Bank Enterprise Survey data, Paul and Isaka (2019) put together an unbalanced panel comprising 146,666 firms from 139 countries and spanning a period from 2002 to 2017. This chapter defines the firm-level labor income share following three alternative approaches and compares these estimates across income groups, regions, firm sizes, and ownership types.

5.1 Data

5.1.1 Data Sources and Coverage

This chapter employs a novel firm-level dataset on the labor income share. Using the World Bank Enterprise Survey data, Paul and Isaka (2019) put together an unbalanced panel of 146,666 firms from 139 countries, spanning a period of 15 years (2002–2017). The survey includes firms spread across 139 countries and collects information on a broad range of topics, including access to finance, corruption, infrastructure, crime, competition, labor, obstacles to growth, and performance measures. The dataset spans the period 2002–2017. Roughly 10% of the firms were successfully re-contacted so that they have more than one year of information, which makes this dataset an unbalanced panel. Table 5.1 provides a description

S. Paul, *Labor Income Share*,
https://doi.org/10.1007/978-981-15-6860-2_5

Table 5.1 Country composition table from World Bank Enterprise Survey data

	Survey year																*Total*
	2003	*2004*	*2005*	*2006*	*2007*	*2008*	*2009*	*2010*	*2011*	*2012*	*2013*	*2014*	*2015*	*2016*	*2017*	*2018*	
Afghanistan	0	0	0	0	0	647	0	526	0	0	0	410	0	0	0	0	1583
Albania	0	0	0	0	304	0	175	0	0	0	360	0	0	0	0	0	839
Angola	0	0	0	425	0	0	0	360	0	0	0	0	0	0	0	0	785
Antigua and Barbuda	0	0	0	0	0	0	0	151	0	0	0	0	0	0	0	0	151
Argentina	0	0	0	1063	0	0	0	1054	0	0	0	0	0	0	991	0	3108
Armenia	0	0	0	0	0	0	374	0	0	0	360	0	0	0	0	0	734
Azerbaijan	0	0	0	0	0	0	380	0	0	0	390	0	0	0	0	0	770
Bahamas	0	0	0	0	0	0	0	150	0	0	0	0	0	0	0	0	150
Bangladesh	0	0	0	0	1504	0	0	0	250	0	1442	0	0	0	0	0	3196
Barbados	0	0	0	0	0	0	0	150	0	0	0	0	0	0	0	0	150
Belarus	0	0	0	0	0	273	0	0	0	0	360	0	0	0	0	0	633
Belize	0	0	0	0	0	0	0	150	0	0	0	0	0	0	0	0	150
Benin	0	197	0	0	0	0	150	0	0	0	0	0	0	150	0	0	497
Bhutan	0	0	0	0	0	0	250	0	0	0	0	0	253	0	0	0	503
Bolivia	0	0	0	613	0	0	0	362	0	0	0	0	0	0	364	0	1339
Bosnia and Herzegovina	0	0	0	0	0	0	361	0	0	0	360	0	0	0	0	0	721
Botswana	0	0	0	342	0	0	0	268	0	0	0	0	0	0	0	0	610
Brazil	1642	0	0	0	0	0	1802	0	0	0	0	0	0	0	0	0	3444
Bulgaria	0	0	0	0	1015	0	288	0	0	0	293	0	0	0	0	0	1596
Burkina Faso	0	0	0	139	0	0	394	0	0	0	0	0	0	0	0	0	533
Burundi	0	0	0	270	0	0	0	0	0	0	0	157	0	0	0	0	427
Cambodia	0	0	0	0	0	0	0	0	0	0	472	0	0	373	0	0	845

Cameroon	0	0	0	207	0	0	363	0	0	0	0	0	0	361	0	0	931
Cape Verde	0	0	0	98	0	0	156	0	0	0	0	0	0	0	0	0	254
Central African Republic	0	0	0	0	0	0	0	0	150	0	0	0	0	0	0	0	150
Chad	0	0	0	0	0	0	150	0	0	0	0	0	0	0	0	153	303
Chile	0	0	0	1017	0	0	0	1033	0	0	0	0	0	0	0	0	2050
People's Republic of China	0	0	0	0	0	0	0	0	0	2700	0	0	0	0	0	0	2700
Colombia	0	0	0	1000	0	0	0	942	0	0	0	0	0	0	993	0	2935
Congo	0	0	0	0	0	0	151	0	0	0	0	0	0	0	0	0	151
Costa Rica	0	0	0	0	0	0	0	538	0	0	0	0	0	0	0	0	538
Croatia	0	0	0	0	633	0	159	0	0	0	360	0	0	0	0	0	1152
Czech Republic	0	0	0	0	0	0	250	0	0	0	254	0	0	0	0	0	504
Côte d'Ivoire	0	0	0	0	0	0	526	0	0	0	0	0	0	361	0	0	887
DRC	0	0	0	340	0	0	0	359	0	0	529	0	0	0	0	0	1228
Djibouti	0	0	0	0	0	0	0	0	0	0	266	0	0	0	0	0	266
Dominica	0	0	0	0	0	0	0	150	0	0	0	0	0	0	0	0	150
Dominican Republic	0	0	0	0	0	0	0	360	0	0	0	0	0	359	0	0	719
Ecuador	453	0	0	658	0	0	0	366	0	0	0	0	0	0	361	0	1838
Egypt	0	0	0	0	0	0	0	0	0	0	2897	0	0	1814	0	0	4711
El Salvador	0	0	0	693	0	0	0	360	0	0	0	0	0	719	0	0	1772
Eritrea	0	0	0	0	0	0	179	0	0	0	0	0	0	0	0	0	179
Estonia	0	0	0	0	0	0	273	0	0	0	273	0	0	0	0	0	546
Eswatini	0	0	0	307	0	0	0	0	0	0	0	0	0	150	0	0	457
Ethiopia	0	0	0	0	0	0	0	0	644	0	0	0	848	0	0	0	1492

(*continued*)

Table 5.1 (continued)

	Survey year																*Total*
	2003	*2004*	*2005*	*2006*	*2007*	*2008*	*2009*	*2010*	*2011*	*2012*	*2013*	*2014*	*2015*	*2016*	*2017*	*2018*	
Fiji	0	0	0	0	0	0	164	0	0	0	0	0	0	0	0	0	164
FYR Macedonia	0	0	0	0	0	0	366	0	0	0	360	0	0	0	0	0	726
Gabon	0	0	0	0	0	0	179	0	0	0	0	0	0	0	0	0	179
Gambia	0	0	0	174	0	0	0	0	0	0	0	0	0	0	0	151	325
Georgia	0	0	0	0	0	373	0	0	0	0	360	0	0	0	0	0	733
Ghana	0	0	0	0	494	0	0	0	0	0	720	0	0	0	0	0	1214
Grenada	0	0	0	0	0	0	0	153	0	0	0	0	0	0	0	0	153
Guatemala	0	0	0	522	0	0	0	590	0	0	0	0	0	0	345	0	1457
Guinea	0	0	0	223	0	0	0	0	0	0	0	0	0	150	0	0	373
Guinea Bissau	0	0	0	159	0	0	0	0	0	0	0	0	0	0	0	0	159
Guyana	0	0	0	0	0	0	0	165	0	0	0	0	0	0	0	0	165
Honduras	450	0	0	436	0	0	0	360	0	0	0	0	0	332	0	0	1578
Hungary	0	0	0	0	0	0	291	0	0	0	310	0	0	0	0	0	601
India	0	0	0	0	0	0	0	0	0	0	0	9281	0	0	0	0	9281
Indonesia	0	0	0	0	0	0	1444	0	0	0	0	0	1320	0	0	0	2764
Iraq	0	0	0	0	0	0	0	0	756	0	0	0	0	0	0	0	756
Israel	0	0	0	0	0	0	0	0	0	0	483	0	0	0	0	0	483
Jamaica	0	0	0	0	0	0	0	376	0	0	0	0	0	0	0	0	376
Jordan	0	0	0	0	0	0	0	0	0	0	573	0	0	0	0	0	573
Kazakhstan	0	0	0	0	0	0	544	0	0	0	600	0	0	0	0	0	1144
Kenya	0	0	0	0	657	0	0	0	0	0	781	0	0	0	0	0	1438
Kosovo	0	0	0	0	0	0	270	0	0	0	202	0	0	0	0	0	472
Kyrgyz Republic	0	0	0	0	0	0	235	0	0	0	270	0	0	0	0	0	505
Lao PDR	0	0	0	0	0	0	360	0	0	379	0	0	0	368	0	0	1107

Latvia	0	0	0	0	0	0	271	0	0	0	336	0	0	0	0	0	607
Lebanon	0	0	0	0	0	0	0	0	0	0	561	0	0	0	0	0	561
Lesotho	0	0	0	0	0	0	151	0	0	0	0	0	0	150	0	0	301
Liberia	0	0	0	0	0	0	150	0	0	0	0	0	0	0	151	0	301
Lithuania	0	0	0	0	0	0	276	0	0	0	270	0	0	0	0	0	546
Madagascar	0	0	0	0	0	0	445	0	0	0	532	0	0	0	0	0	977
Malawi	0	0	0	0	0	0	150	0	0	0	0	523	0	0	0	0	673
Malaysia	0	0	0	0	0	0	0	0	0	0	0	0	1000	0	0	0	1000
Mali	155	0	0	0	490	0	0	360	0	0	0	0	0	185	0	0	1190
Mauritania	0	0	0	237	0	0	0	0	0	0	0	150	0	0	0	0	387
Mauritius	0	0	0	0	0	0	398	0	0	0	0	0	0	0	0	0	398
Mexico	0	0	0	1480	0	0	0	1480	0	0	0	0	0	0	0	0	2960
Micronesia	0	0	0	0	0	0	68	0	0	0	0	0	0	0	0	0	68
Moldova	0	0	0	0	0	0	363	0	0	0	360	0	0	0	0	0	723
Mongolia	0	0	0	0	0	0	362	0	0	0	360	0	0	0	0	0	722
Montenegro	0	0	0	0	0	0	116	0	0	0	150	0	0	0	0	0	266
Morocco	0	0	0	0	0	0	0	0	0	0	407	0	0	0	0	0	407
Mozambique	0	0	0	0	479	0	0	0	0	0	0	0	0	0	0	0	479
Myanmar	0	0	0	0	0	0	0	0	0	0	0	632	0	607	0	0	1239
Namibia	0	0	0	329	0	0	0	0	0	0	0	580	0	0	0	0	909
Nepal	0	0	0	0	0	0	368	0	0	0	482	0	0	0	0	0	850
Nicaragua	452	0	0	478	0	0	0	336	0	0	0	0	0	333	0	0	1599
Niger	0	0	125	0	0	0	150	0	0	0	0	0	0	0	151	0	426
Nigeria	0	0	0	0	1891	0	3157	0	0	0	0	2676	0	0	0	0	7724
Pakistan	0	0	0	0	935	0	0	0	0	0	1247	0	0	0	0	0	2182
Panama	0	0	0	604	0	0	0	365	0	0	0	0	0	0	0	0	969
Papua New Guinea	0	0	0	0	0	0	0	0	0	0	0	0	65	0	0	0	65
Paraguay	0	0	0	613	0	0	0	361	0	0	0	0	0	0	364	0	1338

(*continued*)

Table 5.1 (continued)

	Survey year																*Total*
	2003	*2004*	*2005*	*2006*	*2007*	*2008*	*2009*	*2010*	*2011*	*2012*	*2013*	*2014*	*2015*	*2016*	*2017*	*2018*	
Peru	0	0	0	632	0	0	0	1000	0	0	0	0	0	0	1003	0	2635
Philippines	0	0	0	0	0	0	1326	0	0	0	0	0	1335	0	0	0	2661
Poland	0	0	0	0	0	0	455	0	0	0	542	0	0	0	0	0	997
Romania	0	0	0	0	0	0	541	0	0	0	540	0	0	0	0	0	1081
Russian Federation	0	0	0	0	0	0	1004	0	0	4220	0	0	0	0	0	0	5224
Rwanda	0	0	0	212	0	0	0	0	241	0	0	0	0	0	0	0	453
Samoa	0	0	0	0	0	0	109	0	0	0	0	0	0	0	0	0	109
Senegal	0	0	0	0	506	0	0	0	0	0	0	601	0	0	0	0	1107
Serbia	0	0	0	0	0	0	388	0	0	0	360	0	0	0	0	0	748
Sierra Leone	0	0	0	0	0	0	150	0	0	0	0	0	0	0	152	0	302
Slovak Republic	0	0	0	0	0	0	275	0	0	0	268	0	0	0	0	0	543
Slovenia	0	0	0	0	0	0	276	0	0	0	270	0	0	0	0	0	546
Solomon Islands	0	0	0	0	0	0	0	0	0	0	0	0	151	0	0	0	151
South Africa	603	0	0	0	937	0	0	0	0	0	0	0	0	0	0	0	1540
South Sudan	0	0	0	0	0	0	0	0	0	0	0	738	0	0	0	0	738
Sri Lanka	0	0	0	0	0	0	0	0	610	0	0	0	0	0	0	0	610
St. Kitts and Nevis	0	0	0	0	0	0	0	150	0	0	0	0	0	0	0	0	150
St. Lucia	0	0	0	0	0	0	0	150	0	0	0	0	0	0	0	0	150
St. Vincent and the Grenadines	0	0	0	0	0	0	0	154	0	0	0	0	0	0	0	0	154
Sudan	0	0	0	0	0	0	0	0	0	0	0	662	0	0	0	0	662

Suriname	0	0	0	0	0	0	0	152	0	0	0	0	0	0	0	0	152
Sweden	0	0	0	0	0	0	0	0	0	0	0	600	0	0	0	0	600
Tajikistan	0	0	0	0	0	360	0	0	0	0	359	0	0	0	0	0	719
Tanzania	0	0	0	419	0	0	0	0	0	0	813	0	0	0	0	0	1232
Thailand	0	0	0	0	0	0	0	0	0	0	0	0	0	1000	0	0	1000
Timor-Leste	0	0	0	0	0	0	150	0	0	0	0	0	126	0	0	0	276
Togo	0	0	0	0	0	0	155	0	0	0	0	0	0	150	0	0	305
Tonga	0	0	0	0	0	0	150	0	0	0	0	0	0	0	0	0	150
Trinidad and Tobago	0	0	0	0	0	0	0	370	0	0	0	0	0	0	0	0	370
Tunisia	0	0	0	0	0	0	0	0	0	0	592	0	0	0	0	0	592
Turkey	0	0	0	0	0	1152	0	0	0	0	1344	0	0	0	0	0	2496
Uganda	0	0	0	563	0	0	0	0	0	0	762	0	0	0	0	0	1325
Ukraine	0	0	0	0	0	851	0	0	0	0	1002	0	0	0	0	0	1853
Uruguay	0	0	0	621	0	0	0	607	0	0	0	0	0	0	347	0	1575
Uzbekistan	0	0	0	0	0	366	0	0	0	0	390	0	0	0	0	0	756
Vanuatu	0	0	0	0	0	0	128	0	0	0	0	0	0	0	0	0	128
Venezuela	0	0	0	120	0	0	0	320	0	0	0	0	0	0	0	0	440
Viet Nam	0	0	1150	0	0	0	1053	0	0	0	0	0	996	0	0	0	3199
West Bank and Gaza	0	0	0	0	0	0	0	0	0	0	434	0	0	0	0	0	434
Yemen	0	0	0	0	0	0	0	477	0	0	353	0	0	0	0	0	830
Zambia	0	0	0	0	484	0	0	0	0	0	720	0	0	0	0	0	1204
Zimbabwe	0	0	0	0	0	0	0	0	599	0	0	0	0	600	0	0	1199
Total	3755	197	1275	14,994	10,329	4022	22,819	15,205	3250	7299	26,729	17,010	6094	8162	5222	304	146,666

Source: Author

of countries with survey years covered by the World Bank Enterprise Survey data. It defines the firm-level labor income share following three alternative approaches and compares these estimates across income groups, regions, firm sizes, and ownership types. The estimates of the labor income share average around 0.45, with considerable variation across regions and firm characteristics.

5.1.2 *Alternative Definitions of Labor Income Share*

The labor income share is essentially a macroeconomic concept, defined as the share of national income allocated to labor, and is generally computed from aggregate data by dividing total labor compensation by national income (GDP). The labor compensation should encompass not only wages and salaries but also bonuses and social payments, which are considered non-wage compensation, for the accuracy of calculation. However, even this computation does not give us the labor income share that we seek to obtain because it overlooks contributions from self-employment (Krueger 1998; Gollin 2002). If the earnings of the self-employed are taken as capital income as in the conventional method, then it may underestimate the true value of labor income share and bias international comparisons (Guerriero 2012). Thus, in the macro framework, researchers suffer from the limitation of how to take self-employment into account to gain a less biased labor income share.

In this paper, however, we do not compute the aggregate level of labor income share. Rather, we use the information on compensation at the firm level, which is less susceptible to problems related to the mixed income that arises from self-employment. The Enterprise Survey (ES) asks the same set of questions of enterprises that have employer–employee relationships, so we are not concerned about the comparison within our dataset. However, we should be careful when comparing firm-level and aggregate-level labor income share calculated with national income. At the firm level, little research has been done specifically on the measurement issues. For this reason, we try to estimate the plant-level labor income share using three definitions of the labor income share.

Definition 1
At the national level, the empirical literature usually calculates labor income share (LIS) as a relation of compensation of employees to total value added produced in country *c* in year *t* (GDP):

$$LIS_{c,t} = \frac{Compensation\ of\ employees_{c,t}}{GDP_{c,t}}$$

By contrast, as our dataset is at the firm level, this study follows Gomme and Rupert (2004) for the LIS definition, which takes the following form:

$$LIS_{i,t} = \frac{Compensation\ of\ employees_{i,t}}{Value\ added_{i,t}}$$

The subscript *i* denotes an individual firm. The ES asks a question on the compensation of employees but not on value added directly. In the calculation of value added for each firm, this paper relies on a definition that the World Bank employs in estimating the firm-level total factor productivity by utilizing the same dataset, ES. In its analysis, the difference between the total annual sales of the establishment and total annual cost of inputs acts as a proxy for value added, so that we can finally measure the labor income share such that

$$LIS_{i,t} = \frac{Compensation\ of\ employees_{i,t}}{total\ annual\ sales_{i,t} - total\ annual\ cost\ of\ inputs_{i,t}}$$

Definition 2
Relying on the definition of capital that the World Bank (2018) utilizes in the calculation of total factor productivity, we also define labor income share as follows:

$$LIS_{i,t} = \frac{Compensation\ of\ employees_{i,t}}{compensation\ of\ employees_{i,t} + total\ cost\ of\ capital_{i,t}}$$

Likewise, LIS2 is only available in the manufacturing sector because only firms in that sector are asked a question about the total cost of capital.[1] LIS2 essentially excludes the profits of firms and capitalists and captures how much of the total cost of inputs come from labor.

Definition 3
Following the definition of labor income share that Zhou (2016) employs, LIS3 is defined as

$$LIS_{i,t} = \frac{Compensation\ of\ employees_{i,t}}{total\ sales_{i,t}}$$

The advantage of this definition is that we can use almost all observations in our dataset, including services and other sectors. However, LIS3 could include some undesirable noise. It is possible that firms without any procurement have larger LIS3 than those procuring inputs. Under this definition, the labor income share may encompass not only labor's share of income but also the amount of input used in production, possibly making LIS3 biased against the ideal value, which captures how much value added is allocated to labor.

5.2 Descriptive Evidence

Table 5.2 presents countries in the dataset by region and income group, showing the composition of those in all sectors and the manufacturing sector. The share of high-income countries is relatively small because the objective of ES is to understand how the business environment affects firm performance, particularly in developing countries. Considering the current world population by region, the dataset includes fewer firms from the Middle East and North Africa. The percentages of total firms in all sectors and in the manufacturing sector by region and income group are analogous to each other.

[1] The total cost of capital is measured by variable n7a, with the corresponding question in the ES as follows: "Hypothetically, if this establishment were to purchase [machinery, vehicles, and equipment] it uses now, in their current condition and regardless of whether the establishment owns them or not, how much would they cost, independently of whether they are owned, rented, or leased?"

Table 5.2 Labor income share by income group and regions

Income group: all sectors			*Income group: manufacturing sector*		
	Frequency	*Percent*		*Frequency*	*Percent*
Low income	32,344	22.05	Low income	16,592	21.76
Lower middle income	60,070	40.96	Lower middle income	31,639	41.49
Upper middle income	44,917	30.63	Upper middle income	23,758	31.15
High income	9335	6.36	High income	4274	5.6
Total	146,666	100	Total	76,263	100
Region group: all sectors			Region group: manufacturing sector		
	Frequency	Percent		Frequency	Percent
East Asia and the Pacific	18,348	12.51	East Asia and the Pacific	10,621	13.93
Europe and Central Asia	29,381	20.03	Europe and Central Asia	12,672	16.62
Latin America and the Caribbean	34,715	23.67	Latin America and the Caribbean	18,939	24.83
Middle East and North Africa	9613	6.55	Middle East and North Africa	5926	7.77
South Asia	18,205	12.41	South Asia	13,392	17.56
Sub-Saharan Africa	36,404	24.82	Sub-Saharan Africa	14,713	19.29
Total	146,666	100	Total	76,263	100

Source: Authors' own calculations

Table 5.3 shows the percentage of categorized firms by firm size and ownership. With regard to firm size, there are larger share of micro-sized firms in all sectors than in the manufacturing sector, which implies that service sector is more likely to be operated by a small number of people, probably due to lower initial costs to start a business.[2] Yet micro and small firms are still a majority in the manufacturing sector. The dataset consists of few state-owned firms and a large number of private domestic firms, with the remainder consisting of private foreign firms.[3] The composition appears a little skewed, but it could be justified by the fact that the aim of ES is to focus on private enterprises in the first place.

[2] A firm size is defined as "Micro" for 0–5 employees, "Small" for 6–20, "Medium" for 21–50, and "Large" for 51 or more, following the International Labour Organization (ILO) definition.

[3] We employ Zhou's definition of ownership categorization. Foreign firms are defined as those with the proportion of foreign shareholders being equal to or greater than 10%. Private and state-owned firms are determined by the greater proportion of state-owned and private shareholders.

Table 5.3 Labor income share by firm size and ownership

Firm size: all sectors			*Firm size: manufacturing sector*		
	Frequency	*Percent*		*Frequency*	*Percent*
Micro	15,040	10.32	Micro	5169	6.81
Small	55,621	38.16	Small	26,085	34.37
Medium	32,300	22.16	Medium	17,422	22.95
Large	42,790	29.36	Large	27,223	35.87
Total	145,751	100	Total	75,899	100
Ownership: all sectors			Ownership: manufacturing sector		
	Frequency	Percent		Frequency	Percent
State-owned	1105	0.76	State-owned	444	0.59
Private	126,257	87.35	Private	65,984	87.49
Foreign	17,180	11.89	Foreign	8989	11.92
Total	144,542	100	Total	75,417	100

Source: Authors' own calculation

5.2.1 *Labor Income Share Trends Using Definition 1*

In this section, we employ labor income share definition 1 and thus conduct an analysis only for the manufacturing sector. Before scrutinizing labor income share, some observations are found far beyond its expected range. These values may bias our estimation, so we attempted to detect outliers as follows: First, the LIS values are transformed into ln(*LIS*). Then we apply the three standard deviation rule: observations that are more than three standard deviations away from the mean are then marked as outliers and turned into missing. Finally, we get the LIS1, which we use in this section. The percentage of missing values is shown in Appendix B, including those which are lost during the calculation under definition 1. Panel A of Fig. 5.1 illustrates the distribution for the observation whose value is from 0 to 2 because only 0.88% of them are beyond two the mean value of LIS1 is 0.39, and its distribution is skewed to the left.

In this paper, we utilize weights in calculating the average value of labor income share. The weight is basically the inverse of the probability of the selection of a particular firm and has already been computed by World Bank.[4] In Panel B of Fig. 5.1, high-income countries have the highest

[4] See "Methodology for weight computation" on the World Bank website for more detailed information on the method of the weight computation.

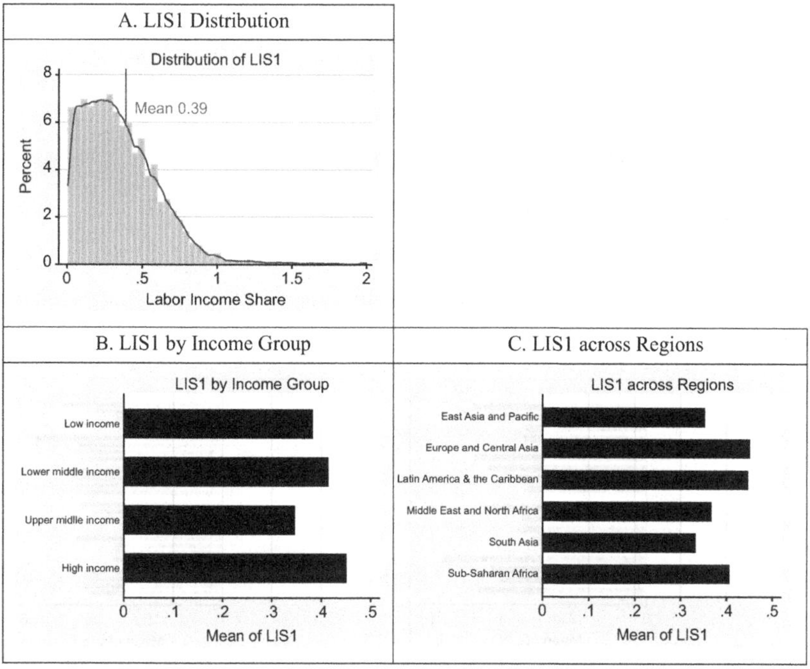

Fig. 5.1 LIS1 distribution and comparison by income group and region

labor income share of all, which is the same result as Guerriero (2012) using a similar definition, but the other countries show different results from hers. LIS1 is the lowest in upper middle-income countries and second lowest in low-income countries. As illustrated in Panel C of Fig. 5.1, Europe and Central Asia as well as Latin America and the Caribbean obtain a relatively high labor income share, followed by sub-Saharan Africa, and, lastly, South Asia. The results are almost comparable to what Oishi and Paul (2018) found from the sector-level labor income share, although North American countries are not included in the ES respondent countries.

In this sub-section, we compare labor income share by firm characteristics: firm size and ownership type. Panel A of Fig. 5.2 indicates that labor income share decreases as the firm size expands. Theoretically, the optimal decision of a firm with market power is to pay workers less than their value of marginal product. Since large firms tend to gain more market power, it

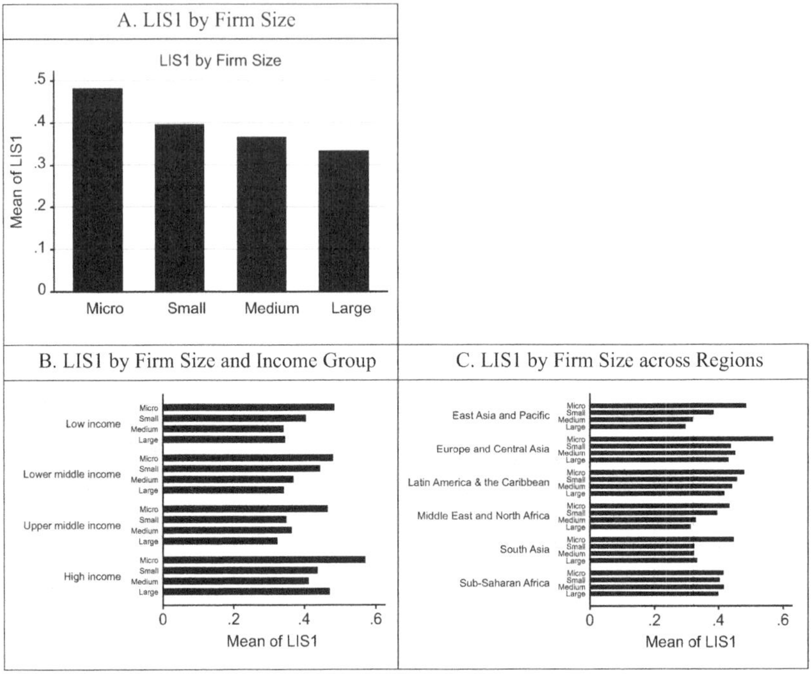

Fig. 5.2 LIS1 by firm size

is understandable that labor income share is negatively correlated with firm size. The correlation is the most conspicuous in low-income and lower middle-income countries, while it becomes less obvious in upper middle-income and high-income countries (Fig. 5.2, Panel B). Across regions, the negative relationship between firm size and labor income share seems to hold, but in sub-Saharan Africa, there is little variation in labor income share by firm size (Fig. 5.2, Panel C).

As illustrated in Panel A of Fig. 5.3, labor income share is highest in domestic private firms, with foreign private firms next, followed by state-owned firms. Zhou (2016) argues that LISs > LISp > LISf (LIS: labor income share, s stands for state-owned, p for private, and f for foreign) should hold when labor productivity is sorted as ys < yp < yf. This is because productive firms, which he assumes are predominantly foreign firms, pay wages based not on labor productivity but on the average productivity of all firms in the economy, whereby foreign ownership is associated with low labor income share. However, while that prediction does not hold here, it seems to hold if we take total factor productivity as a measure of productivity (see Appendix D). There appears to be no consistent and obvious trend between ownership and labor income share by income group (Fig. 5.3, Panel B). As for regions, LIS1 is sorted as LISs > LISp > LISf in Europe and Central Asia, Latin America and the Caribbean, the Middle East and North Africa, and South Asia (Fig. 5.3, Panel C).

LIS1 is calculated as labor compensation over firm-level value added with the average value of 0.39 (Panel A, Fig. 5.1). High-income economies enjoy the highest share of 0.45, as opposed to the Heckscher and Ohlin model or Stolper-Samuelson model, suggesting advanced economies would concentrate on capital-intensive goods and lowering labor income share relative to developing economies. Comparing LIS1 by firm size and type of ownership, LIS1 varies more or less in a predictable way:

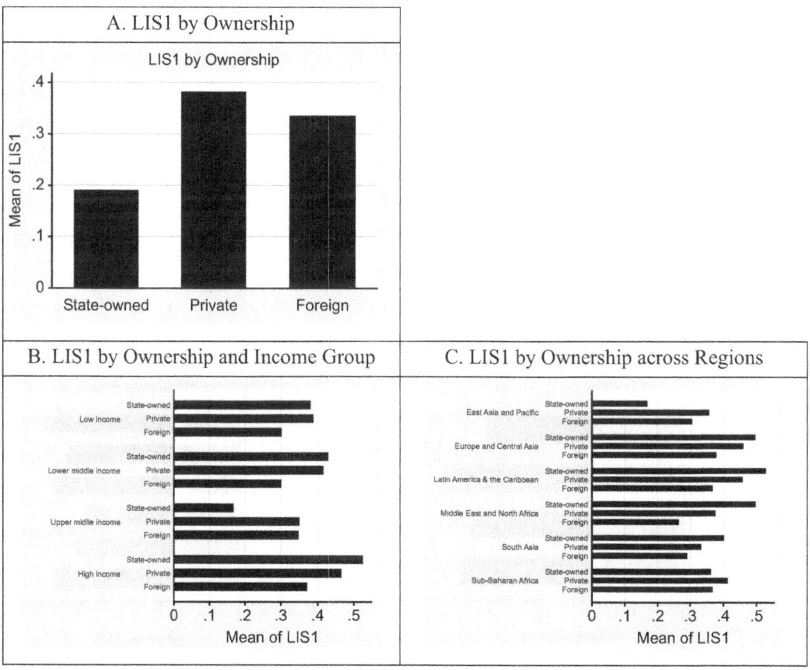

Fig. 5.3 LIS1 by ownership type

smaller firms have lower LIS1 and state-owned firms have higher LIS1. The latter pattern is not observed at the aggregate level because the proportion of state-owned firms with lower LIS in both upper middle-income and East Asia and the Pacific countries is higher than in other regions and economies.

5.2.2 *Labor Income Share Trends Using Definition 2*

This section uses definition 2 to analyze labor income share in the manufacturing sector. We employ the same method of detecting and eliminating the outliers as in definition 1 and get the distribution of LIS2 (Panel A, Fig. 5.4). The mean value is 0.44, and LIS2 is somewhat evenly distributed relative to LIS1 except for the observations bunching up around 1. In definition 2, firms without any capital used in production take the value of 1. Another point to note is that definition 2 lost the most observations

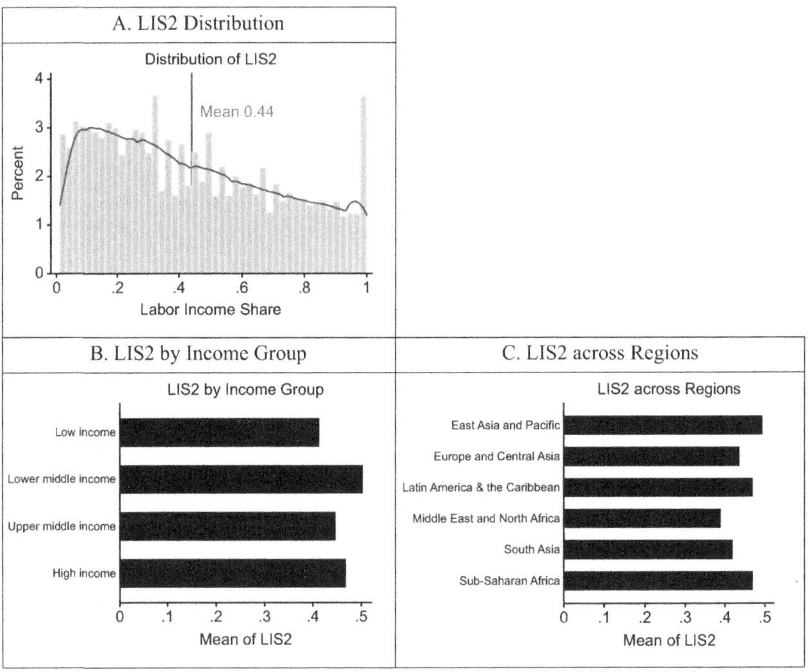

Fig. 5.4 LIS2 distribution and comparison by income group and regions

out of the three definitions during the process of calculating and eliminating outliers, which may make our estimates less representative (See Appendix B). Panel B of Fig. 5.4 shows a different picture from Panel B of Fig. 5.1 in that lower middle-income countries rather than high-income countries have the largest labor income share. The East Asia and the Pacific region, which was second lowest for LIS1, has the highest labor income share in definition 2 (Panel C, Fig. 5.4).

The labor income share is the highest in micro-sized firms but there is almost no difference among the other three sizes under definition 2 (Fig. 5.5, Panel A). In low and lower middle-income economies, the labor income share falls as the firm size grows, whereas the relationship between the two is unclear in high and upper middle-income economies (Fig. 5.5, Panel B). The difference in labor income share across firm sizes is greatest in the East Asia and the Pacific region, where micro firms gain the highest average LIS2 value of 0.68.

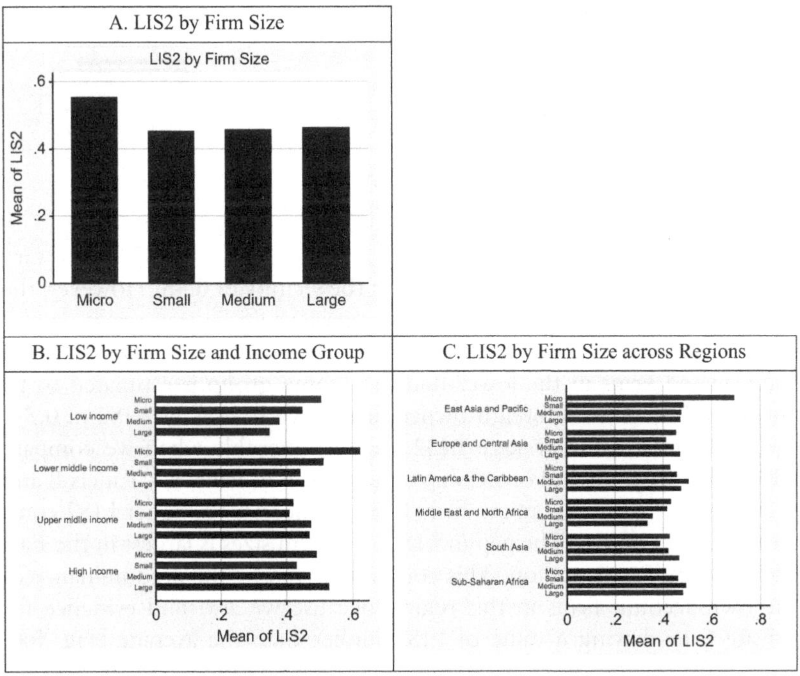

Fig. 5.5 LIS2 by firm size

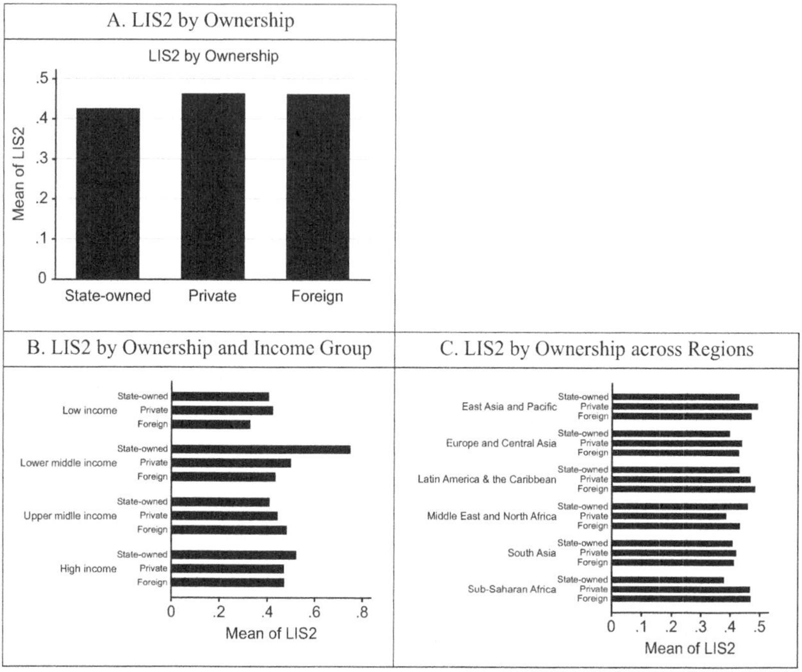

Fig. 5.6 LIS2 by ownership type

As shown in Panel A of Fig. 5.6, the average values of LIS2 do not vary by type of firm ownership and hovers in the vicinity of 0.45. However, the variation is slightly higher when we compare these figures across ownership types and income groups (Fig. 5.6, Panel B). The average LIS2 of state-owned firms in the lower middle-income group is estimated to be around 0.76, whereas foreign-owned firms have an average LIS2 of 0.34.

Differences in the average LIS2 is also noticeable when we compare LIS2 across regions and ownership types (Fig. 5.6, Panel C). Panels B and C of Fig. 5.5 show that micro firms, on average, have a higher LIS2 compared to larger firms. The gap in LIS across firm sizes is largest in the East Asia and the Pacific region. This could be driven by the predominance of the own-account firms in this region because we also find evidence for private firms having a value of LIS2 higher than the average (Fig. 5.6, Panel C). On the other hand, state-owned firms in sub-Saharan Africa have a lower labor income share than private and foreign firms.

5.2.3 Labor Income Share Trends Using Definition 3

5.2.3.1 Firms in the Manufacturing Sector

As mentioned in the Sect. 5.2, LIS3 could be the most biased labor income share out of three. LIS3 is likely to be influenced partly by the amounts of inputs used in production. LIS3 will deviate from the ideal value, which captures how much value added is allocated to labor, unless the proportion of inputs is homogeneous across firms. Even though definition 3 uses samples in our dataset to the full, we should interpret the results conservatively. This definition is also concentrated in the manufacturing sector. We employ the same method of eliminating the outliers as in definitions 1 and 2. Panel A of Fig. 5.7 illustrates the distribution for the observation whose value is from 0 to 1, because only 0.49% of the values are beyond this range. The mean value of LIS1 is 0.22, and its distribution is skewed to the left. In Panel B of Fig. 5.7, high and lower middle-income

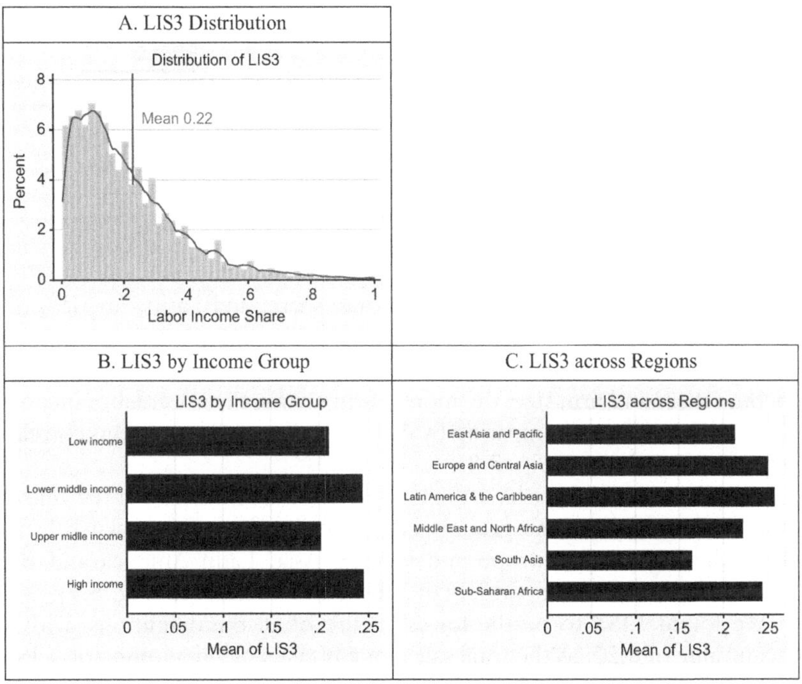

Fig. 5.7 LIS3 distribution and comparison by income group and regions

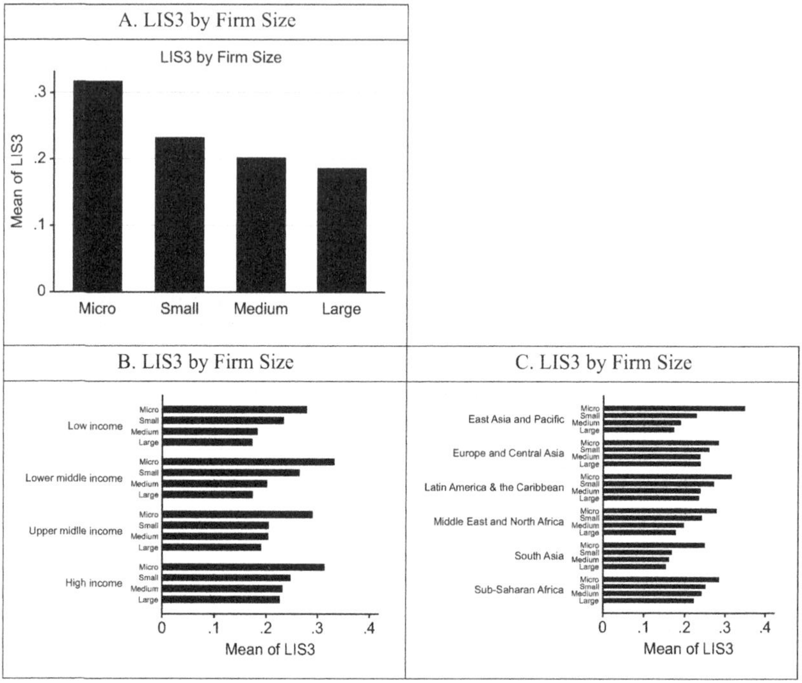

Fig. 5.8 LIS3 by firm size

economies show the highest labor income share, and Latin America and the Caribbean are the highest across regions (Fig. 5.7, Panel C).

Using definition 3, we find a negative relationship between labor income share and firm size: the more a firm grows, the lower labor income share becomes. Even comparing by income group and region, this correlation does not change (Fig. 5.8).

Private domestic firms have the highest labor income share at the aggregate level and by income group while, across regions, state-owned firms show the highest in Europe and Central Asia, Latin America and the Caribbean, Middle East and North Africa, and South Asia (Fig. 5.9).

We found LIS3 to be the lowest figure of all the definitions, with a mean value of 0.22, as the total sale alone is taken as a denominator. LIS3 varies across regions and is the lowest in South Asia, the mean of which is 0.16 (Fig. 5.7, Panel C). This could be because private domestic firms do

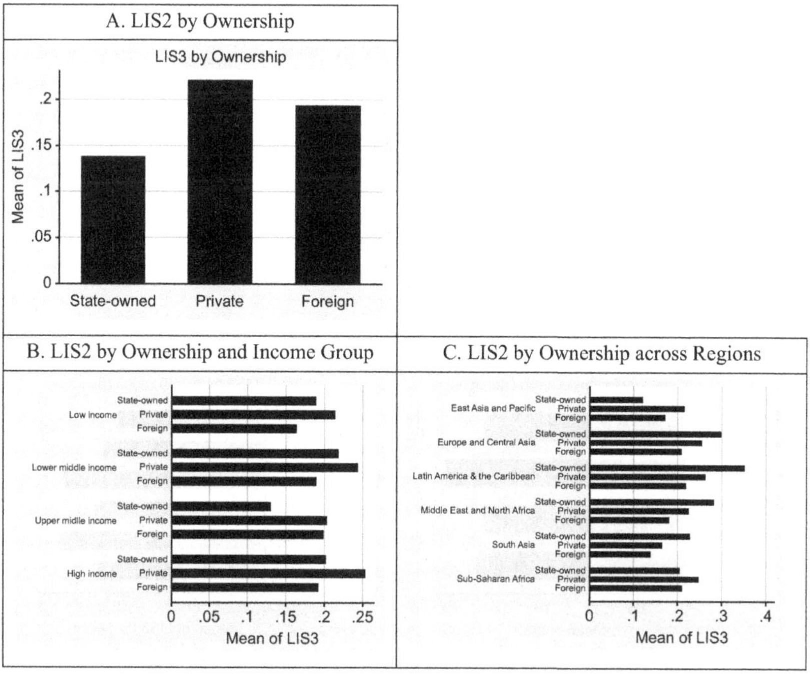

Fig. 5.9 LIS2 by ownership type

not reap a large share of income to labor. As with the other definitions, larger firms tend to enjoy a lower LIS in definition 3, and its variation is the most conspicuous in the East Asia and the Pacific region, with an LIS3 of 0.34 for micro firms and 0.17 for large ones (Fig. 5.8, Panel C).

5.2.3.2 *Firms in the Service Sector*

In this section, we also follow definition 3 but focus on the service sector. The outliers are detected and taken out of the sample through the same methodology used in the previous sections. Panel A of Fig. 5.10 shows that the average of LIS3 in the service sector, 0.23, is almost the same as that in the manufacturing sector, 0.22, although the sector comparison should be cautiously made because the labor income share gap across sectors may merely capture the input effects. If the manufacturing sector procures more materials or intermediate goods than the service sector, which are not deducted from sales in definition 3, LIS3 might reflect the

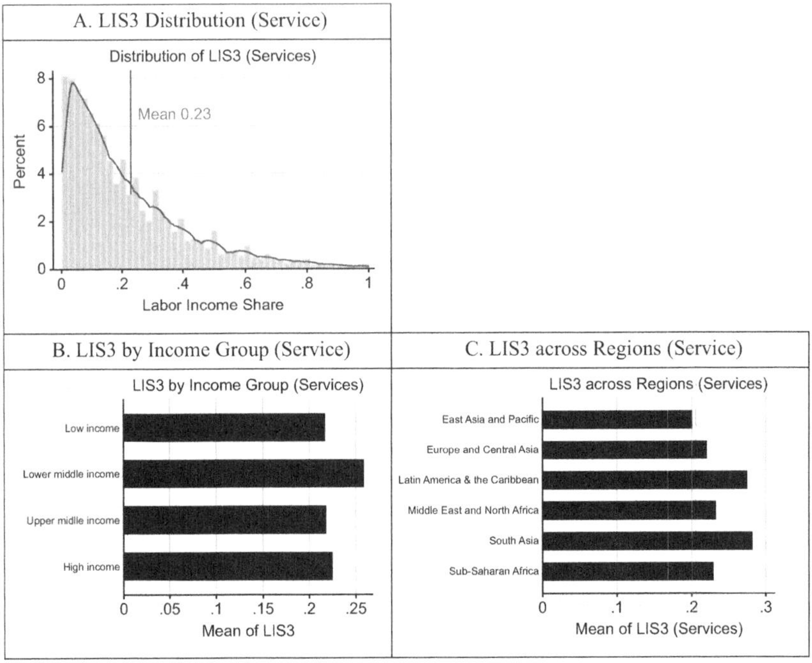

Fig. 5.10 LIS3 distribution and comparison by income group and regions (service)

sector difference in procurement. In the service sector, lower middle-income economies have the highest labor income share, while no obvious differences are not found among the other three economies (Fig. 5.10, Panel B).

LIS3 in the service sector does not seem to vary by firm size, even after dividing the sample into income groups and regions (Fig. 5.11).

Taking a look at ownership, LIS3 in the service sector has the lowest value in state-owned firms and the second lowest in private domestic firms. Moreover, state-owned firms have the highest LIS in high-income economies as well as in South Asia (Fig. 5.12, Panels B and C), where we can observe a heterogeneous ownership–LIS3 relationship in the service sector.

LIS presents a different picture under the third definition in the service sector, even from LIS3 in the manufacturing sector in the previous

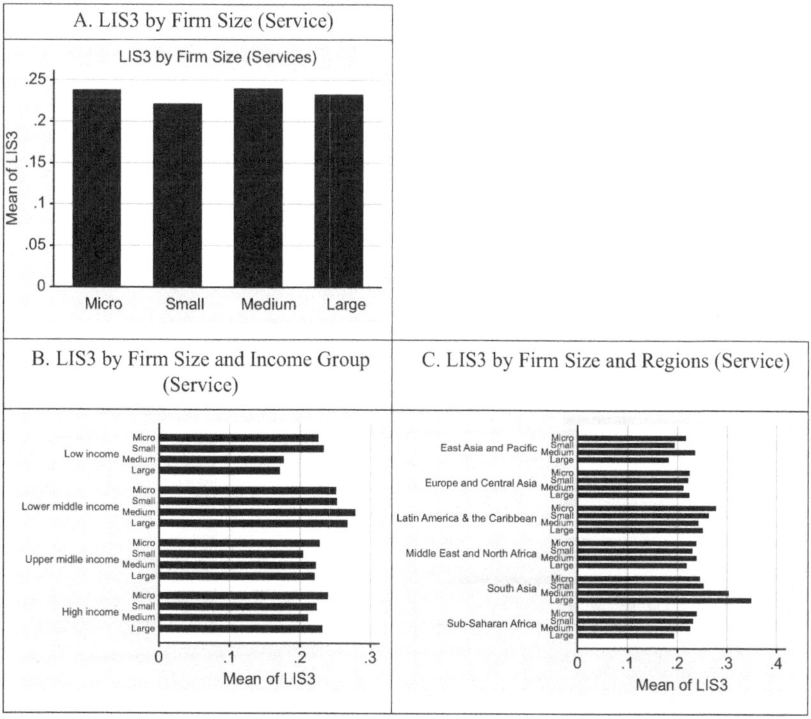

Fig. 5.11 LIS3 by firm size (service)

section. The most striking difference is that LIS3 has little variation across firm sizes, hovering around 0.21 (Fig. 5.11, Panel A). Smaller firms no longer maintain a higher labor income share in the service sector. The gap in LIS across firm sizes is greatest in South Asia (Fig. 5.11, Panel C). At the aggregate level, private foreign firms earn the highest LIS and private domestic firms come second (Fig. 5.12, Panel A), which is also a different pattern from LIS3 in the manufacturing sector, where private domestic firms are the highest. Yet the heterogeneous trends are seen by income group and across regions, such that in high-income and South Asian countries state-owned firms reap by far the highest share of income, with an LIS of 0.56 and 0.81, respectively (Fig. 5.12, Panels B and C).

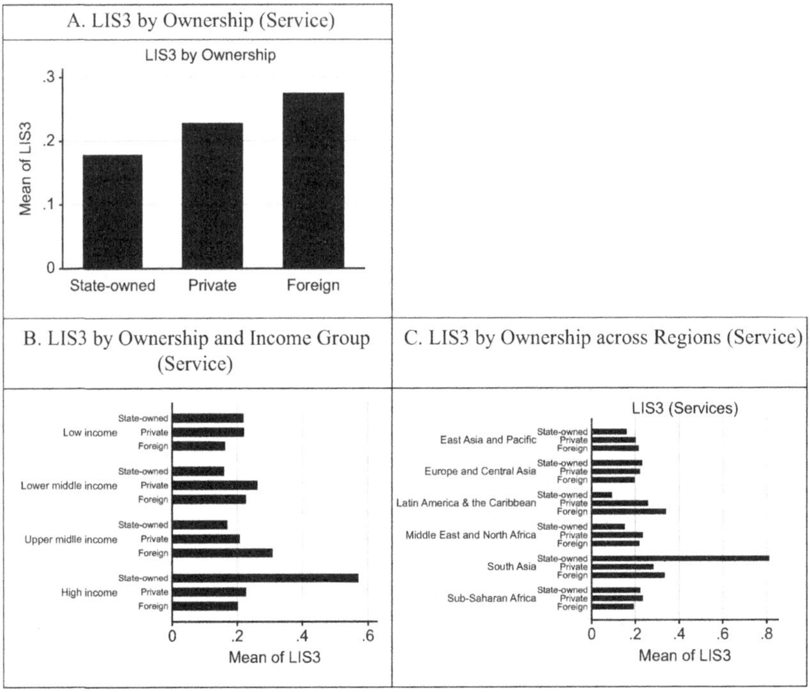

Fig. 5.12 LIS3 by ownership type (service)

5.3 Comparison of LIS1, LIS2, and LIS3

This section highlights the synergies between the four sets of estimates of the labor income share. We first compare the average LIS estimates by income groups (Fig. 5.13, Panel A). The income group averages from the first two definitions (LIS1 and LIS2) are significantly higher than those from the third definition (for both manufacturing and services), and this result is robust across different income groups. We find similar trends when the LIS statistics are compared across regions (Fig. 5.13, Panel B), firm sizes (Fig. 5.13, Panel C), and ownership types (Fig. 5.13, Panel D).

The numerator across different definitions measures compensation of employees; however, in the denominator, we follow alternative approaches

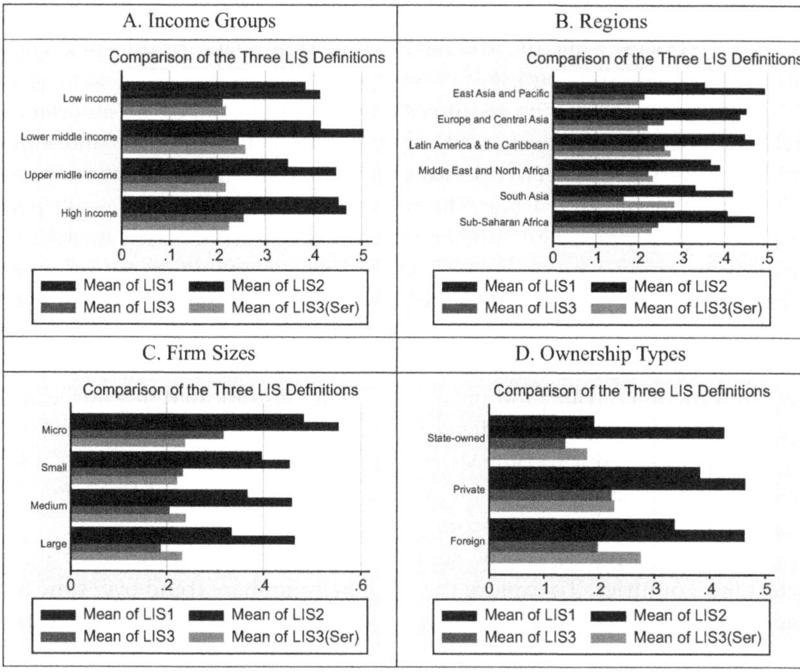

Fig. 5.13 Comparison of LIS estimates

as a proxy for the firm-level value added. We use the gap between the total annual sales on the one hand and the cost of inputs, compensation of employees plus total cost of capital, and total sales, on the other hand, as the denominator for LIS1, LIS2, and LIS3, respectively. The figures for total sales for LIS3, on average, are higher than the estimates of the denominators for LIS1 and LIS2, which broadly explains the gap in the labor income share estimates between different approaches within a particular region, income group, or ownership type. However, the gap between the LIS estimates varies considerably across regions. Firms in South Asia show a much smaller gap compared to firms in East Asia and the Pacific and sub-Saharan Africa. Micro firms clearly top the ranking based on LIS1, LIS2, and LIS3-manufacturing, but there is not a clear leader in the service (LIS3) sector when firms of different sizes are compared. On the other hand, foreign-owned firms top the ranking based on LIS3-services, while the average labor income share for private-owned firms is the highest using LIS1.

Definition 3 allows us to directly compare the labor income share between the manufacturing and service sectors. For medium and large firms, laborers in the service sector enjoy a higher share of income compared to their counterparts in the manufacturing sector. This result particularly holds for foreign and state-owned firms. In contrast, micro and small firms enjoy a higher labor income share in manufacturing than in services. By ownership type, private domestic firms have the highest labor income share in the manufacturing sector. The average labor income share for manufacturing firms is higher than that in services in countries from the high-income group, and most of them are also located in Europe and Central Asia. Overall, the evidence suggests that manufacturing firms tend to have a lower labor income share as the firm size increases. Such causal links can be related to capital-intensive technologies if larger firms tend to use them more with greater economies of scale.

We next compare the time series trends of labor income share for a select few countries. To explore the labor income share trend over time for the three LIS definitions, we selected countries that have at least three years of data. This left us with only 11 countries, out of which nine are from Latin America and the Caribbean. For this reason, we compare the time series trends only for this region (Fig. 5.14). The outcomes show mixed evidence as the time series plots vary across LIS definitions within a country with the exception of Bolivia, Ecuador, and Peru, where the LIS trends are somewhat consistent. We group these countries into five categories. First are countries where most of the LIS measures show an upward trend (Argentina, Ecuador, Nicaragua, and Paraguay). Second are countries with a downward trend based on most of the definitions (El Salvador and Peru). The third group consists of Bolivia, where most of the LIS trends look U-shaped. Uruguay forms the fourth group, where the LIS trends conform to an inverted U-shaped pattern, and the final group consists of Honduras, where the time series plots move in every possible direction. We conclude that the time series trends do not correspond to a regional decline in the labor income share.

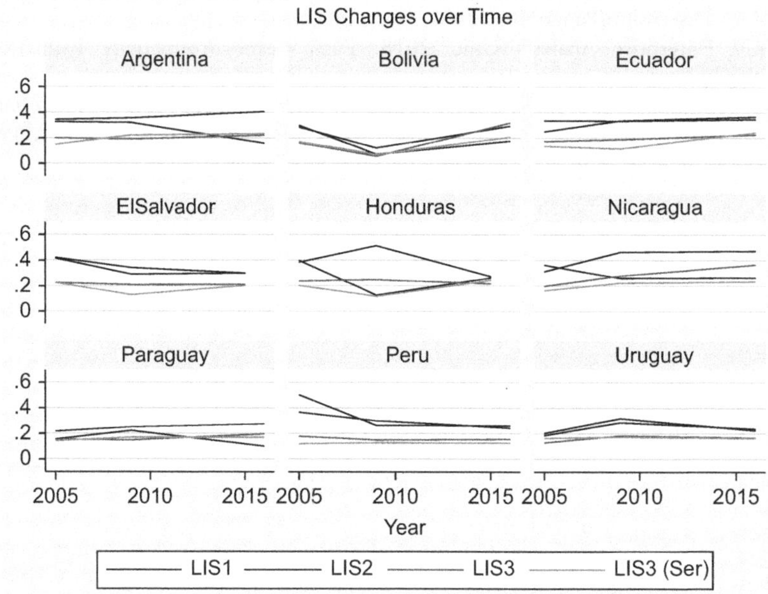

Fig. 5.14 Time series trends for Latin America and the Caribbean

References

Gollin, D. 2002. Getting income shares right. *Journal of Political Economy*, *110*(2), 458–474.

Gomme, P. and P. Rupert. 2004. *Measuring Labor's Share of Income. Policy Discussion Paper* 7. Federal Reserve Bank of Cleveland.

Guerriero, Marta. 2012. The Labour Share of Income Around the World. Evidence from a Panel Dataset. http://piketty.pse.ens.fr/files/Guerriero2012.pdf (accessed 26 November 2018).

Krueger, Alan B. 1998. Measuring Labor's Share. *American Economic Review* 89(2): 45–51.

Oishi, Y. and S. Paul. 2018. "Sectoral Labor Income Share Dynamics: Cross-Country Evidence from a Novel Dataset." ADBI Working Paper 875. Tokyo: Asian Development Bank Institute. https://www.adb.org/publications/sectoral-labor-income-share-dynamics.

Paul, S. and H. Isaka 2019. Labor Income Share at the Firm Level: Global Trends, IZA Discussion Paper No. 12852. [December].

World Enterprise Analysis Unit. 2018. Firm Level Productivity Estimates. World Bank.

Zhou, Minghai. 2016. *Labor's Share of Income: Another Key to Understand China's Income Inequality*. Singapore: Springer. https://www.springer.com/kr/book/9789811001727 (accessed 26 November 2018).

CHAPTER 6

The Economic Forces Behind Labor Income Share: Theory

> The great mystery of the modern theory of distribution
> is why anyone regards the share of wages and profits
> as an interesting problem.
> —*Blaug (1996: 467)*

Economists have always been concerned with the functional distribution of income. David Ricardo's statement, published back in 1817, serves as a testimony to this fact, "*To determine the laws which regulate [this] distribution is the principal problem in political economy.*" As emphasized by both Atkinson (2009) and Glyn (2009), the study of factor income shares plays an important role in understanding the relationship between national income and personal income, the relationship between wage inequality and wealth inequality, and how they link to overall income inequality and concerns for fairness in different sources of income.

A large body of research documents a global decline in the labor income share and offers several theoretical explanations for this phenomenon (Elsby et al. 2013; Piketty 2014). According to the "Accumulation view," a decline in the labor income share is driven by a decline in the relative price of capital (Karabarbounis and Neiman 2014) or a rise in the stock of capital relative to income through a growth in aggregate savings (Piketty 2014). On the other hand, Rognlie (2015) supports the "scarcity view," which assumes an increase in capital share due to the relative scarcity of

S. Paul, *Labor Income Share*,
https://doi.org/10.1007/978-981-15-6860-2_6

some forms of capital, as opposed to the "accumulation view." In either case, the assumption of a non-unitary elasticity of substitution (σ) between capital and labor plays a crucial role in the movement of the labor income share. The crucial role of σ in analyzing the factor income shares has been noted since the seminal work of Hicks (1932) and Robinson (1933). Following the Hicksian partial elasticity of substitution, Elsby et al. (2013) demonstrate the relationship between labor income share (LIS) and σ as $d \ln LIS = -(1 - LIS)\frac{\sigma - 1}{\sigma} dln\left(\frac{K}{L}\right)$. It suggests a drop in LIS when $\sigma > 1$. With $\sigma = 1$, factor income shares remain constant. If capital and labor are gross complements, then a decline in effective capital per unit of effective labor can lead to a more than proportionate increase in the rental rate compared to wages. This mechanism can lead to a lower income share of labor (Alvarez-Cuadrado et al. 2015). At the same time, the "Accumulation view" assumes capital and labor to be gross substitutes. To this extent, either $\sigma > 1$ (capital and labor as gross substitutes) or $\sigma < 1$ (capital and labor as gross complements) can account for changes in the labor income share and rightly so, researchers are widely divided on this issue. We extend the theoretical analysis by considering both homogeneous and heterogeneous labor market and the comparative statics outcomes on the labor income share.

6.1 Production Technology

We begin with a simple two-input production function with technology to understand the role of technological change and factor ratios in productivity growth and factor shares. In Eq. (6.1), output (Y) is produced with capital (K), labor (L), and technological progress (A).

$$Y = f(K, L, A) \tag{6.1}$$

Hicks (1932) defined technological progress that leaves the composition of capital and labor in the production process unchanged. This is known as Hicks-neutral technological progress, which can be expressed as a variant of Eq. (6.1): $Y = Af(K, L)$. Equation (6.1) takes the form of $Y = f(K, AL)$ when technological progress is labor-augmenting. This is also known as Harrod-neutral technological progress (Harrod 1942). And finally, we can write Eq. (6.1) as $Y = f(AK, L)$. This reflects capital-augmenting technological progress and is also known as Solow-neutral technological progress (Solow 1958). Acemoglu (2002) defined factor bias in technological progress when technological progress affects the marginal productivity ratios of input factors.

$$\frac{\partial}{\partial A}\left[\frac{dY}{dL}\Big/\frac{dY}{dK}\right] > 0 \tag{6.2}$$

Constancy of factor income share can be shown using either (1) a Cobb-Douglas production framework or (2) a Constant-Elasticity-of-Substitution (CES) production framework reflecting Harrod-neutral production technology in a neoclassical balanced growth model (Gollin 2002). Since the primary goal of this section is to summarize the key theoretical models that explain changes in the labor income share, we do not elaborate on the theoretical models that show constant factor income shares.

6.2 The Role of Elasticity of Substitution Between Capital and Labor (σ)

The assumption of a non-unitary elasticity of substitution (σ) between capital and labor plays a crucial role in the movement of the labor income share.[1] The discussion of labor income share dates back to David Ricardo (1821). However, the neoclassical economists achieved a significant milestone in the early twentieth century. Marshall's (1920) laws of derived demand provided the foundation, and later the mathematical formulation of the theories of supply and demand (Hicks 1932; Allen 1938) put the discussion of factor income share and the role of factor elasticities and factor substitutions therein at the core.[2] We provide a simple two-factor production function to discuss the link between elasticity of substitution and

[1] The crucial role of σ in analyzing the factor income shares has been noted since the seminal work of Hicks (1932) and Robinson (1933). Following the Hicksian partial elasticity of substitution, Elsby et al. (2013) demonstrate the relationship between labor income share (LIS) and σ as $d\ln LIS = -(1-LIS)\frac{\sigma-1}{\sigma}dln\left(\frac{K}{L}\right)$. It suggests a drop in LIS when $\sigma > 1$. With $\sigma = 1$, factor income shares remain constant.

[2] For a detailed discussion on the evolution of historical thoughts on factor income share, see Kraemer (2010).

factor income shares. Consider a linear homogeneous production function with constant returns to scale,

$$Y = F(K, L), \text{ where } F_i > 0, F_{ii} < 0, \text{ and } F_{ij} > 0 \tag{6.3}$$

Firms maximize profit ($\pi = F(K, L) - rK - wL$) in a competitive market structure, r is return to capital, and w stands for wages. Thus, the ratio of marginal productivities equal factor prices, that is, $\frac{F_L}{F_K} = \frac{w}{r}$. Holding output constant, Allen (1938, 341) defined the elasticity of substitution as

$$\sigma = \frac{dln\left(\frac{K}{L}\right)}{dln\left(\frac{w}{r}\right)} = \frac{dln\left(\frac{K}{L}\right)}{dln\left(\frac{F_L}{F_K}\right)} \tag{6.4}$$

Following Hamermesh 1993, 23–29), we write the price elasticity of labor demand holding the output and the return to capital constant (Marshall's first law of derived demand) as

$$\eta_{LL}^{Compensated} = -(1 - L_S)\sigma < 0 \tag{6.5}$$

where $L_S = \frac{wL}{Y}(>0)$ is the labor income share.

Equation ((6.3) implies that a higher value of σ leads to higher own-price elasticity of labor. Similarly, the cross-price elasticity of demand can be written as follows:

$$\eta_{LK}^{Compensated} = (1 - L_S)\sigma > 0 \tag{6.6}$$

Demand elasticities in Eqs. (6.5) and (6.6) are also known as compensated demand elasticities as they do not allow for the aggregate output to change because of the changes in input prices. Assuming competitive market, we can now introduce the scale effect or Marshall's second law of derived demand, which leads to expressions for the uncompensated demand elasticities. The scale effect implies that a 1% increase in the factor prices raises the cost and product prices by that factor's share. Uncompensated demand elasticities consider this effect.

$$\begin{aligned}\eta_{LL}\text{Uncompensated} &= -\left(1-L_S\right)\sigma - L_S\eta \ \left(\text{own}-\text{price elasticity}\right)\\ \eta_{LK}\text{Uncompensated} &= \left(1-L_S\right)\left(\sigma-\eta\right)\ \left(\text{cross}-\text{price elasticity}\right)\end{aligned} \tag{6.7}$$

From Eq. (6.7) we can infer that the uncompensated labor demand elasticity is higher when the price elasticity of demand for the product goes up. A higher elasticity of substitution produces a similar effect. Finally, the higher the labor share, the higher the uncompensated labor demand elasticity. These rules of derived demand play a key role when movements in the labor income share are explained by changes in wages and the level of employment.[3]

The literature on the estimation of σ is large and still growing[4] but is often plagued by subjective choices on parametric assumptions and functional form of the production (Leon-Ledesma et al. 2010). Two recent studies attempt to overcome these issues. Oberfield and Raval (2014) use a novel micro-level framework to estimate the aggregate elasticity of substitution (σ_{Agg} from here on). They take into consideration the elasticity of substitution between factor inputs within a plant and reallocation of factor inputs across plants. Using plant-level data, they find estimates of σ_{Agg} to be less than one. On the other hand, Chirinko and Mallick (2017) obtain similar findings by using low pass filters in panel data to identify the long-run relations in production technology. Despite these insightful attempts, a consensus on the estimates of the aggregate elasticity of substitution between capital and labor is yet to be reached.

6.2.1 *Changes in the Labor Income Share with Homogeneous Labor Market*

Although the recent literature shows that the skill composition of the labor force is a crucial factor in explaining changes in the labor income share, we begin this section by reviewing a theoretical model that assumes homogeneous labor. Bentolila and Saint-Paul (2003) developed the share capital (SK) model to analyze the drivers of labor income share. They showed that in a CES production function, under the assumption of constant returns to scale and labor-augmenting technological progress,

[3] Schneider (2011) provides a comprehensive summary on this topic in a recent survey article on the labor income share.

[4] See Chirinko (2008) for a comprehensive summary.

perfectly competitive factor markets can produce a stable relationship between the labor income share and capital-output ratio, which they called the "Share capital (SK)" curve. We consider a standard CES production function with two inputs capital (K) and labor (L) as shown in Eq. (6.8):

$$Y = \left[(AK)^{\frac{\sigma-1}{\sigma}} + (BL)^{\frac{\sigma-1}{\sigma}} \right]^{\frac{\sigma}{\sigma-1}} \tag{6.8}$$

From Eq. (6.8), the labor income share can be derived as

$$L_S = \frac{(BL)^{\frac{\sigma-1}{\sigma}}}{(AK)^{\frac{\sigma-1}{\sigma}} + (BL)^{\frac{\sigma-1}{\sigma}}} \tag{6.9}$$

and the capital-output ratio as

$$k = \left[\frac{(AK)^{\frac{\sigma-1}{\sigma}}}{(AK)^{\frac{\sigma-1}{\sigma}} + (BL)^{\frac{\sigma-1}{\sigma}}} \right]^{\frac{\sigma}{\sigma-1}} \tag{6.10}$$

Combining (6.9) and (6.10), we get

$$L_S = 1 - (k)^{\frac{\sigma-1}{\sigma}} \tag{6.11}$$

The expression for the labor income share in Eq. (6.11) is known as the "SK" schedule, which shows a functional relationship between the labor income share and capital-output ratio. For $\sigma > 1$, that is labor and capital are gross substitutes, a higher k reduces the labor share. When $\sigma < 1$, that is, labor and capital are gross complements, a higher k increases the labor income share. However, this relationship remains unaltered in changes in factor prices or quantities, or labor-augmenting technological progress. Any changes on these parameters only produce a movement along the SK curve (movement from E1 to E2), as shown in Fig. 6.1. However, a change in the capital-augmenting technological progress (A) can move the SK curve from E1 to E3, perturbing the stable relationship between the

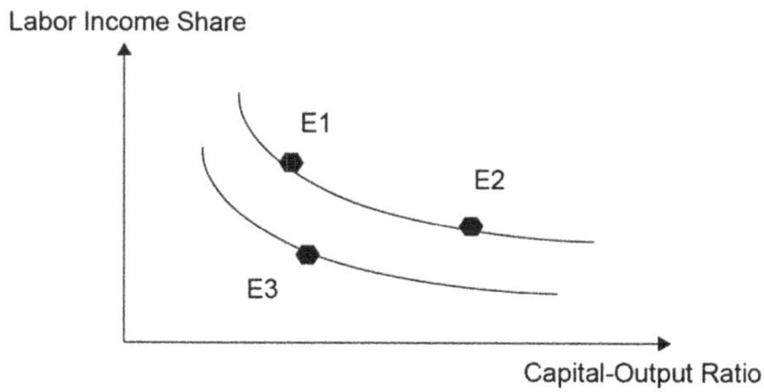

Fig. 6.1 The share-capital (SK) curve

labor income share and capital-output ratio. As Bentolila and Saint-Paul (2003) argue, other factors such as a wedge between the marginal product of labor and the real wage could also make the SK curve shift in a similar manner in the (LIS, k) plane.

6.3 Changes in the Labor Income Share with Heterogeneous Labor Market

The substitutability between capital and labor with heterogeneous labor provides a much richer set of possible distributional outcomes (Atkinson 2009). The relevance of capital-skill substitutability in studying changes in the labor share of income can also be discussed in light of a two-stage production structure. As Goldin and Katz (1998) argued, in the first stage it is plausible to expect that skilled workers adopt new technology and make use of capital efficiently showing high capital-skill complementarity. In the second stage, if unskilled workers take over the routine maintenance of machines and technology, then we can expect a lower level of capital-skill complementarity in the second stage compared to the first stage. To model heterogeneous labor market, a nested-CES production function is generally considered with three inputs: capital (K), skilled labor (S), and unskilled labor (U).[5] With three inputs, the CES production function can be nested in the following ways: $Y = f[(K, S)U]$, $Y = f[(K, U)S]$

[5] Two level bested CES production function was originally developed by Sato (1975), and since then it has been used extensively in many fields, including capital-skill complementarity (Krusell et al. 2000). More recently, Karabarbounis and Neiman (2014) use a similar version of multi-input nested-CES production function to explain changes in the labor income share.

and $Y = f[(S, U)K]$ (nested-inputs are within the first bracket). Since $Y = [(S, U)K]$ boils down to a standard 2-factor CES production. Karabarbounis and Neiman (2014) consider the other two functions to examine the link between capital-skill complementarity and the labor share of income. The literature on capital-skill complementarity relies on the first nesting strategy (Griliches 1969; Fallon and Layard 1975; Krusell et al. 2000) and we present a standard version of $Y = f[(K, S)U]$ in Eq. (6.12).

$$Y = f\left[(K,S)U\right] = \left[\theta\left[\varnothing(AK)^{\frac{\rho-1}{\rho}} + (1-\varnothing)(B_S S)^{\frac{\rho-1}{\rho}}\right]^{\frac{\rho}{\rho-1}\frac{\sigma-1}{\sigma}} + (1-\theta)(B_U U)^{\frac{\sigma-1}{\sigma}}\right]^{\frac{\sigma}{\sigma-1}} \quad (6.12)$$

In Eq. (6.12), Y is output; K, S, and U denote capital, skilled labor, and unskilled labor; θ and $\varnothing$ represent distribution parameters; σ denotes the elasticity of substitution between K and U (similarly, between U and S); and ρ denotes the elasticity of substitution between K and S. Efficiency parameters A, B_S, and B_U represent technological progress in capital, skilled labor, and unskilled labor. The skill-capital complementarity assumes $\sigma > \rho$. It implies that if capital is more substitutable with unskilled labor than skilled labor (Griliches 1969; Berman et al. 1994), then a drop in the share of income is likely to be larger for the unskilled labor compared to the skilled labor resulting from a drop in the relative price of capital.[6] Under the assumption of perfectly competitive factor markets, the labor income share can be written as follows:

$$L_S = \frac{\frac{\partial f}{\partial S}S + \frac{\partial f}{\partial U}U}{f\left[(K,S)U\right]} \quad (6.13)$$

In Eq. (6.13), real wages equal to marginal productivity of each type of laborers. Using this notion of perfectly competitive factor markets, from Eq. (6.13) we derive an expression for the labor income share as follows:

[6] This is also related to a large literature on skill-biased technical change (SBTC). See Griliches (1969); Acemoglu (2002); Autor et al. (2003); Caselli (1999), among others.

$$L_S = 1 - \frac{\varnothing}{1-\varnothing}(Ak)^{\frac{\rho-1}{\rho}}\left[\theta^{\frac{\sigma(\rho-1)}{\rho-\sigma}}(1-\varnothing)^{\frac{\rho(\sigma-1)}{\rho-\sigma}} + (1-\theta)^{\frac{\sigma(\rho-1)}{\rho-\sigma}} l^{\frac{\sigma-1}{\rho-\sigma}} \omega^{\frac{\rho(\sigma-1)}{\rho-\sigma}}\right]^{\frac{\rho-\sigma}{\rho(\sigma-1)}} \quad (6.14)$$

In Eq. (6.14), k denotes the capital-output ratio $\left(\frac{K}{Y}\right)$, l represents the relative supply of skilled labor $\left(\frac{B_S S}{B_U U}\right)$, and ω denotes the skill premium $\left(\frac{\frac{\partial f}{\partial S}/B_S}{\frac{\partial f}{\partial U}/B_U}\right)$. An equation like (6.14) can explain changes in the labor income share driven by capital-augmenting technological progress, changes in the capital-skilled labor ratio, and changes in the skill composition of labor market, that is, changes in the ratio of unskilled labor to skilled labor. Arpaia et al. (2009) also derive an expression for the labor income share in terms of input-ratios (Eq. 6.15). In Sect. 6.2.1, we discussed that labor income share moves along a stable non-linear relationship (SK curve) and certain factors shift the SK curve upward or downward. In Eq. (6.15), heterogeneous labor shifts the labor income share (SK curve) through (a) changes in the relative supply of capital to skilled labor and (b) changes in the relative supply of skilled labor to unskilled labor.

$$LIS = 1 - \phi(Ak)^{\frac{\rho-1}{\rho}}\theta^{\frac{\sigma(\rho-1)}{(\sigma-1)\rho}}\left[1 + \frac{1-\theta}{\theta} l^{\frac{1-\sigma}{\sigma}}\left\{\phi\left(\frac{AK}{B_S S}\right)^{\frac{\rho-1}{\rho}} + (1-\phi)\right\}^{\frac{\rho(1-\sigma)}{\sigma(\rho-1)}}\right]^{\frac{(\rho-1)\sigma+\rho}{\rho(\sigma-1)}} \quad (6.15)$$

6.3.1 *Comparative Statics of* LIS

Following Arpaia et al. (2009), we derive comparative statics results for *LIS*. We differentiate the expression for the labor income share in Eq. (6.15) with respect to the Solow-neutral technological progress (A).

$$\frac{\partial LIS}{\partial A}=-\phi\frac{\rho-1}{\rho}A^{\frac{-1}{\rho}}k^{\frac{\rho-1}{\rho}}\theta^{\frac{\sigma(\rho-1)}{(\sigma-1)\rho}}\left[1+\frac{1-\theta}{\theta}l^{\frac{1-\sigma}{\sigma}}\left\{\phi\left(\frac{AK}{B_S S}\right)^{\frac{\rho-1}{\rho}}+(1-\phi)\right\}^{\frac{\rho(1-\sigma)}{\sigma(\rho-1)}}\right]^{\frac{(\rho-1)\sigma+\rho}{\rho(\sigma-1)}}$$

$$-\frac{(\rho-1)\sigma+\rho}{\rho(\sigma-1)}\phi(Ak)^{\frac{\rho-1}{\rho}}\theta^{\frac{\sigma(\rho-1)}{(\sigma-1)\rho}}\left[1+\frac{1-\theta}{\theta}l^{\frac{1-\sigma}{\sigma}}\left\{\phi\left(\frac{AK}{B_S S}\right)^{\frac{\rho-1}{\rho}}+(1-\phi)\right\}^{\frac{\rho(1-\sigma)}{\sigma(\rho-1)}}\right]^{\frac{(\rho-1)\sigma+\rho}{\rho(\sigma-1)}-1}$$

$$\times\left[\frac{\rho(1-\sigma)}{\sigma(\rho-1)}\frac{1-\theta}{\theta}l^{\frac{1-\sigma}{\sigma}}\left\{\phi\left(\frac{AK}{B_S S}\right)^{\frac{\rho-1}{\rho}}+(1-\phi)\right\}^{\frac{\rho(1-\sigma)}{\sigma(\rho-1)}-1}\right]\phi\frac{\rho-1}{\rho}A^{\frac{-1}{\rho}}\left(\frac{K}{B_S S}\right)^{\frac{\rho-1}{\rho}} \tag{6.16}$$

From Eq. (6.16), $\frac{\partial LIS}{\partial A}<0$ if $\sigma > \rho > 1$. This is a sufficient condition for the labor income share to decrease with capital-augmenting technological progress and capital-skill complementarity ($\sigma > \rho$).

6.3.2 *Comparative Statics of* LIS *Using the Morishima Elasticity of Substitution*

In the previous section, the comparative statics outcomes suggest that if both elasticity parameters are greater than unity, then it is a sufficient condition to have a decline in the labor income share with capital-augmenting technological progress. This condition appears rather strict. Maintaining the assumption of capital-skill complementarity (i.e., $\sigma > \rho$), in this section, we investigate the comparative statics outcomes when $\sigma > 1 > \rho$. Equation (6.9) provides ambiguous results, as the sign of the derivative $\frac{\partial L_S}{\partial A}$ depends on the relative magnitude of the two terms. We take an alternative route. Some recent studies use the Morishima Elasticity of Substitution (MES here on) to measure the degree of substitutability and complementarity between factors for a production function with more than two inputs, and their effects on the changes in the factor shares (Atkinson 2009; Paul 2018). A nested-CES production function (like Eq. 6.12) with three inputs suggests the elasticities of substitution to be different between within-nest (ρ) and across-nest (σ).[7] The MES provides a natural generalization of the Hicksian two-input elasticity of substitution[8] (Blackorby and Russell 1989). The MES holds prices of other factor inputs constant and adjusts the measure of the elasticity of substitution accordingly, which is expressed as a function of own-price and cross-price elasticities of two inputs in the following way

$$MES_{ij} = \frac{dlogx_j}{dlogp_i} - \frac{dlogx_i}{dlogp_i} \tag{6.17}$$

Equation (6.10) provides a direct link between the factors' prices and the ratio of factor input use. Furthermore, Blackorby and Russell (1989) show that changes in the ratio of factor income shares can be directly predicted by MES using Eq. (6.17):

$$\frac{dlog\frac{p_i x_i}{p_j x_j}}{dlog\frac{p_i}{p_j}} = 1 - MES_{ij} \tag{6.18}$$

Following Paul (2018), we derive the similar expressions for MES using a three input nested-CES structure. We rewrite the CES production structure in Eq. (6.12) as a two-stage function consisting of two sub-processes or nests, as follows:

$$Y = f\left[\left(K, S\right)U\right] = N_1\left(K, S\right) + N_2\left(U\right) \tag{6.19}$$

From Eq. (6.12), ρ denotes the intra-nest elasticity of substitution between K and S and σ denotes the inter-nest elasticity of substitution between K and U. The sub-processes N_1 (with inputs K and S), and N_2

[7] ρ and σ could be identical in the special case when the distribution parameters (θ and $\varnothing$) are identical and in the restricted CES structure that allows for Morishima elasticity of substitutions to be symmetric (Blackorby and Russell 1989).

[8] A number of alternative estimates have been developed (Hicks and Allen 1934; Allen 1938; Uzawa 1962; McFadden 1963; Morishima 1967; Mundlak 1968; Blackorby and Russell 1989) to address such issues and to generalize the concept of elasticity of substitution for an arbitrary number of inputs ($i > 2$).

(with only input U) are mutually exclusive and exhaustive. As shown by Anderson and Moroney (1993), for more than two inputs case, we can write the direct link between changes in relative prices of factor inputs and the labor income share for the nested-CES production function, $y = N_1(K,S) + N_2(U)$, as:

$$\frac{dlog\frac{W_S S}{rK}}{dlog\frac{W_S}{r}} = 1 - MES_{SK}\left(=\rho\right) = 1 - \frac{dlogK}{dlogW_S} + \frac{dlogS}{dlogW_S} \tag{6.20}$$

Equation (6.20) suggests that a drop in the relative price of capital (an increase of the ratio $\frac{W_S}{r}$) leads to a lower share of the skilled labor income (i.e., $\frac{dlog\frac{W_S S}{rK}}{dlog\frac{W_S}{r}} < 0$) if $MES_{SK} > 1$. The skilled labor income share declines due to the availability of cheaper capital when capital and skilled labor (intra-nest inputs) are gross substitutes. In a similar way, Eq. (6.14) shows that a drop in the relative price of capital (an increase of the ratio $\frac{W_U}{r}$) leads to a lower share of the unskilled labor income (i.e., $\frac{dlog\frac{W_U U}{rK}}{dlog\frac{W_U}{r}} < 0$) if $MES_{UK} > 1$ or capital and unskilled labor (inter-nest inputs) are gross substitutes.

$$\frac{dlog\frac{W_U U}{rK}}{dlog\frac{W_U}{r}} = 1 - MES_{UK}\left(=\sigma\right) = 1 - \theta\left[\frac{dlogN_2}{dlogP_{N_1}} - \frac{dlogN_1}{dlogP_{N_1}}\right] + \frac{dlogK}{dlogP_K} \tag{6.21}$$

We show the expressions for both ρ and σ for two nested-CES production functions: $\Upsilon = f[(K,S)U]$ and $\Upsilon = f[(K,U)S]$ in Table 6.1. While the intra-nest MES (ρ) is simply the difference in the cross-price and

Table 6.1 MES for two different nested-CES production functions with three inputs

	(1)	*(2)*
	$Y = \left[\theta\left[\varnothing K^{\frac{\rho-1}{\rho}} + (1-\varnothing)S^{\frac{\rho-1}{\rho}}\right]^{\frac{\rho}{\rho-1}\frac{\sigma-1}{\sigma}} + (1-\theta)U^{\frac{\sigma-1}{\sigma}}\right]^{\frac{\sigma}{\sigma-1}}$ $= N_1(K,S) + N_2(U)$	$Y = \left[\theta\left[\varnothing K^{\frac{\rho-1}{\rho}} + (1-\varnothing)U^{\frac{\rho-1}{\rho}}\right]^{\frac{\rho}{\rho-1}\frac{\sigma-1}{\sigma}} + (1-\theta)S^{\frac{\sigma-1}{\sigma}}\right]^{\frac{\sigma}{\sigma-1}}$ $= N_1(K,U) + N_2(S)$
ρ	$\rho = MES_{KS} = \frac{dlogS}{dlogr} - \frac{dlogK}{dlogr}$	$\rho = MES_{KU} = \frac{dlogU}{dlogr} - \frac{dlogK}{dlogr}$
	$\rho = MES_{SK} = \frac{dlogK}{dlogW_S} - \frac{dlogS}{dlogW_S}$	$\rho = MES_{UK} = \frac{dlogK}{dlogW_U} - \frac{dlogU}{dlogW_U}$
σ	$\sigma = MES_{KU}$ $= \theta\left[\frac{dlogN_2}{dlogP_{N_1}} - \frac{dlogN_1}{dlogP_{N_1}}\right] - \frac{dlogK}{dlogr}$	$\sigma = MES_{KS}$ $= \theta\left[\frac{dlogN_2}{dlogP_{N_1}} - \frac{dlogN_1}{dlogP_{N_1}}\right] - \frac{dlogK}{dlogr}$
	$\sigma = MES_{UK}$ $= \theta\left[\frac{dlogN_2}{dlogP_{N_1}} - \frac{dlogN_1}{dlogP_{N_1}}\right] - \frac{dlogU}{dlogW_U}$	$\sigma = MES_{SK}$ $= \theta\left[\frac{dlogN_2}{dlogP_{N_1}} - \frac{dlogN_1}{dlogP_{N_1}}\right] - \frac{dlogS}{dlogW_S}$

Source: Author

Note: At equilibrium, $P_K = r$, $P_S = w_S$ and $P_U = w_U$

own-price elasticities of the factor inputs, for the inter-nest MES (σ) the own-price elasticity factor is replaced by the MES across two nests (N_1 and N_2). Another point to note is that MES estimates vary across different nested-CES production functions and, particularly for inter-nest MES (σ), they vary subject to the relative prices of the factor inputs.

In a recent paper, Paul (2018) derives the necessary and sufficient conditions for a decline in labor income share resulting from a capital deepening or decrease in the relative price of capital to labor. He shows that assuming $\sigma > \rho$ (i.e., capital is more complementary to skilled labor), the necessary condition and the sufficient condition for a decline in the aggregate labor income share with a drop in the relative price of capital are $\sigma > 1$, and $\rho > 1$, respectively. With $\sigma > \rho$, $\rho > 1$ ensures that both elasticities are greater than one.[9] However, a decline in the labor share can also

[9] This is in line with the empirical findings by Karabarbounis and Neiman (2014) and Piketty (2014).

be obtained with a less strict condition when $\sigma > 1 > \rho$ as long as we have

$$\left| \frac{dlog \frac{W_S S}{rK}}{dlog \frac{W_S}{r}} \right| < \left| \frac{dlog \frac{W_U U}{rK}}{dlog \frac{W_U}{r}} \right| \text{ or } |1 - \rho| < |1 - \sigma|.$$

As a final step, following Paul (2018) we consider a numerical example and discuss the possible range of values for which $\sigma_{Agg} < 1$ if $\sigma > 1 > \rho$. In line with the existing literature (Karabarbounis and Neiman 2014; Rognlie 2015), we assume that $\sigma = 1.15$ and $\rho = .9$, then $\frac{dlog\left(\frac{L_S}{1-L_S}\right)}{dlog\left(\frac{\bar{W}}{r}\right)} < 0$ since $|1 - .9| < |1 - 1.15|$. The aggregate elasticity of substitution between capital and labor can be written as a weighted average of σ and ρ (with y and x as weights)

$$\sigma_{Agg} = y\sigma + x\rho \tag{6.22}$$

Imposing the condition for aggregate complementarity between capital and labor, Equation (6.22) becomes an inequality $1 > 1.15y + .9x$ or $y < .869 - .78x$ (after applying the values of $\sigma = 1.15$ and $\rho = .9$). The feasible range of values that satisfies the inequality is plotted in Fig. 6.2. Any point (combination of weights) in the shaded area implies that the weighted average of σ and ρ (with y and x as weights) must be less than the unity for the given values of $\sigma = 1.15$ and $\rho = .9$. This hypothetical example suggests that it is possible to have complementarity between capital and labor ($\sigma_{Agg} < 1$) for a feasible set of values of σ and ρ, which corresponds with a decline in the labor income share. To put it differently, this could imply that a decline of the LIS alongside a drop in the relative price of capital occurs when the loss of income share due to a decrease in the unskilled labor force outweighs the income gained due to an increase in the skilled labor force. The relevance of capital-skill substitutability in studying changes in the labor share of income can also be drawn using a two-stage production structure (Goldin and Katz 1998). In the first stage, skilled workers adopt new technologies and efficiently use capital, thus showing high capital-skill complementarity. In the second stage, unskilled workers continue the mechanical process of machine maintenance indicating a relatively low level of capital-skill complementarity.

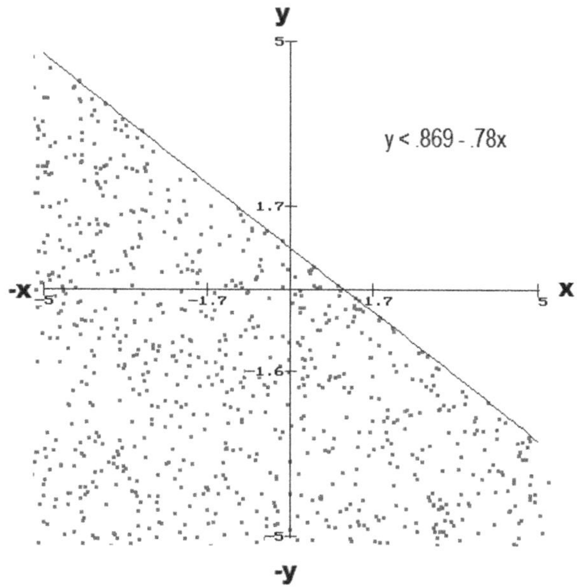

Fig. 6.2 A feasible range of weights for $\sigma_{Agg} < 1$. (Source: Authors. Note: This graph shows a numerical example. It shows the feasible range of value for an equation showing inequality)

References

Acemoglu, Daron. 2002. "Technical Change, Inequality and the Labor Market." *Journal of Economic Literature* 40: 7–72.

Allen, R.G.D. 1938. *Mathematical Analysis for Economists*. London: Macmillan.

Alvarez-Cuadrado, F., N. V. Long, and M. Poschke. 2015. *Capital–Labor Substitution, Structural Change and the Labor Income Share*. IZA Discussion Paper No. 8941.

Anderson, R. K. and J. R. Moroney. 1993. "Morishima Elasticities of Substitution with Nested Production Functions." *Economics Letters* 42: 159–166.

Arpaia, Alfonso, Esther Perez, and Karl Pichelmann. 2009. "Understanding Labour's Income Share Dynamics in Europe." European Economy Economics Paper No. 379, European Commission.

Atkinson, A. B. 2009. "Factor Shares: The Principal Problem of Political Economy?" *Oxford Review of Economic Policy* 25 (1): 3–16.

Autor, D., F. Levy, and R. Murnane. 2003. "The Skill Content of Recent Technical Change: An Empirical Exploration." *Quarterly Journal of Economics* 118: 1279–1334.

Bentolila, Samuel and Saint-Paul, Gilles. 2003. Explaining Movements in the Labor Share. *The B.E. Journal of Macroeconomics*, 3(1), 1–33.

Berman, Eli, John Bound, and Zvi Griliches. 1994. "Changes in the Demand for Skilled Labor within U.S. Manufacturing Industries: Evidence from the Annual Survey of Manufacturing." *Quarterly Journal of Economics* 109(2): 367–397.

Blackorby C. and R. R. Russell. 1989. "Will the Real Elasticity of Substitution Please Stand Up? (A Comparison of the Allen/Uzawa and Morishima Elasticities)." *American Economic Review* 79: 882–888.

Blaug, M. 1996. *Economic Theory in Retrospect*, 3rd ed., Cambridge, Cambridge University Press.

Caselli, F. 1999. Technological Revolutions. *American Economic Review* 89, 78–102.

Chirinko, Robert S. 2008. "The Long and Short of It." *Journal of Macroeconomics* 30: 671–686.

Chirinko, Robert S., and Debdulal Mallick. 2017. "The Substitution Elasticity, Factor Shares, and the Low-Frequency Panel Model." *American Economic Journal: Macroeconomics*, 9(4): 225–253.

Elsby, Michael W., Bart Hobijn, and Ayşegül Şahin. 2013. "The Decline of the US Labor Share." *Brookings Papers on Economic Activity*, 2: 1–63.

Fallon, P. R., and P. R. G. Layard, "Capital-Skill Complementarity, Income Distribution, and Output Accounting," *Journal of Political Economy* 83 (1975), 279–302.

Glyn, A. 2009. "Functional Distribution and Inequality." In W. Salverda, B. Nolan, and T. M. Smeeding (eds.), *Oxford Handbook of Economic Inequality*. Oxford: Oxford University Press. 101–126.

Goldin, Claudia, and Lawrence F. Katz. 1998. "The Origins of Technology-Skill Complementarity." *Quarterly Journal of Economics*, 113 (3): 693–732.

Gollin, D. 2002. Getting income shares right. *Journal of Political Economy*, *110*(2), 458–474.

Griliches, Z. 1969. "Capital–Skill Complementarity." *Review of Economics and Statistics*, 5: 465–468.

Hamermesh, D. 1993. *Labor Demand*. Princeton, NJ: Princeton University Press.

Harrod, R. F. 1942. *Towards A Dynamic Economics: Some Recent Developments of Economic Theory and Their Application to Policy*. London: Macmillan.

Hicks J. R., and R. G. D. Allen. 1934. "A Reconsideration of the Theory of Value, Part II." *Economica* 1: 196–219.

Hicks, John R. 1932. *Theory of Wages*. London: Macmillan.

Karabarbounis, Loukas, and Brent Neiman. 2014. "The Global Decline of the Labor Share." *Quarterly Journal of Economics* 129 (1): 61–103.

Kraemer, Hagen, 2010. "The Alleged Stability of the Labour Share of Income in Macroeconomic Theories of Income Distribution," IMK Working Paper (11).

Krusell, Per, Lee E. Ohanian, José-Victor Ríos-Rull, and Giovanni L. Violante. 2000. "Capital-skill Complementarity and Inequality: A Macroeconomic Analysis." *Econometrica* 68 (5): 1029–1053.

Leon-Ledesma, M., P. McAdam, and A. Willman, "Identifying the Elasticity of Substitution with Biased Technical Change," *American Economic Review*, 100 (2010), 1330.

Marshall, Alfred. 1920. *Principles of Economics*, 8th ed., New York: Macmillan.

McFadden D. 1963. "Constant Elasticity of Substitution Production Functions." *Review of Economic Studies* 31: 73–83.

Morishima M. 1967. "A Few Suggestions on the Theory of Elasticity (in Japanese)." *Keizai Hyoron (Economic Review)*, 16:144–150.

Mundlak Y. 1968. "Elasticities of Substitution and the Theory of Derived Demand." *Review of Economic Studies*, 35: 225–236.

Oberfield, Ezra, and Devesh Raval. 2014. "Micro Data and Macro Technology." NBER Working Paper No. 20452, National Bureau of Economic Research.

Paul, S. 2018. "Capital Skill Substitutability and the Labor Income Share: Identification Using the Morishima Elasticity of Substitution." ADBI Working Paper 839. Tokyo: Asian Development Bank Institute.

Piketty, T. 2014. *Capital in the Twenty-First Century*. Cambridge: Harvard University Press.

Ricardo, David. 1821 [1971]. *Principles of Political Economy*, 3rd ed., ed. R. M. Hartwell. Harmondsworth: Pelican Classics.

Robinson, Joan. 1933. *The Economics of Imperfect Competition*. London: Macmillan.

Rognlie, Matthew. 2015. "Deciphering the Fall and Rise in the Net Capital Share: Accumulation or Scarcity?" *Brookings Papers on Economic Activity* 46 (1): 1–69.

Sato, R. 1975. "The Most General Class of CES Functions," *Econometrica*, 43, 999–1003.

Schneider, D. 2011. "Bargaining, Openness and the Labor Share," Tech. rep., SFB 649 Discussion Paper.

Solow, Robert M. 1958. "A Skeptical Note on the Constancy of Relative Shares." *American Economic Review* 48(4): 618–631.

Uzawa, H. 1962. "Production Functions with Constant Elasticities of Substitution." *Review of Economic Studies* 30: 291–299.

CHAPTER 7

The Economic Forces Behind Labor Income Share: Empirics

In this chapter, we discuss empirical findings on the drivers of labor income share under three broad categories: (a) technological change and capital intensity, (b) structural transformation, and (c) institutional changes.

7.1 Technological Change

Technological advancement, measured by the long-term change in the relative price of investment goods, and the initial exposure to routinization have been the largest contributors to the decline in labor income shares in advanced economies. The empirical analysis suggests that about half of the total decline in labor shares can be traced to the impact of technology. Importantly, for a given change in the relative price of investment, economies with high exposure to routinization experienced about four times the decline in labor income shares than those with low exposure (Dao et al. 2017). This paper also concludes that in the emerging market, there is no discernible rode of technology in the evolution of labor shares. This reflects both a relatively mild decline in the relative price investment goods and, importantly, a much lower exposure to routinization, which has limited labor displacement arising from routine-based technology. While the very extensive literature on skilled-biased technical change provides useful hints, but little evidence exists on the impact of different types of capital on the labor income share

S. Paul, *Labor Income Share*,
https://doi.org/10.1007/978-981-15-6860-2_7

(Koh et al. 2016; O'Mahony et al. 2008) and on their impact on the share of output accruing to different types of labor (European Commission 2007; Lawless and Whelan 2011).

7.1.1 SBTC, Capital-Augmenting, and Labor-Augmenting Technological Change

Technology enables customer to obtain latest and broader information. It also enables customers to choose the goods at the lowest price and enjoy the better quality of goods they consume. At the same time, it allows companies to exploit their competitive advantages. Technology favors large farms, especially if the industry requires a huge fixed cost, which in turn reduces the marginal cost, with the help of technological advancement. In recent years, the advent and growing prominence of social networking services has propelled the network effect, which again enables customers to choose the most popular goods. This also indirectly makes the goods that are technologically savvy more popular. Technological change has been increasingly capital augmenting in recent decades, leading to higher capital-intensive production processes. The relationship between capital-income ratio and the labor income share (Bentolila and Saint-Paul 2003) depends on the elasticity of substitution between capital and labor. With a drop in the price of capital, the labor income share is lower with capital and labor as complements, and it is higher if capital and labor are gross substitutes. However, the recent empirical literature provides mixed results on the value of the elasticity of substitution (Piketty 2014; Piketty and Zucman 2014; Karabarbounis and Neiman 2014; Antras 2001).

The assumption of a non-unitary elasticity of substitution (σ) between capital and labor plays a crucial role in explaining the changes in the labor income share. Research in recent years documents a global decline in the labor income share.[1] With capital and labor as gross substitutes ($\sigma > 1$), the primary drivers of the falling labor income share are, among others, an increasing capital-income ratio (Piketty 2014) and a declining relative price of capital (Karabarbounis and Neiman 2014). It is documented in the literature (Karabarbounis and Neiman 2014; Piketty 2014) that gross substitutability between capital and labor (aggregate, skilled, and unskilled)

[1] Elsby et al. (2013); Karabarbounis and Neiman (2014); Piketty (2014); Piketty and Zucman (2014); Bentolila and Saint-Paul (2003); Blanchard and Giavazzi (2003); Gollin (2002).

can explain a decline in the aggregate labor income share with the availability of cheaper capital. To this extent, both Piketty (2014) and Karabarbounis and Neiman (2014) estimate the values of elasticity of substation between capital and labor to be greater than unity. At the same time, many studies find an estimate of σ to be less than one (Leon-Ledesma et al. 2010; Oberfield and Raval 2014; Chirinko and Mallick 2017).[2] With $\sigma < 1$, these causal mechanisms in fact predict a rise in the labor income share. In a recent study, Alvarez-Cuadrado et al. (2015) argue that if capital and labor are gross complements, then a decline in capital per unit of effective labor can lead to a more than proportionate increase in the rental rate compared to wages. This mechanism can lead to a lower income share of labor. Overall, these findings point to an apparent puzzle. The decline of labor income share resulting from capital deepening or capital-augmenting technological progress (availability of cheaper capital) is not feasible if capital and labor are gross complements ($\sigma < 1$).

We discuss two very recent studies that address this puzzle. The first study is by Grossman et al. (2017). Their theoretical model relies on the human capital accumulation in a standard framework of neoclassical growth model. Let us denote three elasticity parameters as follows: (1) between human capital and physical capital as $\sigma_{HC,\ PC}$, between human capital and raw labor as $\sigma_{HC,\ RL}$, and between total labor and physical capital as $\sigma_{L,\ PC}$. They show that if $\sigma_{HC,\ PC} < \sigma_{HC,\ RL}$ and $\sigma_{L,\ PC} < 1$, then holding the level of schooling constant, the movement in the share of labor in national income and the rate of labor productivity growth will be positively correlated across steady states. This way a slowdown in labor productivity growth implies a drop in the labor income share. Then the authors discuss this mechanism by considering the case of a drop in the interest rate relative to growth rate of wages. This prompts individuals to achieve a higher level of human capital for any steady state level of technology and the size of capital stock. Since, $\sigma_{HC,\ PC} < \sigma_{HC,\ RL}$ (i.e., human capital is more complementary to physical capital than raw labor), this generates a shift in the relative factor demand in favor of a rise in the capital-income share. Thus, in their model, they show that a decline in the labor income share is feasible with $\sigma < 1$ if there is a slowdown of labor productivity growth.

The second study by Paul (2018) addresses this puzzle by arguing for proper identification of the elasticity of substitution parameters. Drawing

[2] Using sectoral-level data, Herrendorf et al. (2015) show elasticity of substitution to be 1.58 in agriculture, 0.80 in manufacturing, and 0.75 in services.

insights from the micro-level estimation of the σ_{Agg} (Oberfield and Raval 2014) and the literature on differential capital-skill substitutability (Krusell et al. 2000; Karabarbounis and Neiman 2014), he shows that it is possible to have a decline in the labor income share resulting from a fall in the relative price of capital when $\sigma_{Agg} < 1$. This paper proposes a framework to identify and estimate the elasticity of substitution parameters (ρ and σ) using a three-input nested-CES production structure. In a production structure with more than two inputs, the primary identification problem emerges from the simultaneous changes in prices of factor inputs apart from the two directly used to estimate elasticities of substitution. Paul (2018) uses the concept of Morishima Elasticity of Substitution (MES, here on),[3] which holds prices of other factor inputs constant and adjusts the measure of the elasticity of substitution accordingly. He then shows that both ρ and σ can be approximated by the differences in own-price and cross-price elasticities in a nested-CES production framework. Moreover, MES directly links the changes in relative factor input prices to labor income share trends. Using this framework with capital-skill complementarity ($\sigma > \rho$), the necessary and the sufficient condition for a decline in the aggregate labor income share with a drop in the relative price of capital are $\sigma > 1$ and $\rho > 1$, respectively. However, a decline in the labor share can also be obtained with a less strict condition when $\sigma > 1 > \rho$ and as long as we have $\left|\frac{dlog\frac{W_S S}{rK}}{dlog\frac{W_S}{r}}\right| < \left|\frac{dlog\frac{W_U U}{rK}}{dlog\frac{W_U}{r}}\right|$ or $|1 - \rho| < |1 - \sigma|$. And, in this case, it is feasible to expect the value of σ_{Agg} to be less than unity.

To estimate the empirical model (Eq. 31), in an extended version of Paul (2018), Paul (2019a) creates a new dataset by combining data available from Karabarbounis and Neiman (2014) (KN, hereon), Buera et al. (2015) (BKR, hereon), the Penn World Tables (PWT, Mark 7.1), and the World Development Indicators (WDI) from the World Bank. Constrained by the availability of data, the empirical analysis is restricted to the United States for the period from 1977 to 2005. KN measure labor income share by combining national income and product accounts data across various sources, including data collected from country-specific national

[3] Morishima Elasticity of Substitution is the natural multi-input generalization of Hicksian two-input elasticity of substitution (Blackorby and Russell 1989 and Anderson and Moroney 1993).

accounting sources on the Internet, the OECD, the UN, and physical books. The aggregate LIS is simply measured as compensation of employees divided by GDP. The second set of the aggregate LIS data comes from a combined OECD-UN database. The second dataset does not include the country-specific information that KN collected from other sources. As KN documents at length, the price of capital (investment) relative to consumption goods also declined alongside a global decline in the labor income share. Paul (2019a) uses data on the relative price of capital from two sources, PWT and WDI, and merges it with BKR containing data on wages by different skill levels to compute the factor prices for capital, skilled, and unskilled labor.

To compute data on skilled and unskilled labor income share, Paul (2019a) follows the definition of BKR on high-skill share of labor income in high-skill and low-skill sectors. The high-skill sectoral shares are generated by adding up the percentage of labor compensation across all age and gender for high-skill from four industries (financial intermediation, real estate and business services, education, and health and social work) available in the EU KLEMS database. Also, the sector shares are calculated as compensation-weighted averages of the industry-specific shares. I multiply the aggregate LIS data with sectoral shares of the high-skill labor for each sector and sum them up to generate the aggregate income shares for both types of skills. Figure 7.1 plots the LIS trends. Both capital-income share and the LIS for skilled workers show an upward trend, whereas the unskilled workers predominantly drive a decline in the aggregate LIS. This is consistent with capital-skill complementarity and a declining cost of capital. The own-price demand elasticities, calculated based on the estimated parameters, range between −0.15 and −0.65. The cross-price elasticities due to changes in the price of capital are positive, suggesting both relationships, between skilled labor and capital, and unskilled labor and capital, as substitutes. However, the magnitude of the effect of changes in the capital price on the stock of unskilled labor is three-times higher than that for skilled labor. This again broadly supports the notion of capital-skill complementarity.

The empirical outcomes from Paul (2019a) are listed in Table 7.1. Panel A (Table 7.1) reports the computed values of the MES. The MES is calculated using the cross-price and the own-price demand elasticities. Both MES_{UK} and MES_{KU} are candidate measures for σ, whereas ρ can be approximated by either MES_{SK} or MES_{KS}. The empirical support for the asymmetric property of the MES is strong, as $MES_{KU} \neq MES_{UK}$ and

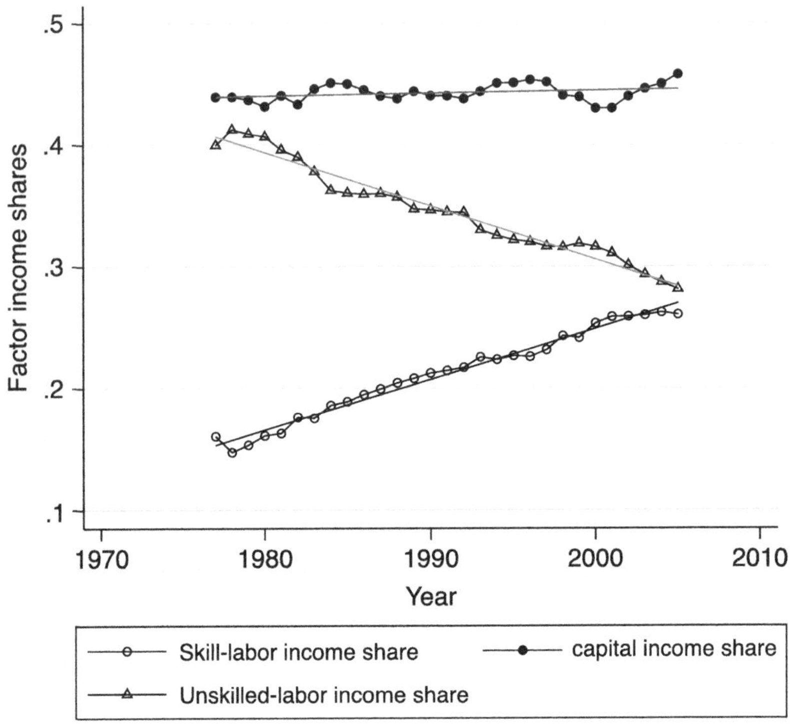

Fig. 7.1 Factor income shares in the United States, 1977–2005. (Note: Authors' calculation based on a combined data set using data sets from Karabarbounis and Neiman (2014) and Buera et al. (2015))

$MES_{KS} \neq MES_{SK}$. The estimated MES follow an order of hierarchy $MES_{KU} > MES_{SK} > MES_{UK} > MES_{KS}$, which is consistent across all the models. The estimated value of MES_{KU} suggests that capital and unskilled labor are Morishima substitutes, that is, $\sigma > 1$, whereas the rest of the MES measures suggest Morishima complementarity between factor inputs. This leaves us with two possible combinations (MES_{SK}, MES_{KU}) and (MES_{KS}, MES_{KU}) from each model, with a total of eight out of 16 possible cases that satisfy the first part of the necessary condition ($\sigma > 1 > \rho$). Panel B of Table 7.2 shows the comparative statics outcomes. The condition

Table 7.1 The MES and the comparative statics outcomes

	1	*2*	*3*	*4*
	KN-BK-PWT	*KN-BK-WDI*	*UN/ OECD-BK-PWT*	*UN/ OECD-BK-WDI*
A. Morishima elasticity of substitutions				
MES_{SK}	0.635	0.799	0.840	0.971
MES_{UK}	0.200	0.193	0.692	0.580
MES_{KS}	−0.004	0.137	0.284	0.421
MES_{KU}	1.214	1.245	1.568	1.595
$2 - MES_{SK} - MES_{KU}$	> 0	< 0	< 0	< 0
$2 - MES_{KS} - MES_{KU}$	> 0	> 0	> 0	< 0

Source: Author

Note: Panel A shows the Morishima elasticity of substitutions using estimated parameters for four models. Panel B shows the comparative statics outcomes for the sample with combination of the MES that meets the necessary condition: $\sigma > 1 > \rho$ and $2 - \sigma - \rho < 0$ (or $|1 - \rho| < |1 - \sigma|$). If $2 - \sigma - \rho < 0$, then it implies a drop in the labor income share with a decline in the relative price of capital

$2 - \sigma - \rho < 0$ is met in four (MES_{SK}, MES_{KU}; MES_{SK}, MES_{KU}; MES_{SK}, MES_{KU}; and MES_{KS}, MES_{KU}) out of eight cases suggesting a drop in the labor income share with a decline in the relative price of capital. Taken together, four out of the 16 cases show a drop in the relative price of capital forces the aggregate labor income share to decline when the necessary condition is met.

7.1.2 *Labor Income Share Dynamics with Variable Elasticity of Substitution*

The Constant Elasticity of Substitution (CES) production technology has been a dominant model choice for researchers studying the labor income share. The CES production framework, with constant returns to scale and perfectly competitive factor markets, predicts a stable relationship between the labor income share and capital accumulation where the constant σ_{KL} forces a decrease (increase) in the labor income share with capital accumulation when it is greater than (less than) unity. Empirical evidences, however, do not always support this accumulation principle. For example, both capital-output ratio and the labor income share increased in a majority of the Japanese industrial sectors between 1970 and 2012 but the CES model estimates of σ_{KL} are predominantly greater than unity across sectors.

Table 7.2 Comparison of the estimated elasticity of substitution parameters

Industry code	*Industry name*	$\hat{\sigma}_{CES}$	$\hat{\sigma}_{VES}\big\|_{\theta=\hat{\theta}}$	$\hat{\sigma}_{VES}\big\|_{\theta_t=e^{-\left(\frac{k_t-\gamma}{\kappa}\right)^{\alpha}}}$
1	Agriculture	1.408	1.050	1.075
2	Mining	0.787	0.782	0.714
3	Food	0.766	1.061	1.215
5	Paper	0.975	0.990	0.986
6	Chemicals	1.202	0.655	0.802
7	Petroleum	1.383	1.052	1.116
8	Ceramics	1.183	0.963	0.956
9	Basic metal	1.198	0.416	0.610
10	Processed metals	−0.712	0.952	0.987
11	Machinery	1.116	0.337	0.485
12	Electrical	1.058	0.496	0.633
13	Transport equipment	1.089	0.441	0.697
14	Precision instruments	1.517	1.036	1.032
15	Other manufacturing	0.827	0.663	0.792
16	Construction	0.532	0.699	0.723
17	Utilities	1.037	1.101	12.838
19	Finance	1.093	0.666	0.840
20	Real estate	0.204	1.000	1.162
21	Transport	2.282	1.953	1.556
22	Non-government services	1.684	0.488	0.627

Source: Author's calculation based on the Regional-level Japanese Industrial Productivity (R-JIP) database https://www.rieti.go.jp/en/database/R-JIP2017/index.html#09

Note: The figures for the VES models are averages over the period from 1970 to 2012

As an alternative strategy, Paul (2019b) analyzes the relationship between capital accumulation and the labor income share using a variable elasticity of substitution framework. He defines the share parameter as a cumulative distribution function of a three-parameter Weibull distribution of the capital-labor ratio.[4] The share parameter as a monotonic transformation of the capital-labor ratio implies that a higher capital-labor ratio leads to a higher share of the capital-output ratio following the explicit parameters of the Weibull distribution of the capital-labor ratio. He extends the variable elasticity framework of Lu and Fletcher (1968) to incorporate time-variant σ_{KL} and time-variant share parameter as non-linear functions of the capital-labor ratio, which he then uses to

[4] Taking stock of the growing literature on productivity levels driven by an explicit set of technology (Kortum 1997; Jones 2005; Growiec 2008).

theoretically derive the full set of parameters. This model is referred as the VES-W model. Using annual data from 20 Japanese industrial sectors over a period of 43 years (1970–2012), Paul (2019b) tests the evidence of a variable σ_{KL} and estimate a full set of parameters in both CES and VES-W models.

The empirical findings suggest that the labor income share increased in 18 out of the 20 industrial sectors (leaving transport and non-government services) between 1970 and 2012. The capital-labor ratio plays a consistent and statistically significant role in explaining the variation the elasticity of substitution between capital and labor. The estimated values of the elasticity of substitution in the VES-W model fluctuate around unity in most of the sectors with an overall average of 0.91, but do not show any consistent relationship with the capital-labor ratio across sectors. The calibration outcomes based on a full set of estimated parameters do not suggest that VES-W must be a preferred choice of model over CES. Both models fit the actual output and factor income shares reasonably well, but the most striking difference lies in the estimated values of σ_{KL}: an average $\hat{\sigma}_{VES-W} = 0.91$ against $\hat{\sigma}_{CES} = 1.03$. Table 7.2 shows a significant discrepancy in the estimated values of σ_{KL} between both models where 14 out of the 20 industrial sectors show a lower average $\hat{\sigma}_{VES-W}$ than $\hat{\sigma}_{CES}$. In the production process, capital and labor show complementarity in most of the industrial sectors based on the VES-W model, whereas the CES model estimates suggest more substitutability between capital and labor. This way the VES-W model accounts for the same labor income share dynamics but with complementary factor inputs at the sectoral level.

Table 7.2 compares the estimates of the elasticity of substitution from three models: CES, VES, and VES-W. The CES estimates suggest that capital and labor are substitutes in 13 out of 20 industrial sectors, whereas in both VES models this number drops to only seven (comparing with the average σ_{KL} for each sector). Notably, the elasticity of substitution in the VES-W model shows an increasing trend in 10 out of 20 sectors. However, there is no consistent relationship observed between the elasticity of substitution and labor income share over time. In fact, in most of the cases, no relationship exists between these two factors. For example, the labor income share declined the most in processed metal and real estate industries. The elasticity of substitution in processed metal decreases over time whereas in real estate it shows a slight upward trend.

Figure 7.2 compares the calibrated output levels from the CES, VES, and VES-W models with the actual level of output for 20 industrial

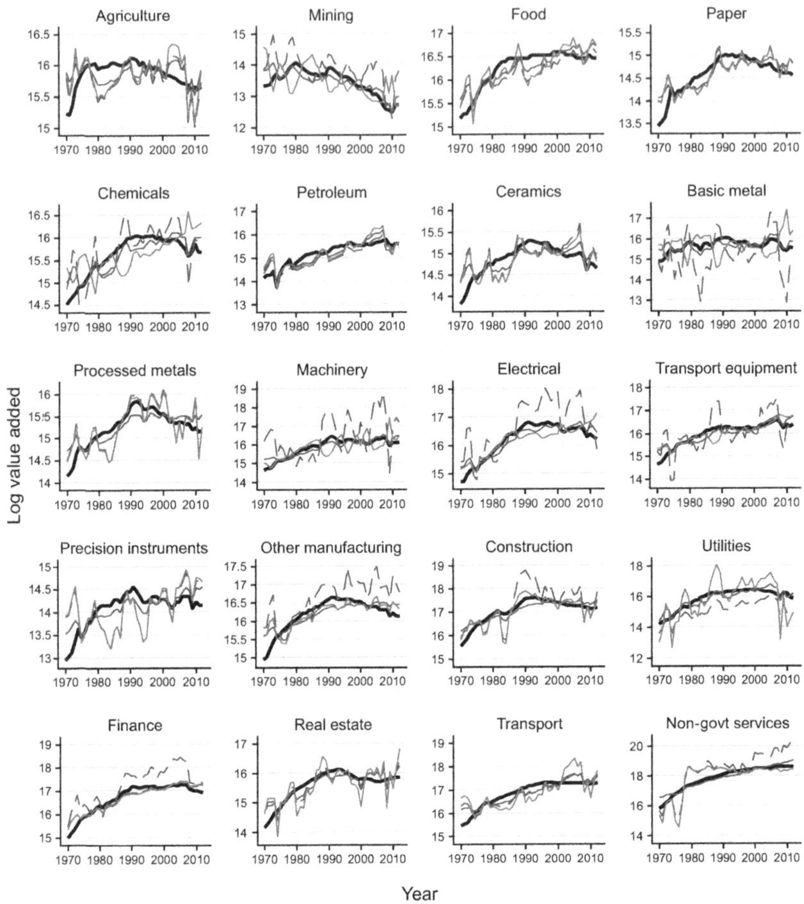

Fig. 7.2 Actual versus calibrated value added by industrial sectors. (Note: The solid black lines measure the actual value-added figures. The solid-blue lines, dashed-blue lines, and -brown lines show calibrated value-added figures using CES model, VES model, and VES-W model. The Kormogorov-Smirnov test for goodness of fit suggests that the distribution of actual output level is similar to the calibrated output figures from the CES and the VES-W models. Source: Author's calculation based on the Regional-level Japanese Industrial Productivity (R-JIP) database https://www.rieti.go.jp/en/database/R-JIP2017/index.html#09)

sectors. The log of output levels are plotted against time variable. The sectoral averages of log output are measured as 15.75, 15.84, and 15.75 in from the CES, the VES, and the VES-W models. The Kormogorov-Smirnov goodness of fit test statistics suggest a reasonably good fit between the actual values of the output and the calibrated results from the CES and the VES-W model. Finally, Table 7.5 compares the estimated labor income shares from the three models with the actual labor income share. The Kormogorov-Smirnov goodness of fit test statistics suggest a reasonably good fit between the actual values of the labor income share and the calibrated results from the CES and the VES-W model. For both models, the test statistics reject the null hypothesis that the distributions are identical in only 7 out of 20 industrial sectors. On the other hand, the VES model performs poorly relative to the other two models. The calibrated results of VES-W model provide a much better fit to the actual data compared to VES model, which supports the approximation of the share parameters with extreme value distribution of the capital-labor ratio.

7.2 Globalization

7.2.1 Trade Liberalization and Labor Income Share: Country Level

Globalization has been broadly defined to include everything from falling prices for goods that use low-skill labor (such as garments) to increasing outsourcing by multinationals (Harrison 2002). The owners of capital have greater bargaining power over laborers, ostensibly because capital is footloose and can quickly relocate to wherever it can find the highest returns (Harrison 2002; Rodrik 1997). Slaughter (2001) argues that trade can make labor demand more elastic in two main ways: by making output markets more competitive and by making domestic labor more substitutable with foreign factors. Trade can generate these effects without also generating product-price changes and, via the Stolper-Samuelson theorem, factor price changes.[5] Classical trade theories predict patterns of

[5] For example, in a Heckscher-Ohlin trade model, if an economy's autarky relative endowment equals that of the rest of the world, then when that country opens to trade it experiences no change in product prices and thus (via the Stolper-Samuelson theorem) no change in wages. But this opening can make foreign factors more substitutable with domestic ones. If product markets are imperfectly competitive in autarky, opening can also make product markets more competitive.

specialization and specific factor demand drive relative factors endowment. Factor reallocation in the production function induced by trade also crucially deepens on the wage flexibility/rigidity regimes as shown by Decreuse and Maarek (2015). Decreuse and Maarek (2015) assume a frictional labor market with productive heterogeneity and claim that foreign direct investment (FDI) has two opposite effects on the labor income share. The first is a negative effect originated by technological advancement and then a positive effect due to an increasing labor market competition between firms. Using data from 98 developing countries over the period from 1980 to 2000, they find a U-shaped relationship between labor income share and the proportion of foreign firms. Furthermore, they argue that the magnitude of the relationship is governed by the technological gap between foreign and local firms. In addition, the effect of trade openness on the labor income share also depends on the elasticity of substitution between different types of labor and capital (Guscina 2006; European Commission 2007). Foreign direct investment (FDI) or offshoring can also have a negative effect on the labor income share by providing firms an outside option with decreasing workers' bargaining power (especially for the low-skilled workers) (Guscina 2006; Harrison 2002; Jaumotte and Tytell 2007; Jayadev 2007).

New trade theories emphasize the role of firm heterogeneity in production. The factors such as capital intensity, skills, among others drive productivity and determine the impact of increasing openness on the labor income share of different types of workers. Elsby et al. (2013) noted that increased import penetration would be expected to depress labor's share of domestic income if imported intermediates were more substitutable with labor than with capital from the perspective of an aggregate production technology. The same authors argue that for the more labor-intensive part of US production, the remaining production in the US economy would be expected to become more capital intensive by offshoring. If, in addition, capital is more than unit-elastic with respect to labor, then applying the concept of Hicksian elasticity (Hicks 1932) this will imply that the labor income share in the United States will fall.

The rise of superstar firms can also contribute to a decline in the labor income share as shown by Autor et al. (2017). They analyze micro panel data from the US Economic Census since 1982, and international sources and document empirical patterns to assess a new interpretation of the fall in the labor income share based on the rise of "superstar firms." If globalization or technological changes advantage the most productive firms in each industry, product market concentration will rise as industries become increasingly dominated by superstar firms with high profits and a low share of labor in firm value added and sales. As a result, as the importance of superstar firms increases, the aggregate labor share will tend to fall. In a related study, Kehrig and Vincent (2017) also ascribe the growing dominance of superstar firms as an explanation for a fall in the labor income share. As studies show, global integration has also played a key role, largely by lowering labor shares in tradables sectors (Dao et al. 2017). To this extent, the empirical literature suggests that rising trade shares reduce labor share from their country-level panel data analysis (Stockhammer Engelbert 2013; Harrison 2005; Jayadev 2007). The impact from trend changes in the participation in global value chain on the decline in labor income share is homogeneous across the emerging market, while the impact from exposure to the routinization and relative price decline contain significant differences among individual economies (Dao et al. 2017).

One of the drivers that explain the global decline of labor share, according to a study by Elsby et al. (2013), is the offshoring of tasks that are more capital intensive relative to the other tasks in the receiving countries. Analogously, Feenstra and Hanson (1997) argue that offshored, low-skill tasks from advanced countries actually require skilled labor in the recipient countries. In an earlier study, Diwan (2001) shows that financial crises have systemically led to a decline in labor share relative to capital but does not address the role of globalization directly. Harrison (2005) conducted panel data analysis using data from more than 100 countries. In the period from 1960 to 1997, she finds that labor income share in low-income countries fell, while the share in high-income countries increased. She also finds that rising trade shares and exchange rate crises reduce labor income share, while capital controls and government spending increase labor income share. In addition, foreign investment inflows are associated with a fall in labor income share.

Rodrik (1997) and Slaughter (2001) argue that globalization is affecting labor by increasing the elasticity of labor demand. However, Slaughter (2001) finds that there is no strong relationship between globalization and change in labor elasticity using the data of the United States from 1961 to 1991. Jaumotte and Tytell (2007) show that though technological change, especially in the information and communications sectors, has a large magnitude to the labor income share, especially for the unskilled sectors, globalization, which includes aspects such as trade prices, offshoring, and immigration, reduces the labor income share in 18 developed countries over 1982–2002. Jaumotte and Tytell (2007) also find that countries that have enacted reform to lower the cost of labor to business and improve labor market flexibility have generally experienced a smaller decline in the labor income share.

7.2.2 *Trade Liberalization and Labor Income Share: Country Level*

The recent protectionist trade policies of some industrialized countries have provoked a debate on the impact of globalization on income inequality within countries. The neoclassical trade theory predicts that trade will benefit all countries, but this does not mean that individual income always increases. There could be both winners and losers from trade. In this section, we explore the dynamics of the labor income share over the course of trade liberalization. This sheds light on whether the production factor is key in determining the fate among individuals within countries. Theoretically, there is no consensus on how trade liberalization affects the labor income share. Two possible channels have been proposed through which trade liberalization impacts the dynamics of the labor income share: the traditional trade theory and the bargaining game framework. The traditional trade theory, the Heckscher-Ohlin model, predicts that a country will have comparative advantages in industries where a relatively abundant production factor is intensively utilized. When a country opens up to trade, the country specializes in industries with comparative advantages. Accordingly, trade changes the relative factor price such that the abundant factor gains and the scarce factor loses. Therefore, the theory predicts that trade will reduce the labor income share in capital-abundant advanced economies but raise it in labor-abundant developing economies.

On the other hand, the bargaining framework predicts that the income share between labor and capital will depend on the bargaining power of population groups. Reductions in trade and FDI barriers after liberalization would increase the relative bargaining power of capital owners as they can relocate their resources to destinations with higher returns. Moreover, reductions in migration barriers would make it possible to substitute imported labor for domestic labor, leading to further decreases in the bargaining power of workers. Under this framework, liberalization decreases the labor income share in both developed and developing countries.

As a measure of trade openness, we use a binary indicator from Wacziarg and Welch (2008). Their indicator was initially constructed by Sachs and Warner (1995) and later extended, updated, and revised by Wacziarg and Welch (2003, 2008). This indicator regards a country closed in any given year if at least one of the following conditions is satisfied: (a) average tariffs exceed 40%; (b) nontariff barriers cover more than 40% of its imports; (c) it has a socialist economic system; (d) the black-market premium on the exchange rate exceeds 20%; and (e) many of its exports are controlled by a state monopoly. Wacziarg and Welch (2008) cover the years from 1950 to 2001. Therefore, we exclude the data after 2001 from our sample for the countries recorded as closed as of 2001, since they might liberalize their economy after 2001, but we cannot know whether it happens, and if so, when. In terms of the countries that opened their economy before 2001, we assume that they did not close the country after 2001. We keep the data for 80 countries that have neither extrapolated nor interpolated labor income share data after 2001.

Among the 133 countries with labor income share data provided by the Penn World Tables (PWT), we analyze countries for which the trade liberalization indicator is available and whose labor income shares are estimated based on actual observed values. In the PWT, about 66.7% of labor income share data are either extrapolated or interpolated for the years for which observed data are not available. The extrapolation assumes that the labor income shares are constant over time and missing values are replaced by the closest year's labor income share. Interpolation is applied for missing years between two calculated values. It employs linear approximation and replaces the missing labor income share value, inserting a value from trajectories of the connected closest two points. As those non-observed data are not appropriate for analyzing the impact of trade liberalization on the labor income share, we exclude them and focus on countries and years with labor income shares neither extrapolated nor interpolated. Those eliminations of the data leave 108 countries for our analysis of trade liberalization.

Table 7.3 presents the summary statistics of the labor income share and the trade liberalization variable. When we see the year of trade liberalization, about 38% of the sample countries open their economy in the late 1980s to early 1990s (from 1985 to 1994). However, we can observe the regional tendency. For example, some countries open their economy in the 1960s, and they are mainly observed in East Asian and European regions. We have five countries that open their economies before 1950

Table 7.3 Overview of labor share measures for low- and middle-income countries since 1990

Data set	*Obs.*	*Years*	*Ctry*	*Mean*	*Median*	*Min*	*Max*	*SD*
SNA unadj.	1421	15.3	93	35.3	35.5	5.4	90.7	11.8
SNA G1	508	13.4	38	56.5	56.1	26.2	87	10.4
SNA G2	508	13.4	38	45.6	46	21	73.4	8.5
SNA G3	766	10.5	73	62	55.5	21.5	658.4	33.8
ILO unadj.	1044	14.3	73	39.6	39.9	3.4	93.8	14
ILO adj.	1044	14.3	73	56.9	56.2	3.4	231.7	25.1
PWT	2298	24.7	93	52	52.6	9	86.6	13.1
Trapp	1421	15.3	93	46.8	47	6	90.7	12.5
WIOD unadj.	258	16.1	16	42.3	44.5	22.2	61.8	8.5
WIOD adj.	258	16.1	16	53.2	53.4	31.5	104.5	11.3
UNIDO	1072	11.2	96	29.9	28.3	1.7	140.9	14

Data set	Adj. approach	Data sources	Authors
SNA unadj.	Unadj.	UN SNA	UN (2017)
SNA G1	G1	UN SNA	UN (2017)
SNA G2	G2	UN SNA	UN (2017)
SNA G3	G3	UN SNA, KILM	UN (2017), ILO (2017)
ILO unadj.	Unadj.	UN SNA, KILM, OECD, China NBS, SNA Brazil	
ILO adj.	G3	UN SNA, KILM, OECD, China NBS, SNA Brazil	Charpe et al. (2014)
PWT	G2 (47%), G1[a] (47%), G3 (3%), unadj. (3%)	UN SNA, WIOD	Feenstra et al. (2015)
Trapp	G3[b] full (50%), G3[b] 2/3 (18%), G1 (4%), G2 (21%), unadj. (6%)	UN SNA, FAOStat, WB WDI	Trapp (2015)
WIOD unadj.	Unadj.	WIOD SEA	Timmer et al. (2015)
WIOD adj.	G3	WIOD SEA	Timmer et al. (2015)
UNIDO	Corp. manuf. sector	INDSTAT2	UNIDO (2015)

Source: van Treeck (2017)

[a]Agricultural value added used as proxy for mixed income

[b]Agricultural employment share used as proxy for self-employment share

and 19 countries are characterized as being closed as of 2001. PWT 9.0 data cover the period 1950–2014, but only France and the United States have the labor income share data, which were calculated based on the observed values from 1950. Other countries have data from 1970 at the earliest. This allows the United States to have the longest sample period and the largest observation, from 1950 to 2014 and 65, respectively. In contrast, Kenya, Togo, and the Russian Federation have only one observation each. Wacziarg and Welch (2008) report on the temporal trade openness for 13 countries. However, due to the data availability of calculated labor income shares, only four countries experienced temporal liberalization in our sample years.[6] The right-hand column of Table 7.1 shows the unweighted labor income share for each country and region, though it is not comparable as it is not adjusted for the number of observations for each country, and nor are the sample years. The largest average labor income share is observed in Togo (0.852) followed by Rwanda (0.773) and Barbados (0.746), while the smallest is Iraq (0.138) followed by Nigeria (0.303) and Botswana (0.318). As regards the regional average, South Asia (0.694) has the largest unweighted average, while the smallest is Latin America and the Caribbean (0.519).

To assess the impact of trade liberalization on the labor income share, we cover a period of five years before and ten years after trade liberalization. This left 56 countries with us: 5 from East Asia and the Pacific, 18 from Europe and Central Asia, 17 from Latin America and the Caribbean, 5 from Middle East and North Africa (MENA) and South Asia, and 11 from sub-Saharan Africa. Figures 7.1–7.10 show time trends of the labor income share for each country over a period of five years of pre- and ten years of post-liberalization. As indicated below in Figs. 7.3–7.12, the year of trade liberalization varies from country to country. Thus, in Figs. 7.1–7.10, the year of trade liberalization for each country is normalized to 0, and the preceding five years and the following ten years are numbered −5 to −1 and 1 to 10, respectively.

Among East Asia and Pacific countries, New Zealand experiences a moderate decline in the labor income share after the liberalization (Fig. 7.3). The labor income shares of the other countries are observed only after the liberalization, but overall, they kept constant trends. Among the first group of European and Central Asian countries, France has a moderate declining trend since five years before the liberalization.

[6] Bolivia, Sri Lanka, Ecuador, and Jamaica.

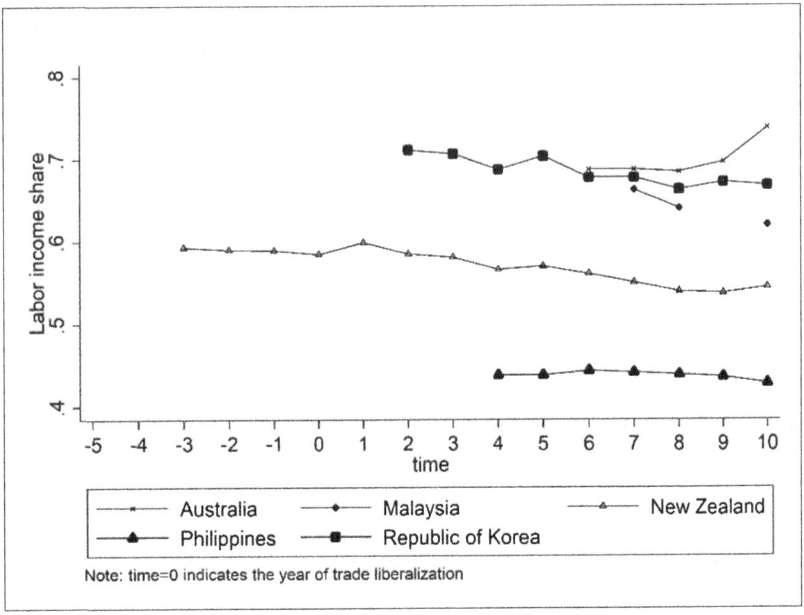

Fig. 7.3 Trade liberalization and labor income share in East Asia and Pacific. (Note: The period for each country is 1970–1974 (Australia); 1970–1971, 1973 (Malaysia); 1983–1996 (New Zealand); 1992–1998 (Philippines); and 1970–1978 (Republic of Korea))

Although the labor income share data before the liberalization are not available, Georgia experienced a steep decline in the labor income share after it opened up to trade (Fig. 7.4).

Trends of the labor income shares of the second group of European and Central Asian countries are shaky (Fig. 7.5). The Kyrgyz Republic experienced a steep decline from four years to two years before the liberalization, a rapid increase from two years before to two years after the liberalization, and then a sharp decrease afterward.

Among the third group of European and Central Asian countries, Serbia witnessed a sharp decline in the labor income share from four to one year before the liberalization, a slight increase right after the liberalization, and then a moderate decline from two years after the liberalization (Fig. 7.6).

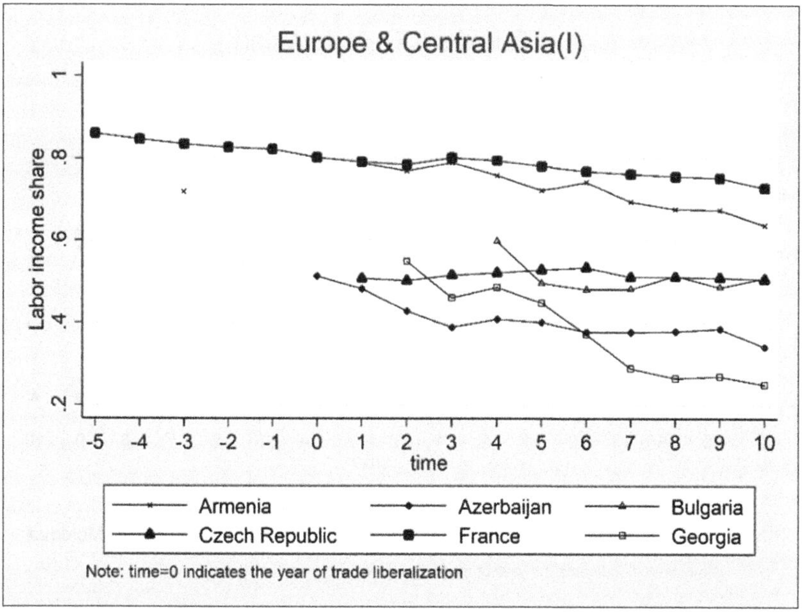

Fig. 7.4 Trade liberalization and labor income share in Europe and Central Asia (I). (Note: The period for each country is 1992, 1996–2005 (Armenia); 1995–2005 (Azerbaijan); 1995–2001 (Bulgaria); 1992–2001 (Czech Republic); 1954–1969 (France); and 1998–2006 (Georgia))

Among the first group of Latin American and Caribbean countries, Costa Rica had a relatively constant trend in the labor income share (Fig. 7.7). Argentina experienced a decline after the liberalization, while Brazil witnessed an increase after the liberalization.

Among the second group of Latin American and Caribbean countries, Panama witnessed a slight decline in the labor income share after the liberalization. The labor income share of Ecuador had a declining trend before the liberalization, while its post-liberalization data are not available (Fig. 7.8). Among the third group of Latin American and Caribbean countries, Trinidad and Tobago and Peru had decreasing trends for four to five years prior to liberalization and continued to decrease after opening up to trade (Fig. 7.9). The labor income share of Venezuela was shaky, but it had a long-term declining trend after the liberalization.

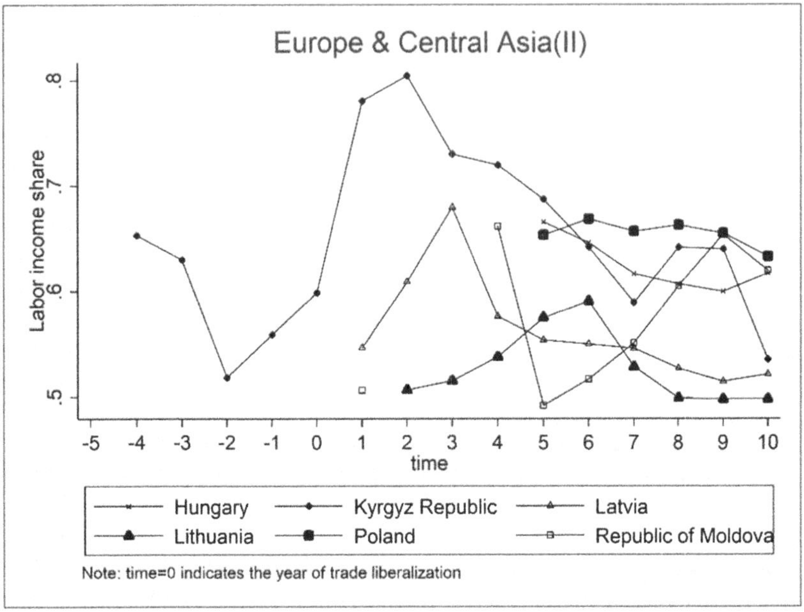

Fig. 7.5 Trade liberalization and labor income share in Europe and Central Asia (II). (Note: The period for each country is 1995–2000 (Hungary); 1990–2004 (Kyrgyz Republic); 1994–2003 (Latvia); 1995–2003 (Lithuania); 1995–2000 (Poland); and 1995*, 1998–2004 (Republic of Moldova). *denotes a year in which the adjustment method used for calculating labor income share differs from the one applied for the other years)

Among MENA and South Asian countries, Sri Lanka experienced a long-term declining trend after the period that predated the liberalization (Fig. 7.10). The labor income share was relatively constant for Egypt after the liberalization.

Among the first group of sub-Saharan African countries, Ivory Coast witnessed a drop in the labor income share in the year of liberalization (Fig. 7.11). Burundi experienced a sharp decline from six to seven years after the liberalization.

Among the second group of sub-Saharan African countries, South Africa followed a decreasing trend, which predated the trade liberalization (Fig. 7.12). Tanzania experienced a decline in the labor income share after

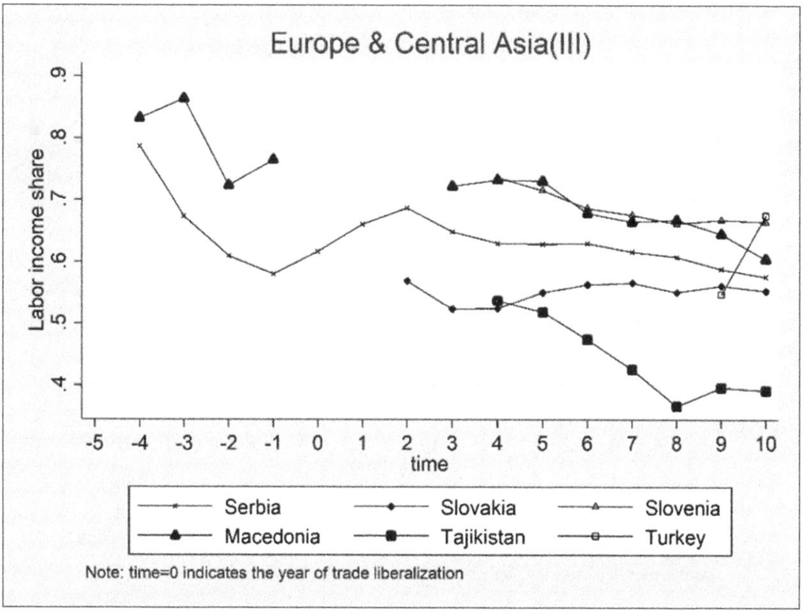

Fig. 7.6 Trade liberalization and labor income share in Europe and Central Asia (III). (Note: The period for each country is 1997–2001 (Serbia); 1993–2001 (Slovakia); 1995–2001 (Slovenia); 1990*–1993*, 1997–2004 (Macedonia); 2000–2006 (Tajikistan); and 1998–1999 (Turkey). *denotes years in which the adjustment method in calculating labor income share differs from the one applied for the other years)

the liberalization, while Niger witnessed an increase after three years of trade liberalization.

The time series plots of the labor income share for most of the countries suggest a downward trend following the episode of trade liberalization. However, from this bivariate analysis it is difficult to identify whether a fall in labor income share was driven entirely by trade openness, as for some countries the labor income share started declining before they embraced the trade reform measures. Such causal links are difficult to discern unless we look at the sectoral labor income shares and understand the sectoral dynamics of labor income share associated with trade reforms. We take this up in the following section.

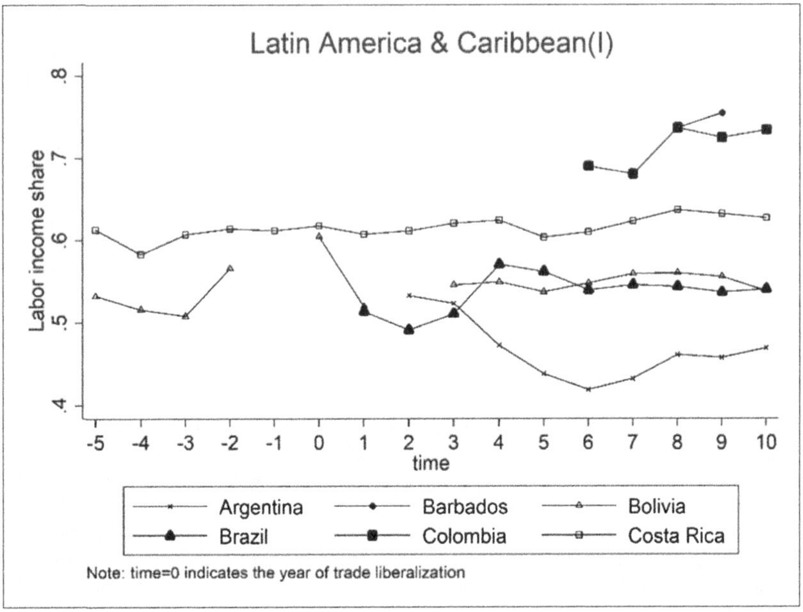

Fig. 7.7 Trade liberalization and labor income share in Latin America and the Caribbean (I). (Note: The period for each country is 1993–2001 (Argentina); 1974–1975 (Barbados); 1980–1983, 1985–1986, 1988–1995 (Bolivia); 1992–2001 (Brazil); 1992–1996 (Colombia); and 1981–1996 (Costa Rica))

7.2.3 *Trade Liberalization and Labor Income Share: Sectoral Level*

In this section, we discuss some stylized facts about the labor income share at the sectoral level. For this purpose, we rely on the sectoral-level labor income share data computed by Oishi and Paul (2018) for 54 countries across five regions based on the most recent World Bank classification of countries (9 from East Asia and the Pacific, 28 from Europe and Central Asia, 8 from Latin America and the Caribbean, 2 from the Middle East and North Africa, 2 from North America, and 5 from sub-Saharan Africa). In Fig. 7.13, we show cross-country scatter plots between the sectoral labor income share and trade share of GDP. In the left-hand column, the plots show labor income shares for three key sectors (agriculture,

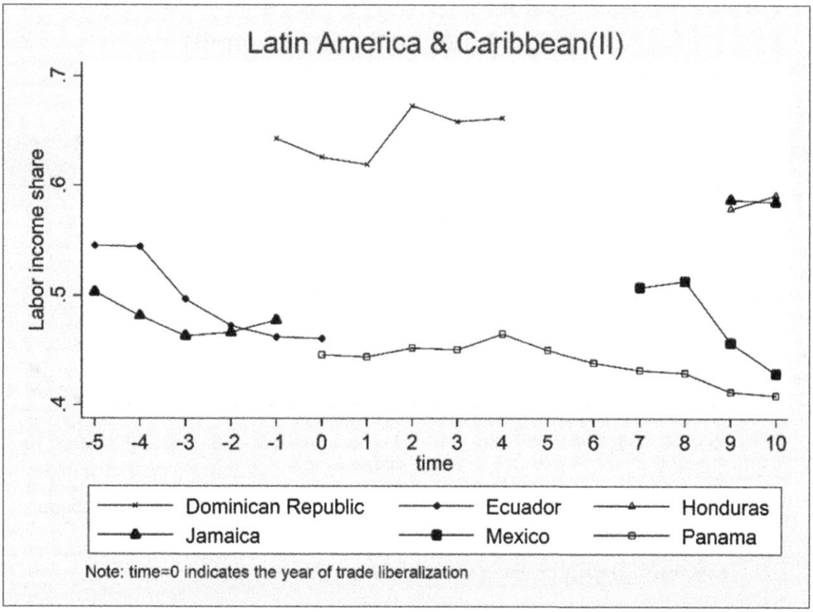

Fig. 7.8 Trade liberalization and labor income share in Latin America and the Caribbean (II). (Note: The period for each country is 1991–1996 (Dominican Republic); 1986–1991 (Ecuador); 2000–2001 (Honduras); 1984–1988, 1998–1999 (Jamaica); 2003–2006 (Mexico); and 1996–2006 (Panama))

manufacturing, and services)[7] and trade share of GDP averaged over the period from 1995 to 1999. In the right-hand column, we plot the same variables, but averages are taken for the period from 2000 to 2004. In each plot countries from different regions are demarcated by different colors.

Overall, the results show a negative correlation between the volume of trade (as a share of GDP) and labor income shares at the key sectoral levels. The negative correlation in the manufacturing sector is somewhat weaker than in other sectors; however, such sectoral patterns of trade and factor income shares do not change over time, except for agriculture, where it almost doubled from −0.14 in the period 1995–1999 to −0.22 in the period 2000–2004. Countries like Turkey, Poland, and Botswana

[7] Services include five disaggregated sectors: WRT, TRA, FIRE, GOV, and OTH.

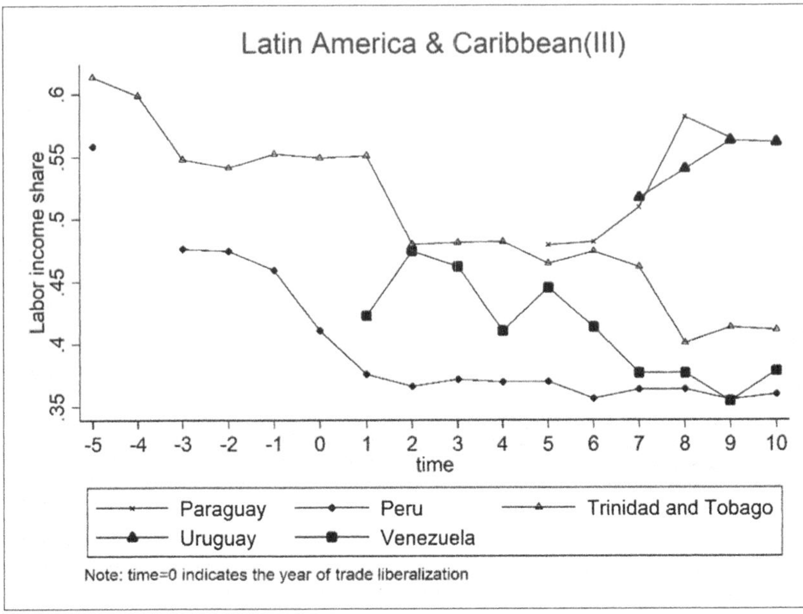

Fig. 7.9 Trade liberalization and labor income share in Latin America and the Caribbean (III). (Note: The period for each country is 1994–1998 (Paraguay); 1986, 1988–2001 (Peru); 1987–2002 (Trinidad and Tobago); 1997–2000 (Uruguay); and 1997–2006 (Venezuela))

show a relatively higher share of labor income in agriculture, whereas Brazil and Austria have the highest labor income share in manufacturing. We do not find any regional bias. The same holds for the services sector, where Denmark and the Netherlands continue to have the highest labor income share.

We next show the dynamic (changes over time) relationship between sectoral labor income share and trade. The plots in the left-hand column of Fig. 7.14 compare the changes in the average values of labor income share and trade share of GDP between two periods: 1995–1997 and 2001–2003. And in the right-hand column, the plots compare the same relationship between 2001–2003 and 2007–2009. The correlation between changes in the sectoral labor income share and trade share of GDP is negative for all the sectors and periods, except in agriculture between 2001–2003 and 2007–2009 where we find a positive association

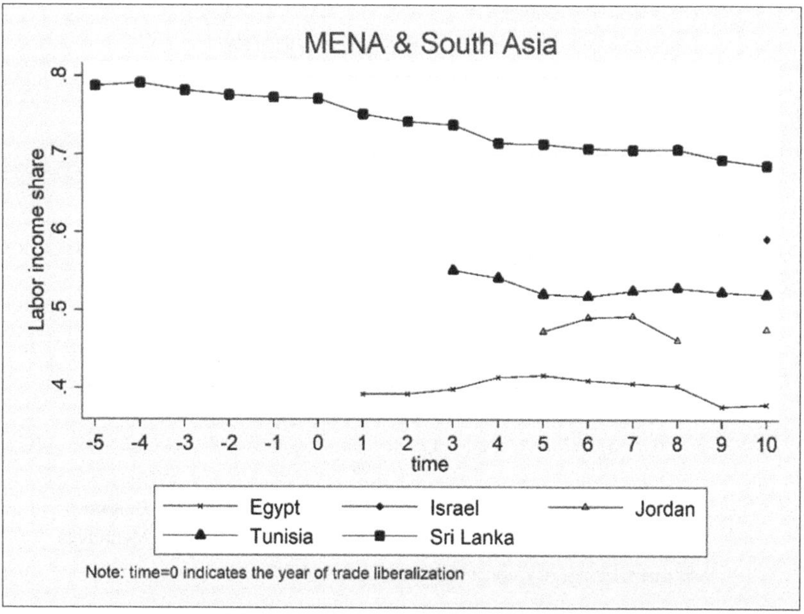

Fig. 7.10 Trade liberalization and labor income share in MENA and South Asia. (Note: The period for each country is 1996–2005 (Egypt); 1995 (Israel); 1970–1973, 1975 (Jordan); 1992–1999 (Tunisia); and 1986–2001 (Sri Lanka))

between changes in the labor income shares in agriculture and changes in the trade share of GDP. Since the plots show a dynamic relationship considering different time periods, it is difficult to directly compare the results with that at the level. However, the negative correlation observed both at the level and dynamics over time provide some robustness from across time and space. The bivariate plots suggest a negative correlation between labor income share at the sectoral level and trade volume, which is in line with many of the studies on this topic.

Finally, we examine the time series plots at the country level. Figure 7.15 shows labor income share trends for three sectors and the trade GDP ratio for four countries: the PRC (manufacturing and services), Brazil (manufacturing and services), Egypt (agriculture, manufacturing, and services), and Botswana (agriculture, manufacturing, and services). Let us first compare the trade performance of these countries. The PRC outperforms other countries in terms of the growth in trade share of GDP. While the

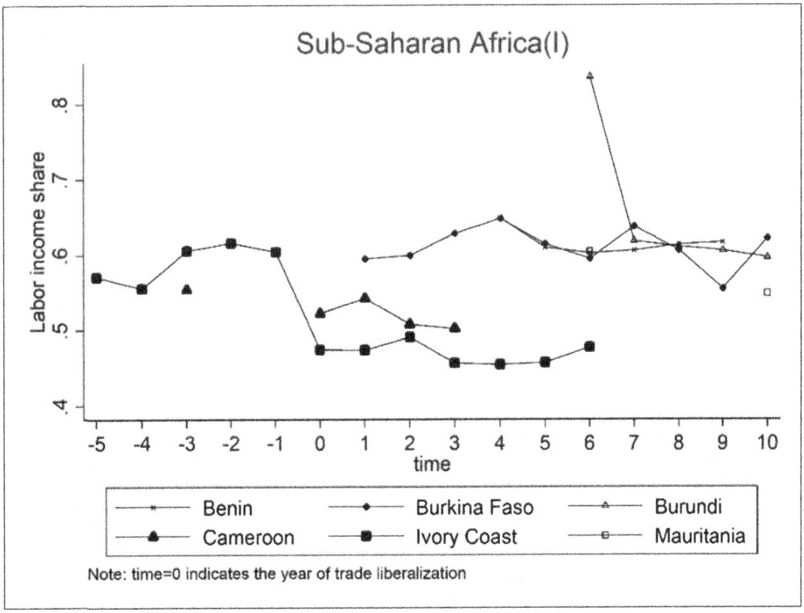

Fig. 7.11 Trade liberalization and labor income share in sub-Saharan Africa (I). (Note: The period for each country is 1994–1999 (Benin); 1999–2008 (Burkina Faso); 2005–2009 (Burundi); 1990, 1993–1996 (Cameroon); 1989–2000 (Ivory Coast); and 2001, 2005 (Mauritania))

data from the period available for these countries differ, both Brazil and Egypt show stronger trade performance from the early 2000s whereas it did not change much for Botswana and the trade share of GDP oscillated around 1. In the PRC, the labor income shares in manufacturing remained constant around 0.3, whereas the same in services steadily grew from the early 2000s and reached about 0.5 by 2008. On the other hand, in Brazil, the labor income shares trends for both sectors are similar with a slight decline in the labor income share in the manufacturing sector since 1994. For Egypt and Botswana, the labor income share in agriculture is higher than in the other sectors. In Egypt, the trade volume and labor income share in agriculture show a strong positive correlation. Overall, the time series plots from country cases suggest a more diverse picture of the relationship between trade and sectoral labor income shares.

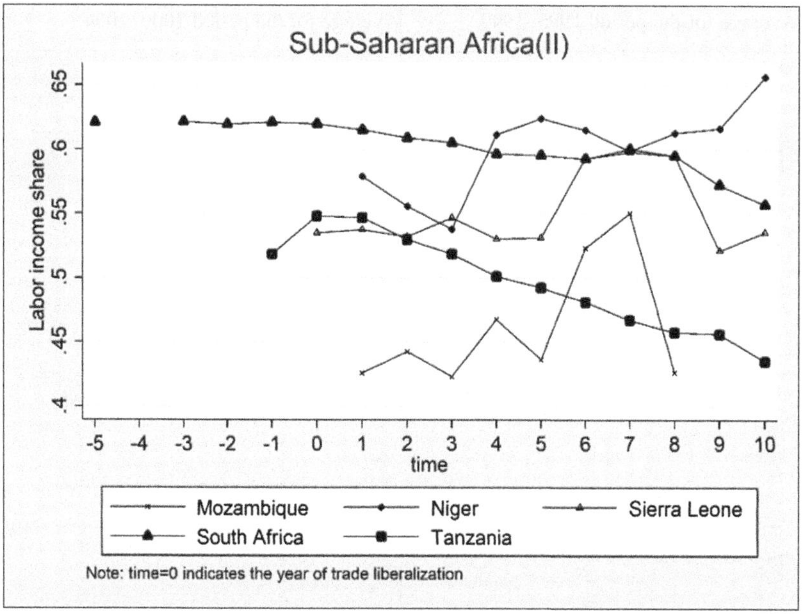

Fig. 7.12 Trade liberalization and labor income share in sub-Saharan Africa (II). (Note: The period for each country is 1996–2003 (Mozambique); 1995–2004 (Niger); 2001–2011 (Sierra Leone); 1986 and 1988–2001 (South Africa); and 1994–2005 (Tanzania))

To conclude, based on the descriptive analysis we find mild support for a negative correlation between labor income share and trade openness at the cross-country level. Evidence at the sectoral level provides a more nuanced picture and suggests a possible association between sectoral labor income share and trade. This prompts us to dig deeper and examine the process of structural transformation at the sectoral level as a causal mechanism between trade reforms and the labor income share.

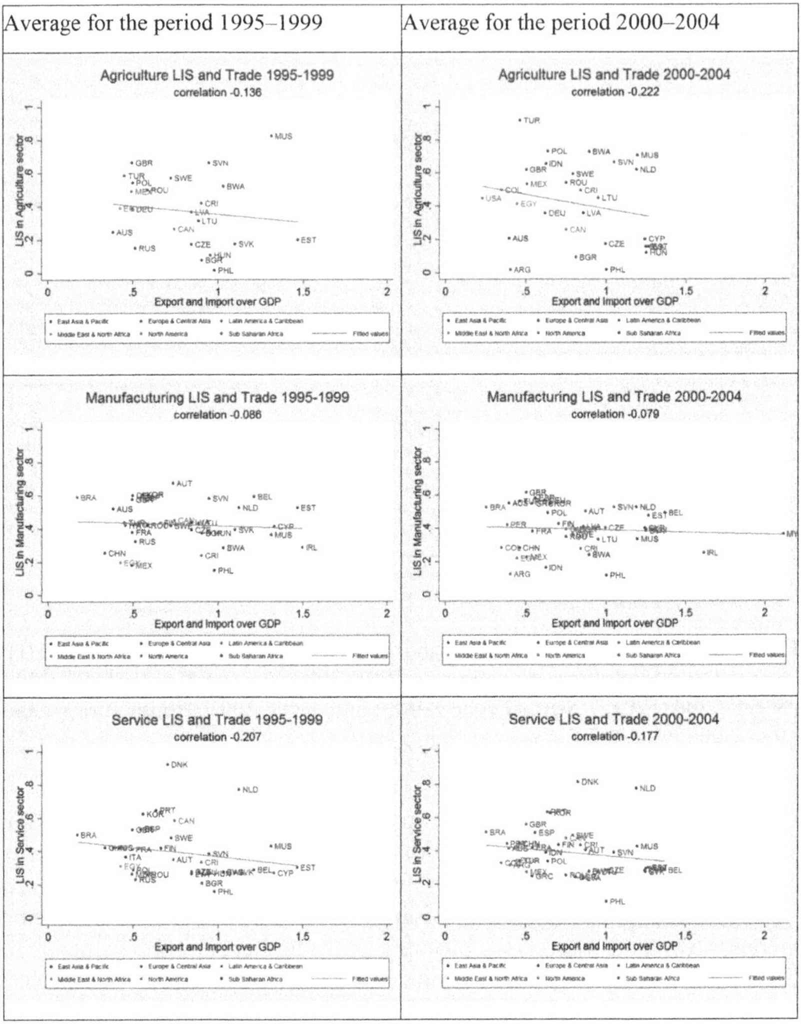

Fig. 7.13 Sectoral labor income share (broad categories) and trade share of GDP. (Source: Authors' own calculations)

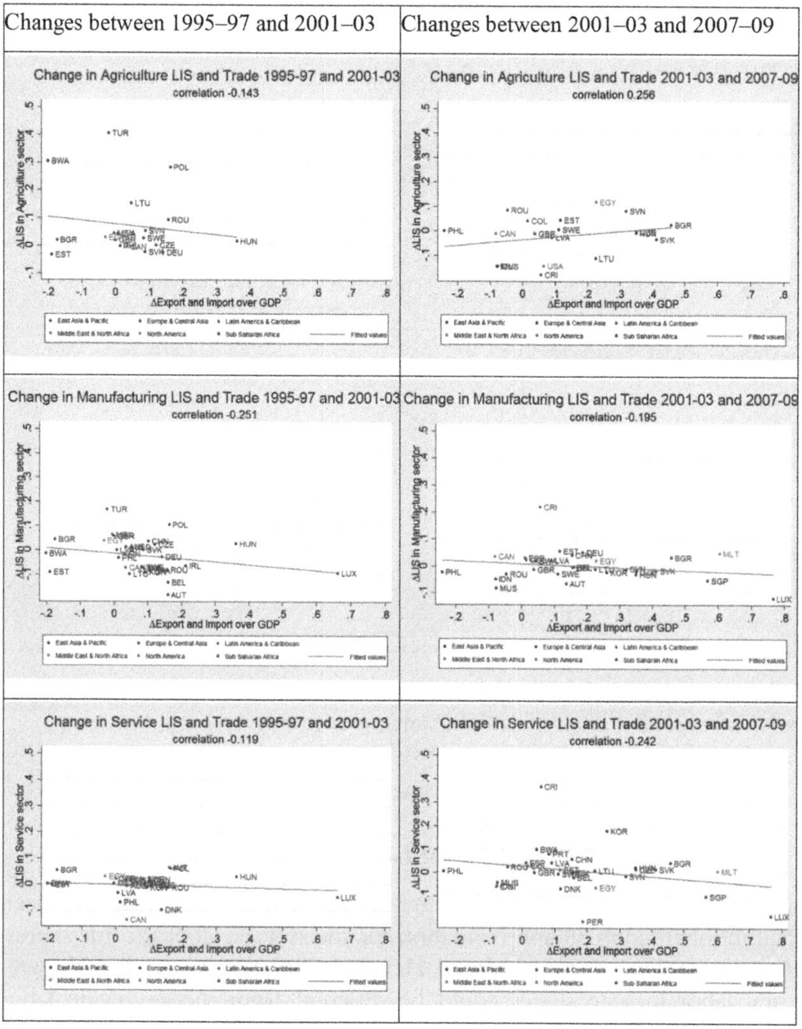

Fig. 7.14 Changes in sectoral labor income share and trade share of GDP. (Source: Authors' own calculations)

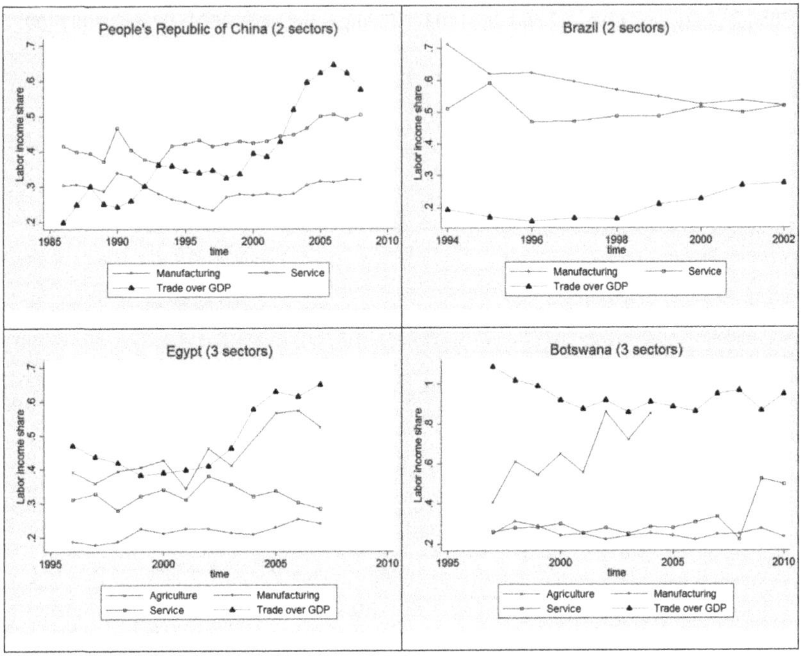

Fig. 7.15 Changes in sectoral labor income share and trade share of GDP: selected countries. (Source: Authors' own calculations)

7.3 Structural Transformation

7.3.1 Sectoral Labor Income Share

In the literature, the national (aggregate) labor income share has been commonly used as an approximation for the sectoral labor income shares. A recent paper by Valentinyi and Herrendorf (2008) shows that the sectoral labor income shares could be different from the aggregate labor income share. In this section, we elaborate on the importance of sectoral labor income share trends. We provide a snapshot of the existing literature available at the disaggregated level including both industries and sectors and some novel insights for future research. In one of the early papers, Bentolila and Saint-Paul (2003) studied the labor income shares in the value added of the 13 industries in the business sectors in 12 OECD countries during 1972–1993. Two other papers (Young, 2006 and Zuleta and Young 2013) also looked at the labor income shares of 35 industries (value added) in the United States for the period from 1958 to 1996. In another study on the United States, Valentinyi and Herrendorf (2008) find that the smallest labor income share is in agriculture, followed by manufactured consumption, services, equipment, and construction. Moreover, the labor income share of agriculture is less than two times that of construction and more than 50% smaller than that of the aggregate economy. They aggregate the factor income shares in the industry outputs to get the sectoral level.

To highlight the role of structural transformation behind the link between sectoral (or industry-specific) labor income shares and the aggregate labor income share, we next discuss the shift-share decomposition framework. Following a variant of the canonical shift-share decomposition methodology (see Fabricant 1942, for the original decomposition; de Vries et al. 2013; and Arpaia et al. 2009, for the variant) we write changes in the aggregate labor income share between t and $t + 1$ as follows (Eq. 7.1):

$$\Delta LIS = \sum_i \left(\theta_i^t\right)\left(\Delta LIS_i\right) + \sum_i \left(\Delta\theta_i\right)\left(LIS_i^t\right) \tag{7.1}$$

where LIS_i is the labor income share in sector i, and LIS denotes the aggregate labor income share. Labor is reallocated across sectors between two points in time, t and $t + 1$, and θ_i^t denotes the sectoral labor share of sector i in period t. The first term on the right-hand side of Eq. (7.2) measures the contribution of within-sector effect (changes in the labor income share within a sector) whereas the second term measures the contribution of between-sector effect (changes in the weights of the sector) or structural transformation. In the absence of structural transformation, the aggregate labor income share trend would simply be a weighted average of the sectoral labor income share trends. Many studies (Lawrence 2015; Elsby et al. 2013; Rodrigues and Jayadev 2010) find that the change in the aggregate labor income share is driven by declines in within-industry labor shares rather than the process of structural transformation through an increasing flow of activities from high to low labor share industries. In another study, Dao et al. (2017) find that almost 90% of the changes in the aggregate labor income shares in PRC come from within-industry changes rather than sectoral reallocation. In addition, reallocation from agriculture to other industries accounts for most of the decline in the labor share of income in People's Republic of China, from 1993 to 2014 (Dao et al. 2017). Arpaia et al. (2009) examine the role of structural transformation for a panel of OECD countries and find similar evidences on the dominance of within-sector effects. However, in a separate paper, de Serres et al. (2002) estimate that about 50% of the variation in the labor share is due to structural transformation in the United States.

7.3.2 *Labor Share in Manufacturing and Service Sectors*

Next, we compare the labor income share trends between two broad sectors, manufacturing and services. If the elasticity of substitution between factor inputs is different from one, and varies across sectors (e.g., manufacturing vs. services), then sectoral labor income share trends could follow different trajectories. In a recent study on the United States, Alvarez-Cuadrado et al. (2015) show that a larger decline in labor income share in manufacturing relative to that in services is partly driven by a larger elasticity of substitution (or in other words a higher elasticity of substitution between capital and labor) in manufacturing associated with a much faster labor-augmenting productivity growth relative to services. Alvarez-Cuadrado et al. (2015) use Jorgenson's 35-sector KLEM database for 16 developed economies. They calculate the labor income share for two broad sectors, manufacturing and services, computed as compensation of employees over value added. In Fig. 7.16, we compare the average labor income share between manufacturing and services sectors across 16 developed economies for the period from 1970 to 2007.

On average, the labor income share in manufacturing sectors was higher than that in the services sectors. In countries like Hungary, Japan, and

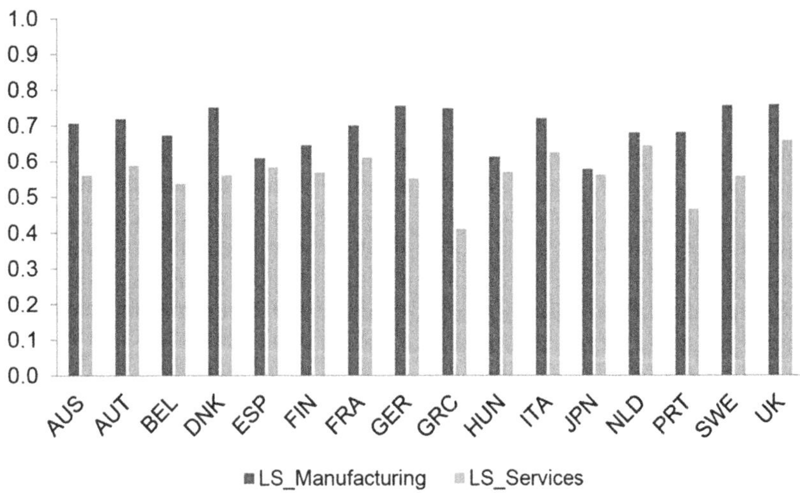

Fig. 7.16 Average sectoral labor income share for 16 developed countries, 1970–2007. (Source: Authors' elaborations based on Alvarez-Cuadrado et al. (2015); original data source: http://www.euklems.net)

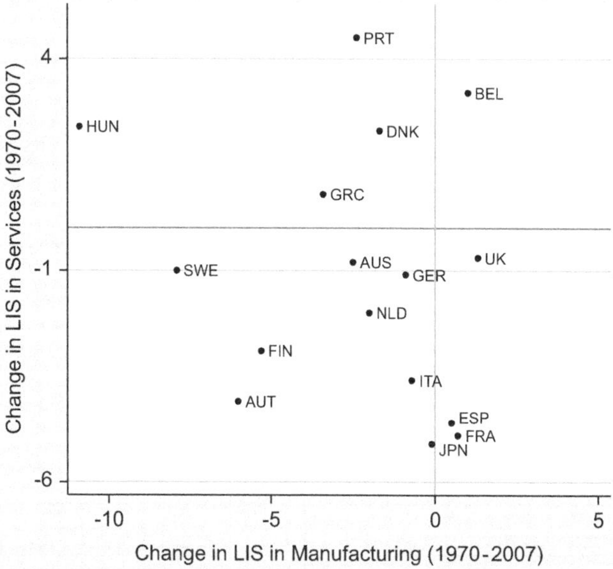

Fig. 7.17 Changes in labor income shares: manufacturing versus services, 1970–2007. (Source: Authors' elaborations based on Alvarez-Cuadrado et al. (2015); original data source: http://www.euklems.net)

Spain, the sectoral gap in labor income share between manufacturing and services was less than 3 percentage points, whereas in countries like Greece, Denmark, and Portugal the gap was more than 15 percentage points. As a next step, we examine how a change in the sectoral labor income share is related to the observed global decline in the aggregate labor income share. This also helps us understand the role of structural transformation in the decline in the labor income share better. Figure 7.17 shows a scatterplot of 16 countries between changes in the labor income shares in manufacturing and changes in the labor income share in services. We find four categories of countries. Belgium is the only country that had an increase in the labor income share in both sectors. Then we have the next category consisting of Greece, Hungary, Denmark, and Portugal, where the labor income share declined only in the manufacturing sector.

Spain, France, and the UK made up the next group of countries that had a drop in the labor income share only in services. Finally, the largest group of countries (Australia, Austria, Finland, Japan, Italy, Germany, Sweden, and the Netherlands) shows declining labor income shares in

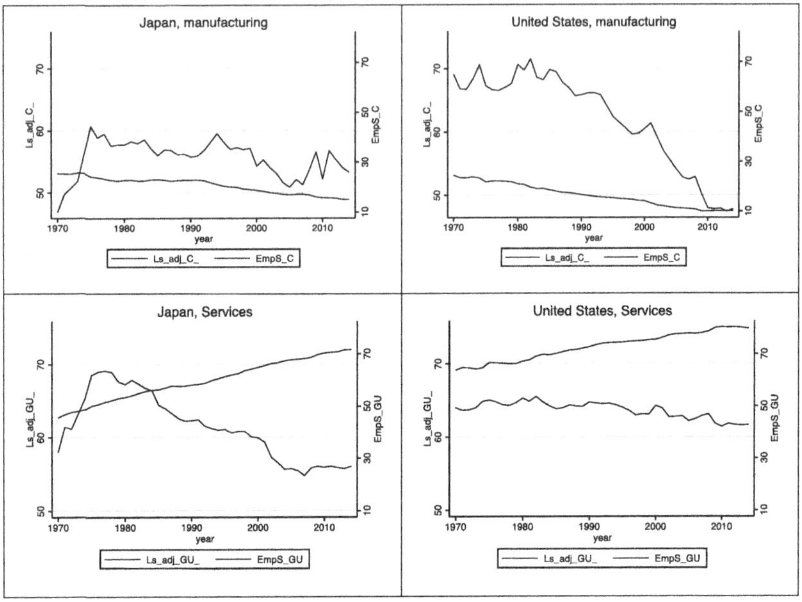

Fig. 7.18 Changes in sectoral labor income shares: Japan versus the United States. (Source: Authors' elaborations on Ameco data)

both sectors. These four groups of countries demonstrate heterogeneous relationships between structural transformation and movements in the labor income share. The highest decline in labor income share (in terms of percentage point differences) in services and manufacturing was in Japan and Portugal, respectively. Moving on, we next compare the labor income share trends in manufacturing and services between the United States and Japan using annual data from Ameco[8] for the period from 1970 to 2014 (Fig. 7.18). Manufacturing labor income share in Japan shows an upward trend since the early 1990s, whereas labor income share in services steadily declined since the early 1980s, contributing to a declining total labor share in Japan over the last two decades. This is in sharp contrast to sectoral labor income share trends observed in the United States, where labor income share declines faster in manufacturing compared to services (Alvarez-Cuadrado et al. 2015).

[8] https://ec.europa.eu/info/business-economy-euro/indicators-statistics/economic-databases/macro-economic-database-ameco/ameco-database_en.

7.3.3 Skill-Biased Structural Transformation and Labor Income Share

It is well documented in the literature that there has been a dramatic increase in the supply and relative wages of skilled labor over time (Acemoglu and Autor 2011). While the literature on skill-biased technical change (SBTC) argues for an increase in the demand for skill as a potential driver (Acemoglu and Autor 2011), the availability of cheaper capital equipment could also increase the demand for skilled labor with or without SBTC (Krusell et al. 2000). Extending the literature that argues for an increase in the relative demand for skilled labor, Buera et al. (2015) argue for a systematic reallocation of value-added shares toward high-skill-intensive sectors, which they term the "skill-biased structural change" (SBSC from hereon). They develop a two-sector model of the SBSC process and use it to examine the rise in the skill premium in the United States, and a broad panel of advanced economies, over the period 1977–2005. Their empirical findings across a broad panel of advanced economies suggest that increases in GDP per capita are associated with a shift in the composition of value added to sectors that are intensive in high-skill labor.

We use the labor income share data compiled by Buera et al. (2015) from the EU KLEMS database to compare the labor income shares for high-skilled labor (college graduates and above) for the ten key sectors (Fig. 7.8). Overall, the labor income shares of high-skilled workers show rising trends across the board, which supports the role of SBSC (Buera et al. 2015) in sectoral labor income share movements. We also find three parallel trends clearly emerging:

high $LIS^{Skilled}$ sectors—finance, insurance, real estate, and other business; community, social, and personal services.

medium $LIS^{Skilled}$ sectors—electricity, gas and water, manufacturing, wholesale and retail trade, mining and quarrying, transport, storage, and communication.

low $LIS^{Skilled}$ sectors—agriculture, hotels and restaurants, construction.

In a recent paper, Buera and Kaboski (2012) argue that this rising return to skill is closely related to the structural transformation from manufacturing to services. They show that it is useful to model the different roles of human capital to various activities to understand some key features of structural transformation, and labor income share trends, as we find in

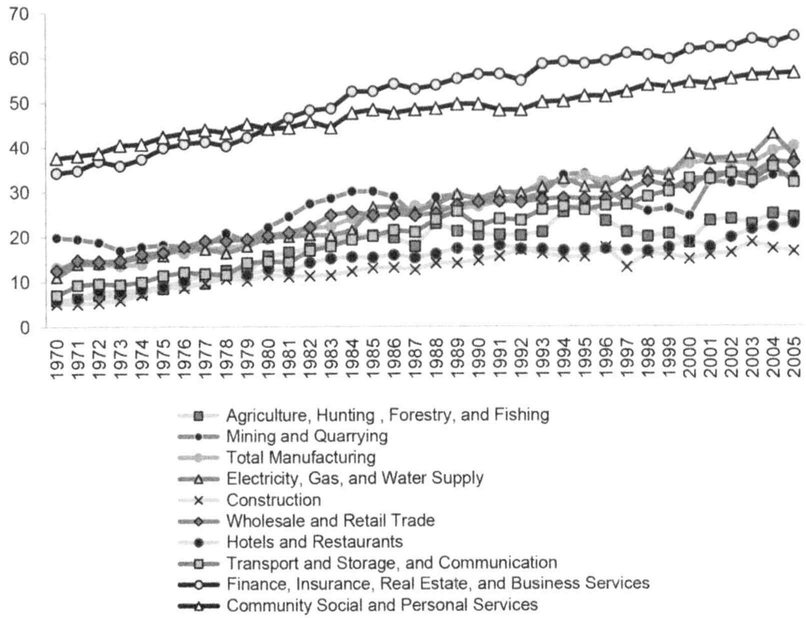

Fig. 7.19 Sectoral labor income share trends for high-skilled workers, 1970–2005. (Source: Authors' calculation based on data compiled by Buera et al. (2015). Original data source is EU KLEMS. Note: EU KLEMS data cover the following countries: Australia, Austria, Belgium, Cyprus, the Czech Republic, Denmark, Estonia, Spain, Finland, France, Germany, Greece, Hungary, Ireland, Italy, Japan, the Republic of Korea, Lithuania, Latvia, Luxembourg, Malta, the Netherlands, Poland, Portugal, the Slovak Republic, Slovenia, Sweden, the United Kingdom, and the United States)

Fig. 7.19. As the economy develops, it produces services that are complex, which also creates additional incentives for market production skill accumulation. As the authors assume an upward sloping supply curve for skilled workers, the skill premium also increases.

7.4 Structural Transformation, Trade, and Labor Income Share

7.4.1 Regression Outcomes

We conduct regression analyses using cross-country unbalanced panel data. We use sectoral labor income shares (both at the broad and disaggregated levels) as the dependent variables. The summary statistics for these variables are available in Table 7.8. The sectoral data are available for 10 Groningen Growth and Development Centre (GGDC) disaggregated sectors and following the World Development Indicators (WDI) database we create the broad sectors in the following manner: (1) agriculture consisting of AGR; (2) manufacturing sector consisting of MAN; and (3) services consisting of WRT, TRA, FIRE, GOV, and OTH. The average (unweighted) figures (across all countries) for these broad sectors and 10 disaggregated sectors are shown in Table 7.3. On average, employees in the agriculture, manufacturing, and services sectors enjoy about 40% of the total income. At a more disaggregated level, GOV shows the highest share of labor income (46%) followed by MAN (41%), AGR, WRT, and TRA, each with an average of 40%. On the other hand, PU (16%) and MIN (20%) are the sectors with the lowest share of labor income. Other country characteristics that potentially impact the labor income share and are correlated with trade openness are taken from the World Development Indicators (WDI) of the World Bank. These control variables include GDP per capita, population, the share of export and import to GDP, and the share of manufacturing, agriculture, and service value added to GDP. Since available data periods differ across countries, the constructed panel data are unbalanced. Summary statistics of these variables are also reported in Table 7.4. We use trade share of GDP as a proxy for trade openness or trade intensity. To examine the effect of structural transformation, we use sectoral value-added shares of GDP. The regression models for both the baseline and alternative specification are discussed below. We also run regressions on the different components of the sectoral labor income share measure to understand the causal channels better. With the help of panel data methods, we can address both cross-country and temporal effects.

To identify the impact of trade liberalization, we carry out fixed-effect (FE) estimations. We prefer the fixed-effects (or within) estimation in this analysis because it allows us to address the issues of endogeneity in a limited manner. We accept the fact that the correlation between the unobserved heterogeneity and the explanatory variables, caused for example by institutional factors at the sectoral level, cannot be directly measured. In addition, with FE estimation we can remove any time-invariant variable, which helps eliminate country-specific idiosyncrasies in the data used to compute the labor income share. We regress the labor income share on the

Table 7.4 Summary statistics (unweighted)

	Observations	*Mean*	*Standard deviation*	*Min*	*Max*
Labor income share					
Agriculture	330	0.40	0.24	0.01	0.97
Manufacturing	505	0.41	0.14	0.07	0.97
Service	495	0.39	0.16	0.06	0.97
AGR	330	0.40	0.24	0.01	0.97
MIN	493	0.20	0.15	0.00	0.95
MAN	505	0.41	0.14	0.07	0.97
PU	499	0.16	0.11	0.03	0.74
CON	451	0.32	0.22	0.03	1.00
WRT	432	0.40	0.16	0.04	0.97
TRA	468	0.40	0.16	0.09	0.97
FIRE	405	0.28	0.19	0.03	0.99
GOV	320	0.46	0.14	0.16	0.93
OTH	82	0.33	0.18	0.10	0.99
Employment (logarithm)					
AGR	545	12.62	2.19	6.28	17.58
MIN	538	9.85	2.15	1.79	14.14
MAN	549	13.36	1.79	7.74	16.49
PU	538	10.39	1.83	3.50	14.62
CON	549	12.44	1.77	6.25	15.57
WRT	549	13.41	1.86	7.26	16.92
TRA	549	12.34	1.82	5.94	15.71
FIRE	549	12.50	1.89	5.34	15.77
GOV	529	13.46	1.85	6.67	16.68
OTH	482	12.43	1.66	8.52	16.09
GDP per capita in 2010 (logarithm)	541	9.51	1.12	5.45	11.63
Trade to GDP ratio	540	0.93	0.65	0.10	4.42
Service trade to GDP ratio	510	0.23	0.28	0.02	2.12
Agriculture value added to GDP	527	5.42	5.44	0.04	41.17
Manufacturing value added to GDP	520	16.48	6.07	0.00	32.45
Service value added to GDP	495	57.17	7.67	33.37	76.02
Other sector value added to GDP	488	21.16	6.10	8.58	53.87

Source: Authors' own calculations

indicators of trade liberalization, structural transformation, and other controls. The baseline model takes the form of Eq. (7.2):

$$LIS_{ijt} = \alpha + \varphi_i + \delta_t + \beta_1 Trade\_open_{jt} + \beta_2 StrucTrans_{ijt} + X_{jt}^{¢\,3} + \varepsilon_{i,t}, \tag{7.2}$$

where φ_i are country fixed effects, δ_t capture time fixed effects, $X^{'}_{i,t}$ includes GDP per capita (in log form) and other controls, $Trade\_open_{jt}$ is measured by the share of trade (export plus import) to GDP, $StrucTrans_{ijt}$ are proxied by sectoral value-added shares to GDP, and $\varepsilon_{i,t}$ is an error term.

As a next step, we shed light on potential channels through which trade liberalization and structural transformation impact the labor income share. The labor income share is the ratio between the total income earned by the laborers and the total income generated in the economy. The total income earned by the laborers in a sector can be affected in two ways: (a) changes in the average sectoral wages and (b) changes in the size of sectoral employment. Since wages are not PPP adjusted and as a result are more likely to generate bias in the estimation, we decide to examine the sectoral employment as a possible causal mechanism channel. In other words, our second set of regressions use log employment in each sector to find potential channels through which trade and structural transformation affect the labor income share (Eq. 7.3).

$$logEmp_{ijt} = \alpha + \varphi_i + \delta_t + \beta_1 Trade\_open_{jt} + \beta_2 StrucTrans_{ijt} + X_{jt}^{¢\,3} + \varepsilon_{i,t} \tag{7.3}$$

In Table 7.5 we show the baseline model outcomes for broad sectors: agriculture, manufacturing, and services. FE estimation results suggest that trade share of GDP is negatively correlated to labor income share in all sectors; however, the estimates are statistically significant for manufacturing and services. We control for sectoral value-added shares (agriculture, services, and other) with manufacturing as the omitted group. The pace of structural transformation is low in a country with a higher agriculture value-added share of GDP. The labor income share in agriculture and services is negatively correlated with the agriculture value-added share of GDP. This implies that countries at an advanced stage of structural transformation, on average, are more likely to enjoy a higher labor income share in these sectors. This could be due to a higher bargaining power for the workers. However, such effects could be dampened by the negative effect of trade, which could also be associated with substitution of labor by capital as discussed in Sect. 4.1. Richer countries enjoy a higher labor

Table 7.5. Baseline models (broad sectors) of the labor income share

	Labor income share		
	Agriculture	*Manufacturing*	*Service*
	(1)	*(2)*	*(3)*
GDP per capita in 2010 (logarithm)	−0.147***	−0.112***	0.0606**
	(0.0451)	(0.0219)	(0.0257)
Trade to GDP ratio	−0.00783	−0.0602***	−0.0900***
	(0.0449)	(0.0165)	(0.0188)
Agriculture value added to GDP	−0.0226***	0.00253	−0.00907***
	(0.00573)	(0.00302)	(0.00350)
Service value added to GDP	0.00506	0.00464***	−0.00374*
	(0.00399)	(0.00171)	(0.00198)
Other sector value added to GDP	−0.00516	0.00943***	−0.00650***
	(0.00429)	(0.00195)	(0.00228)
Constant	1.734***	1.066***	0.298
	(0.409)	(0.219)	(0.256)
Observations	297	445	437
R-squared	0.137	0.206	0.079
Countries	33	47	48

Standard errors in parentheses $^{***}p < 0.01$, $^{**}p < 0.05$, $^{*}p < 0.1$

income share in services, but we find opposite results for agriculture and manufacturing. Services value-added share of GDP is positively correlated with manufacturing labor income share. This could be driven by complementarity between manufacturing and services sectors in some countries.

In Table 7.6, we extend the baseline model to disaggregated sectors. It shows outcomes for eight sectors: MIN, PU, CON, WRT, TRA, FIRE, GOV, and OTH. The last five sectors are included in services. Labor income share in GOV is higher in richer countries, but it is significantly lower in countries where services value-added share of GDP is higher. This suggests that the opposite channels are at work, and the net effect depends on how large the services sector in a rich country is. At the disaggregated level, the effect of trade is mostly negative but statistically insignificant, except for MIN and WRT. We do not find any consistent trend or relationship between structural transformation and labor income shares at the disaggregated sectoral level.

Table 7.7 shows the same baseline model outcomes with alternative specification. We use service trade share of GDP instead of trade share of GDP as the proxy for trade openness. Overall, the results conform to the baseline model outcomes with original specification. Service trade share of

Table 7.6 Baseline models (disaggregated sectors) of the labor income share

	MIN	*PU*	*CON*	*WRT*
	(2)	*(4)*	*(5)*	*(6)*
GDP per capita in 2010	−0.0174	−0.0132	0.0145	−0.0310
(logarithm)	(0.0282)	(0.0268)	(0.0257)	(0.0264)
Trade to GDP ratio	−0.0869***	−0.0195	−0.00942	−0.0478**
	(0.0229)	(0.0214)	(0.0186)	(0.0188)
Agriculture value added to GDP	−0.00550	−0.00645*	−0.0110***	−0.0111***
	(0.00387)	(0.00372)	(0.00348)	(0.00358)
Service value added to GDP	−0.00592***	−0.00624***	−0.0113***	−0.00322
	(0.00224)	(0.00215)	(0.00198)	(0.00210)
Other sector value added to GDP	−0.00901***	−0.00238	−0.0107***	−0.000424
	(0.00253)	(0.00244)	(0.00229)	(0.00246)
Constant	1.005***	0.738***	1.111***	0.992***
	(0.287)	(0.278)	(0.256)	(0.262)
Observations	435	442	431	379
R-squared	0.112	0.036	0.091	0.064
Countries	46	47	45	44
	TRA	FIRE	GOV	OTH
	(7)	(8)	(9)	(10)
GDP per capita in 2010	0.00495	0.0480	0.0969***	0.0292
(logarithm)	(0.0309)	(0.0340)	(0.0214)	(0.146)
Trade to GDP ratio	−0.0308	−0.0159	0.0142	0.0405
	(0.0276)	(0.0304)	(0.0207)	(0.195)
Agriculture value added to GDP	0.00524	−9.08e−05	−0.00597*	0.0771***
	(0.00416)	(0.00466)	(0.00313)	(0.0226)
Service value added to GDP	−0.00352	0.00591**	−0.00505***	0.0338**
	(0.00264)	(0.00281)	(0.00175)	(0.0127)
Other sector value added to GDP	−0.000643	0.00113	−0.0107***	0.0138
	(0.00279)	(0.00325)	(0.00212)	(0.00877)
Constant	0.566*	−0.515	0.0625	−2.580*
	(0.294)	(0.330)	(0.213)	(1.524)
Observations	410	347	272	67
R-squared	0.053	0.075	0.200	0.268
Countries	47	41	33	14

Standard errors in parentheses $^{***}p < 0.01$, $^{**}p < 0.05$, $^{*}p < 0.1$

GDP is negatively correlated with labor income share in TRA, which suggests possibilities of outsourcing of jobs, in turn lowering the labor income share in TRA in the home country. The estimated coefficients of the sectoral value-added shares of GDP are now statistically significant for more sectors at the disaggregated level.

Table 7.7 Alternative specification: service trade as a share of GDP

	Labor income share				
	AGR	*MIN*	*MAN*	*PU*	*CON*
	(1)	*(2)*	*(3)*	*(4)*	*(5)*
GDP per capita in	−0.150***	−0.0482*	−0.119***	−0.0147	0.0222
2010 (logarithm)	(0.0401)	(0.0259)	(0.0191)	(0.0254)	(0.0225)
Service trade to	−0.0322	−0.156***	−0.0371	0.00142	−0.0138
GDP ratio	(0.0652)	(0.0324)	(0.0230)	(0.0304)	(0.0260)
Agriculture value	−0.0219***	−0.00134	0.00610**	−0.00663	−0.00906***
added to GDP	(0.00570)	(0.00401)	(0.00301)	(0.00403)	(0.00347)
Service value added	0.00565	−0.00290	0.00693***	−0.00652***	−0.0103***
to GDP	(0.00395)	(0.00237)	(0.00175)	(0.00239)	(0.00199)
Other sector value	−0.00479	−0.00723***	0.0112***	−0.00226	−0.00987***
added to GDP	(0.00419)	(0.00259)	(0.00189)	(0.00261)	(0.00220)
Constant	1.722***	1.022***	0.891***	0.749***	0.951***
	(0.406)	(0.286)	(0.210)	(0.288)	(0.246)
Observations	298	420	416	417	411
R-squared	0.138	0.136	0.169	0.031	0.085
Countries	34	47	48	48	46
	Labor income share				
	WRT	TRA	FIRE	GOV	OTH
	(6)	(7)	(8)	(9)	(10)
GDP per capita in	−0.0551**	−0.00527	0.0390	0.101***	0.0598
2010 (logarithm)	(0.0240)	(0.0276)	(0.0311)	(0.0200)	(0.190)
Service trade to	−0.0276	−0.124***	−0.0231	0.0186	0.442
GDP ratio	(0.0269)	(0.0342)	(0.0378)	(0.0227)	(1.116)
Agriculture value	−0.00907**	0.00840**	0.000799	−0.00663**	0.0758***
added to GDP	(0.00368)	(0.00417)	(0.00474)	(0.00312)	(0.0234)
Service value added	−0.00162	−0.000678	0.00668**	−0.00555***	0.0333**
to GDP	(0.00217)	(0.00265)	(0.00284)	(0.00178)	(0.0127)
Other sector value	0.00167	0.00110	0.00191	−0.0109***	0.0143
added to GDP	(0.00244)	(0.00270)	(0.00319)	(0.00211)	(0.00947)
Constant	1.026***	0.448	−0.503	0.0800	−2.888
	(0.260)	(0.293)	(0.334)	(0.214)	(1.910)
Observations	364	399	336	264	59
R-squared	0.046	0.084	0.074	0.195	0.273
Countries	44	47	41	33	14

Standard errors in parentheses ***$p < 0.01$, ** $p < 0.05$, *$p < 0.1$

Moving on, we next analyze the effects of structural transformation and trade on sectoral employment as a possible channel of the relationship between these factors and the sectoral labor income share. As expected, employment in agriculture is lower in richer countries. Employment in all the service sectors (such as WRT, TRA, FIRE, GOV, and OTH) is positively correlated per capital GDP of a country. Increase in trade intensity is negatively correlated with the size of employment in most of the sectors; the estimated coefficients are statistically significant for MIN, MAN, and CON (Table 7.8). The results do not alter when we consider the alternative specification as shown in Table 7.9. Employment is positively correlated with sectoral value-added shares of GDP.

The outcomes from Tables 7.8 and 7.9 provide mild support for the employment channel of the link between trade and labor income share. Trade affects firm productivity and employment through different channels. Differences in trade costs and trade imbalances (Smitkova 2018), lower cost of innovation with the availability of new foreign inputs (Goldberg and Pavcnik 2007), resource allocation through more productive firms through export opportunities and competition (Melitz 2003; Melitz and Ottaviano 2008)—such processes of trade adjustment also vary across countries and regions as countries open up and become a part of different trade agreements. All these point to the development of more capital-intensive technologies as the trade intensity increases, which in turn could cause a lower share of labor income if labor and capital are gross substitutes in the production function.

To conclude, the empirical evidence at the sectoral level does not allow us to claim any strong causal relationship between trade and labor income share. We find support for a negative correlation between trade openness and sectoral labor income share; however, the evidence on the relationship between the process of structural transformation and labor income share is at best mixed. Skill-biased structural transformation is likely to be positively correlated with the share of labor income predominantly in the service sectors.

7.4.2 *Case Study: Japan*

In this section we provide a snapshot of the sectoral trends in the labor income and employment share in Japan for the period from 1970 to 2010. In this period structural transformation in Japan mainly came through the

Table 7.8 Channels of change in labor income share (baseline model specification)

	Size of employment (logarithm)				
	AGR	*MIN*	*MAN*	*PU*	*CON*
	(1)	*(2)*	*(3)*	*(4)*	*(5)*
GDP per capita in 2010 (logarithm)	−0.557***	0.0874	−0.0200	−0.165*	0.825***
	(0.0530)	(0.125)	(0.0328)	(0.0850)	(0.0538)
Trade to GDP ratio	−0.105**	−0.274***	−0.0663***	−0.107	−0.169***
	(0.0412)	(0.101)	(0.0247)	(0.0686)	(0.0406)
Agriculture value added to GDP	0.00762	0.0581***	−0.0156***	0.0102	0.0249***
	(0.00721)	(0.0170)	(0.00443)	(0.0116)	(0.00727)
Service value added to GDP	−0.00713*	−0.000570	−0.0203***	0.00627	0.00652
	(0.00409)	(0.00967)	(0.00249)	(0.00660)	(0.00410)
Other sector value added to GDP	0.00597	0.0260**	−0.00522*	0.00979	0.0264***
	(0.00465)	(0.0111)	(0.00286)	(0.00757)	(0.00469)
Constant	18.33***	8.493***	15.05***	11.56***	3.687***
	(0.537)	(1.264)	(0.331)	(0.862)	(0.543)
Observations	483	476	487	476	487
R-squared	0.486	0.095	0.227	0.040	0.525
Countries	50	49	50	49	50
	Number of employments (logarithm)				
	WRT	TRA	FIRE	GOV	OTH
	(6)	(7)	(8)	(9)	(10)
GDP per capita in 2010 (logarithm)	0.351***	0.355***	1.007***	0.288***	0.452***
	(0.0347)	(0.0409)	(0.0758)	(0.0448)	(0.0538)
Trade to GDP ratio	−0.0192	−0.0428	0.0323	0.124***	0.0600
	(0.0261)	(0.0309)	(0.0571)	(0.0358)	(0.0426)
Agriculture value added to GDP	0.00933**	0.0193***	0.0181*	0.0280***	0.0147*
	(0.00468)	(0.00553)	(0.0102)	(0.00647)	(0.00784)
Service value added to GDP	0.00741***	0.000974	0.0223***	0.0147***	0.00693*
	(0.00264)	(0.00312)	(0.00577)	(0.00343)	(0.00415)
Other sector value added to GDP	0.0154***	0.0122***	0.0205***	0.0124***	0.0127***
	(0.00302)	(0.00357)	(0.00661)	(0.00397)	(0.00475)
Constant	9.359***	8.655***	1.112	9.452***	7.192***
	(0.350)	(0.413)	(0.765)	(0.464)	(0.554)
Observations	487	487	487	467	449
R-squared	0.417	0.231	0.551	0.277	0.333
Countries	50	50	50	48	46

Standard errors in parentheses ***$p < 0.01$, **$p < 0.05$, *$p < 0.1$

Table 7.9 Channels of change in labor income share (alternative specification)

	Number of employments (logarithm)				
	AGR	*MIN*	*MAN*	*PU*	*CON*
	(1)	*(2)*	*(3)*	*(4)*	*(5)*
GDP per capita in	−0.604***	−0.0722	−0.0373	−0.221***	0.722***
2010 (logarithm)	(0.0490)	(0.118)	(0.0300)	(0.0810)	(0.0498)
Trade to GDP ratio	−0.000306	−0.000757	−0.00166***	4.43e–06	−0.000526
	(0.000591)	(0.00142)	(0.000361)	(0.000979)	(0.000600)
Agriculture value	0.0114	0.0687***	−0.00938**	0.00986	0.0321***
added to GDP	(0.00760)	(0.0182)	(0.00464)	(0.0125)	(0.00770)
Service value added to	−0.00410	0.00813	−0.0160***	0.00649	0.0117***
GDP	(0.00441)	(0.0106)	(0.00268)	(0.00732)	(0.00445)
Other sector value	0.00876*	0.0311***	−0.00206	0.00998	0.0311***
added to GDP	(0.00480)	(0.0117)	(0.00293)	(0.00807)	(0.00486)
Constant	18.47***	9.207***	14.90***	12.03***	4.186***
	(0.544)	(1.296)	(0.331)	(0.892)	(0.550)
Observations	454	447	458	447	458
R-squared	0.476	0.086	0.237	0.033	0.505
Countries	51	50	51	50	51
	Number of employments (logarithm)				
	WRT	TRA	FIRE	GOV	OTH
	(6)	(7)	(8)	(9)	(10)
GDP per capita in	0.341***	0.294***	0.995***	0.306***	0.452***
2010 (logarithm)	(0.0318)	(0.0361)	(0.0715)	(0.0420)	(0.0507)
Trade to GDP ratio	0.000179	−0.000743*	0.00123	0.000992**	0.000469
	(0.000383)	(0.000436)	(0.000862)	(0.000500)	(0.000600)
Agriculture value	0.0143***	0.0246***	0.0175	0.0232***	0.00767
added to GDP	(0.00491)	(0.00559)	(0.0111)	(0.00684)	(0.00830)
Service value added to	0.0103***	0.00542*	0.0220***	0.0116***	0.00276
GDP	(0.00284)	(0.00323)	(0.00639)	(0.00375)	(0.00451)
Other sector value	0.0178***	0.0149***	0.0211***	0.00824**	0.00863*
added to GDP	(0.00310)	(0.00352)	(0.00698)	(0.00415)	(0.00500)
Constant	9.26^{2}***	8.950***	1.334*	9.717***	7.690***
	(0.351)	(0.399)	(0.791)	(0.473)	(0.570)
Observations	458	458	458	438	422
R-squared	0.422	0.208	0.533	0.220	0.301
Countries	51	51	51	49	47

Standard errors in parentheses ***$p < 0.01$, **$p < 0.05$, *$p < 0.1$

growth of commerce and private sector services[9] (Fukao and Paul 2017). Between 1970 and 1990, the primary gainers in employment shares were construction, commerce and services, and machinery. However, the rate of productivity growth slowed down compared to the previous period in all sectors including commerce and services. For the first time in Japan's history, labor was moving out of most manufacturing sector industries to private sector services. At the same time, compared to the early 1970s, the aggregate labor income share in Japan decreased by approximately 10 percentage points in the following three decades. This decline was primarily driven by services as the labor income share in manufacturing sectors remained almost constant (Fukao and Perugini 2018). This section aims to reconcile some of these facts using a sectoral-level analysis.

7.4.2.1 Descriptive Evidence Using Japan Industrial Productivity (JIP) Data

We use the Japan Industrial Productivity (JIP) and the Regional-level Japan Industrial Productivity (R-JIP) databases compiled by RIETI (Research Institute of Economy, Trade and Industry) and Hitotsubashi University, Tokyo.[10] The latest round of the JIP database (2015) covers 108 industries for the period 1970–2012. Following Fukao and Perugini (2018), we construct the labor income share by sector (industry) as the ratio of nominal total labor compensation to nominal value added (at current prices). Since nominal total labor compensation includes all types of remuneration, such as employee compensation and mixed income (i.e., for labor supplied by self-employed and family workers), it automatically adjusts for labor compensation of non-workers (employees). This makes our labor income share measure less susceptible to measurement errors as highlighted by many researchers (Gollin 2002; Guerriero 2012). In addition, we use the Regional-level Japan Industrial Productivity (R-JIP) database,[11] which consists of 23 sectors (agriculture, mining, food,

[9] Private services include private medical services, private education services, private hygiene services, private research services, information and Internet-based services, work in eating and drinking places, automobile maintenance, and so on.

[10] See https://www.rieti.go.jp/en/database/JIP2015/#01. For a detailed account of the JIP database, see Fukao et al. (2007). JIP sectors can be easily translated into international industry classifications such as ISIC and KLEMS.

[11] http://www.rieti.go.jp/en/database/r-jip.html. (It should be noted that data are missing for Okinawa for the period 1955–1970.)

textiles, pulp, chemicals, petroleum, nonmetallic minerals, primary metals, fabricated metals, machinery, electrical machinery, transport equipment, precision instruments, other manufacturing, construction, utilities (electricity, gas, and water supply), wholesale and retail trade, finance and insurance, real estate, transport and communication, private services, and government services). We merge this data set into the JIP database, mainly to facilitate the creation of the classification of sectors.

We divide 108 industries into six broad categories of sectors. *Agri* consists of agriculture, forestry, and fisheries. *Heavy manufacturing* comprises mining, chemicals, petroleum, fabricated metals, machinery, construction, and electrical machinery. *Light manufacturing* consists of food, textiles, pulp, nonmetallic minerals, primary metals, transport equipment, precision instruments, and other manufacturing. *Utilities* include electricity, gas, and water supply. *Commerce* consists of wholesale and retail trade, finance and insurance, real estate, transport, and communication. We include both private services and government services in *Services*. The left-hand panel of Fig. 7.19 shows labor income share trends for these six broad sectors. The labor income shares remained almost constant in heavy manufacturing and light manufacturing whereas the other sectors showed downward trends in the period from 1970 to 2010. During the same period, we observe the secular trends of structural transformation: employment shares rising in services, falling in agriculture, and remaining unchanged in manufacturing.

Despite a growth in employment shares, services experienced a decline in labor income share. To gain more insights into this topic, we compare the labor income share trends between two groups of sectors: (a) sectors that experienced rapid expansion and (b) sectors that experienced contraction in terms of employment shares between 1970 and 2010. The right-hand panel of Fig. 7.21 confirms the rising trend in employment shares for three fast-growing sectors: eating and drinking places, private medical services, and other business services. However, the labor income shares decline for both the eating and drinking places and private medical sectors. An increase in the employment share is likely to increase the labor income share unless the wages dramatically fall. As a next step, we examine some other factors that could be correlated with a fall in labor income share in these sectors.

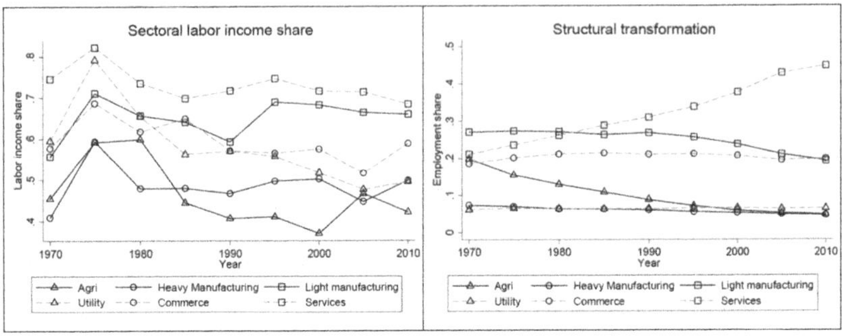

Fig. 7.20 Sectoral labor income and employment share in Japan, 1970–2010. (Note: Authors' calculation based on the Japan Industrial Productivity (JIP) database, https://www.rieti.go.jp/en/database/JIP2015/#01, and Regional-level Japan Industrial Productivity (R-JIP) database, http://www.rieti.go.jp/en/database/r-jip.html. The latter data set consists of 23 sectors. We divide them into six broad categories)

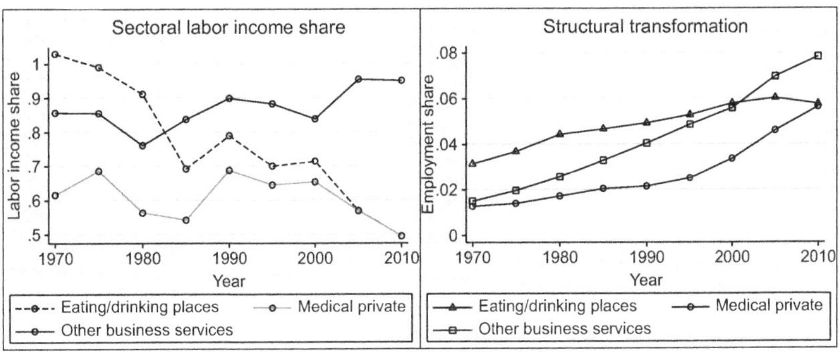

Fig. 7.21 Labor income and employment share in some fast-growing sectors. (Note: Authors' calculation based on the Japan Industrial Productivity (JIP) database, https://www.rieti.go.jp/en/database/JIP2015/#01)

In the left-hand panel of Fig. 7.22, we compare the part-time employment shares. The part-time employment share in eating and drinking places rose from about 10% to nearly 50% between 1970 and 2010. The other two sectors also show an increasing trend for part-time workers but to a somewhat lesser extent. At the same time, female employment shares had been very high and became more than 75% in 2010 in private medical

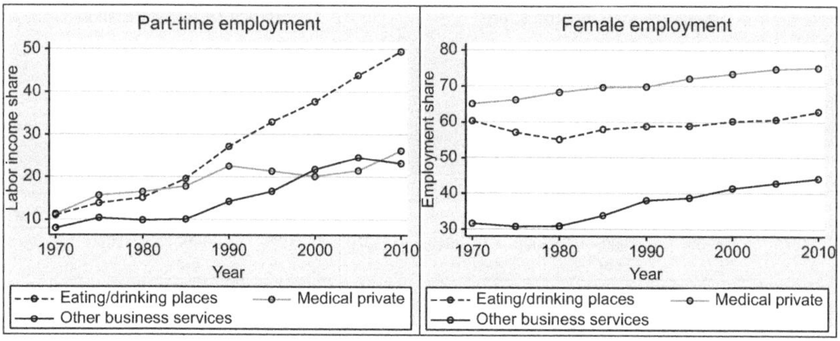

Fig. 7.22 Part-time and female employment shares in some fast-growing sectors. (Note: Authors' calculation based on the Japan Industrial Productivity (JIP) database, https://www.rieti.go.jp/en/database/JIP2015/#01)

services. Taken together, if one can argue that if part-timers get paid less per hour and female employees face gender discrimination in wages, then a fall in labor income share in these sectors despite a growth in employment is conceivable. To conclude, a drop in the labor income share in eating and drinking places could be driven by a significant increase in part-time workers whereas a drop in the labor income share in private medical services could be due to a combination of the growth in part-time workers and an increase in the female labor force participation rate.

We finally look at the labor income share trends in some shrinking sectors. As is evident from the right-hand panel of Fig. 7.23, lumber industries, printing businesses, and household appliances industries experienced a significant drop in employment shares over the period from 1970 to 2010. However, the labor income shares in household appliances industries in fact rose after 1990. The other two sectors, lumber and printing, experienced a drop in the labor income share. One can use the same logic to reconcile the puzzling outcomes on employment shares and labor income share in household appliances industries.

7.4.2.2 A Shift-Share Decomposition Analysis

In this section, we provide some results from a shift-share decomposition of labor income share changes between 1970 and 2010. We use a variant of the canonical shift-share decomposition methodology (Fabricant 1942; de Vries et al. 2013) and write changes in the aggregate labor income

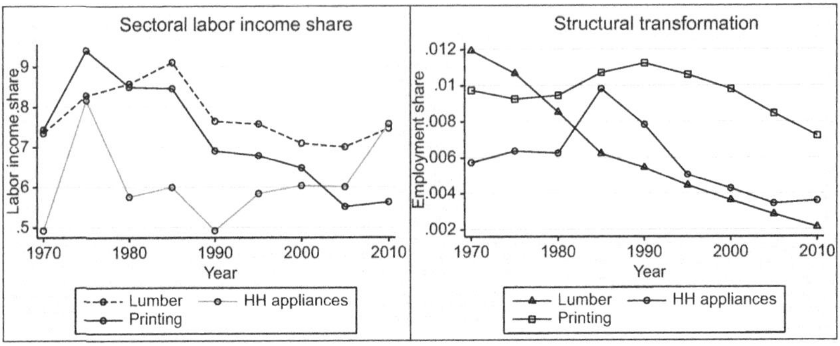

Fig. 7.23 Labor income and employment share for some shrinking sectors. (Note: Authors' calculation based on the Japan Industrial Productivity (JIP) database, https://www.rieti.go.jp/en/database/JIP2015/#01)

share between t and $t + 1$ as $\Delta LIS = \sum_i \left(VA_i^t\right)\left(\Delta LIS_i\right) + \sum_i \left(\Delta VA_i\right)\left(LIS_i^t\right)$, where LIS_i is the labor income share in sector i, and LIS denotes the aggregate labor income share. Labor is reallocated across sectors between two points in time, t and $t + 1$, and VA_i^t denotes the value-added share of sector i in period t. The first term on the right-hand side of Eq. (7.2) measures the contribution of changes in the sectoral labor income share over time whereas the second term measures the contribution of structural transformation (to put it simply, the changes in the weights of the sector). Thus, in the absence of structural transformation, the aggregate labor income share trend would simply be a weighted average of the sectoral labor income share trends.

We describe the decomposition outcomes in Fig. 7.24. A decomposition exercise is performed for four time periods, 1970–1980, 1980–1990, 1990–2000, and 2000–2010, and for 23 main sectors based on the R-JIP database. As is clear from Fig. 7.24, the contribution of structural transformation to changes in the labor income share over time for most of the sectors is negligible. Structural transformation explains a sizable variation in the labor income share only for sectors like private and government services, and to a lesser extent for wholesale and retail trade, and finance and insurance. These services sectors also experienced employment growth in recent years. So, we find mild support for the fact that the role of

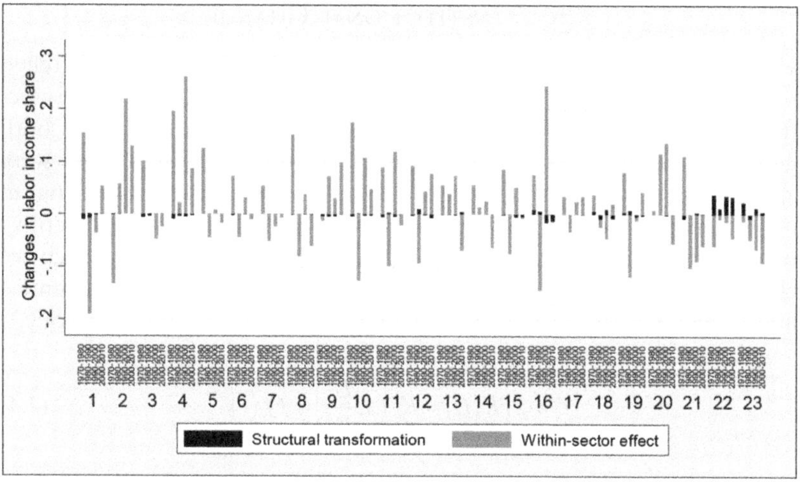

Fig. 7.24 Shift-share decomposition outcomes. (Authors' calculation based on the Regional-level Japan Industrial Productivity (R-JIP) database, http://www.rieti.go.jp/en/database/r-jip.html. Note: The R-JIP data set consists of 23 sectors (1 = agriculture, 2 = mining, 3 = food, 4 = textiles, 5 = pulp, 6 = chemicals, 7 = petroleum, 8 = nonmetallic minerals, 9 = primary metals, 10 = fabricated metals, 11 = machinery, 12 = electrical machinery, 13 = transport equipment, 14 = precision instruments, 15 = other manufacturing, 16 = construction, 17 = utilities (electricity, gas, and water supply), 18 = wholesale and retail trade, 19 = finance and insurance, 20 = real estate, 21 = transport and communication, 22 = private services, and 23 = government services))

structural transformation in explaining the variation in sectoral labor income share also depends on the level of structural transformation in that sector.

The main goal of this section is to highlight the role of structural transformation in labor income share trends using a case study on Japan. We used JIP data to provide some descriptive evidence and analytical evidence supporting the role of change in the sectoral employment share behind changes in the sectoral labor income share. Overall, the findings suggest a limited role of structural transformation in the movement of labor income share in Japan, and the direction of changes in certain sectors is driven by part-time employment.

7.5 Institutional Change

Until this point, the analysis of the drivers of labor income share has relied primarily on the assumption of a perfectly competitive market. In this section we discuss, the role of imperfect competition, which arises in both goods and labor market. Kalecki's seminal studies (1938, 1954) were among the first ones to analyze the labor income share considering an imperfectly competitive market. Essentially, in an imperfectly competitive market, the price contains a mark-up over the marginal cost, which we elucidate with the help of a simple production function below. Assume a lineal homogeneous production function with constant returns to scale,

$$Y = f(K,L) = Kf\left(1,\frac{L}{K}\right) = Ff(l) \tag{7.4}$$

Firms maximize profit = $pK(fl) - wKl - rk$ and goods market clear when $\frac{w}{p} = f'(l)$. This prompts us to write the labor income share (LIS) as

$$LIS = \frac{wL}{pY} = \frac{lf'(l)}{f(l)}. \tag{7.5}$$

A price mark-up (∅) can enter the profit maximization condition in an imperfectly competitive market as $\varnothing\frac{w}{p} = f'(l)$, which results in a slightly different expression for the labor income share as shown in Eq. (7.6), which suggests a countercyclical movement in the labor income share if the movement in the mark-up is procyclical.

$$LIS = \frac{wL}{pY} = \varnothing^{-1}\frac{lf'(l)}{f(l)}. \tag{7.6}$$

On the other hand, the main source of imperfect competition in the labor market arises from the bargaining power of trade unions and other related institutional factors (Blanchard and Giavazzi 2003; Autor et al. 2017; Barkai 2016). In many countries, trade unions exhibit bargaining power to set the wages different from the marginal product of labor (leaving the paradigm of the competitive market). Consider an effective bargaining model (Blanchard et al. 1997), then the first order condition of the profit maximization (goods market clearing condition) defines the real wage as a weighted sum of the average product of labor and the real reservation wage. The weight reflects the bargaining power of the workers (Eq. 7.7.).

$$\frac{w}{p} = \theta \frac{f(l)}{l} + (1-\theta)\frac{\bar{w}}{p}. \tag{7.7}$$

Like Eq. (7.6), we can write the labor income share assuming the effective bargaining model as

$$LIS = \frac{wL}{pY} = \frac{wl}{pf(l)} = \theta + (1-\theta)\frac{\bar{w}l}{pf(l)}. \tag{7.8}$$

Equation (7.8) suggests that a higher bargaining power of trade union (a higher value of θ) lowers the sensitivity of the labor income share to capital-output ratio. Both Eq. (7.6) and Eq. (7.8) can shift the SK curve, a movement from point E1 to E3 in Fig. 7.1.

In the presence of imperfectly competitive markets, the extent to which emerging rents accrue to labor or to capital becomes crucial to explain the dynamics in factors income shares (Blanchard and Giavazzi 2003). However, the extent of this phenomenon also depends on workers' bargaining power, shaped by macroeconomic conditions and labor market institutional settings (European Commission 2007). Many studies provide evidence of the decline of labor union organizations (union density and collective bargaining systems) and labor market regulations (employment protection and minimum wage provisions), which might have contributed to the decreasing trend in the labor share (Bentolila and Saint-Paul 2003; OECD 2011). The net effect on the labor income share, however, depends on the bargaining models and, once again, on the elasticity of substitution between production factors (Zuleta and Young 2013). Globalization has reduced labor bargaining power (Lawrence 2015).

An emerging strand of the labor share literature emphasizes the role of rising concentration and markups. Institutional settings shape rent-sharing patterns: if price markups are larger than wage markups, a lower degree of competition is expected to decrease the labor share (Autor et al. 2017; Barkai 2016). The quantitate impact of changes in policies and institutions and reforms in product and labor markets appears to be limited but may reflect in part the difficulty of empirically separating trends in global integration and de-unionization (Dao et al. 2017). Blanchard and Giavazzi (2003) consider labor market regulation as a determinant of the bargaining power of workers, and they show that the decrease in the labor share in Europe during the 1980s was primarily caused by a decrease in the bargaining power of workers. On the other hand, in a recent study, Rognlie (2015) shows that capital share is higher because higher markups came alongside increased globalization.

Another recent study by Grullon et al. (2016) uses firm-level data to document that most US industries became more concentrated over time because the most successful firms made large profits and realized the most outstanding stock returns as well as profitable mergers and acquisitions. Barkai (2016) shows that markups have grown over time, lowering both the labor and capital shares. This paper shows a negative relationship between changes in the concentration of firms and changes in the labor income share using the industry level data. In this study, a Cobb-Douglas production function for the representative firm at the industry level implicitly assumes that a decline in the labor income share is driven by within firms as the fall in relative factor prices is shared within the industry.

References

Acemoglu, D., and D. H. Autor. 2011. Skills, Tasks and Technologies: Implications for Employment and Earnings. In Handbook of Labor Economics Volume 4, Orley Ashenfelter and David E. Card (eds.), Amsterdam: Elsevier.

Alvarez-Cuadrado, F., N. V. Long, and M. Poschke. 2015. *Capital–Labor Substitution, Structural Change and the Labor Income Share*. IZA Discussion Paper No. 8941.

Anderson, R. K. and J. R. Moroney. 1993. "Morishima Elasticities of Substitution with Nested Production Functions." *Economics Letters* 42: 159–166.

Antras, P. 2001. Is the U.S. Aggregate Production Function Cobb-Douglas? New Estimates of the Elasticity of Substitution. Contributions to Macroeconomics 4 (1): Article 4.

Arpaia, Alfonso, Esther Perez, and Karl Pichelmann. 2009. "Understanding Labour's Income Share Dynamics in Europe." European Economy Economics Paper No. 379, European Commission.

Autor, David H., David Dorn, Lawrence F. Katz, Christina Patterson, and John Van Reenen. 2017. "Concentrating on the Fall of the Labor Share." NBER Working Paper 23108, National Bureau of Economic Research, Cambridge, MA.

Barkai, S. 2016. *Declining Labor and Capital Shares.* University of Chicago, November.

Bentolila, Samuel and Saint-Paul, Gilles. 2003. Explaining Movements in the Labor Share. *The B.E. Journal of Macroeconomics*, 3(1), 1–33.

Blackorby C. and R. R. Russell. 1989. “Will the Real Elasticity of Substitution Please Stand Up? (A Comparison of the Allen/Uzawa and Morishima Elasticities).” *American Economic Review* 79: 882–888.

Blanchard, O., and Giavazzi, F. 2003. “Macroeconomic Effects of Regulation and Deregulation in Goods and Labor Markets.” *The Quarterly Journal of Economics*, 118(3): 879–907.

Blanchard, O., W. Nordhaus, and E. Phelps. 1997. “The Medium Run.” *Brookings Papers on Economic Activity*, 2: 89–158.

Buera, F. J., and J. P. Kaboski. 2012. The Rise of the Service Economy. *American Economic Review*, 102 (6): 2540–69.

Buera, F. J., J. P. Kaboski, and R. Rogerson. 2015. *Skill Biased Structural Change.* NBER Working Paper No. 21165.

Charpe, M., S. Lee, D. Arias, and S. Bridji. 2014. Does income distribution matter for development? Trends in labour share of income and their economic impacts in developing countries. World of Work Report: ILO, Chap. 8.

Chirinko, Robert S., and Debdulal Mallick. 2017. “The Substitution Elasticity, Factor Shares, and the Low-Frequency Panel Model.” *American Economic Journal: Macroeconomics,* 9(4): 225–253.

Dao, M. C., M. M. Das, Z. Koczan, and W. Lian. 2017. *Why is Labor Receiving a Smaller Share of Global Income? Theory and Empirical Evidence.* International Monetary Fund.

de Serres, Alain, Stefano Scarpetta, and Christine de la Maisonneuve. 2002. “Sectoral Shifts in Europe and the United States: How They Affect Aggregate Labour Shares and the Properties of Wage Equations,” OECD Economics Department Working Papers 326, OECD Publishing, April.

de Vries, Gaaitzen J., Marcel P. Timmer, and Klaas de Vries. 2013. “Structural Transformation in Africa: Static Gains, Dynamic Losses.” *Groningen Growth and Development Centre Research Memorandum* GD-136.

Decreuse, B., and P. Maarek. 2015. “FDI and the Labor Share in Developing Countries: A Theory and Some Evidence.” *Annals of Economics and Statistics/ Annales d’Économie et de Statistique*, 119/120: 289–319.

Diwan, I. 2001. “*Debt as Sweat: Labor, Financial Crises, and the Globalization of Capital*”, The World Bank, Mimeo.

Elsby, Michael W., Bart Hobijn, and Ayşegül Şahin. 2013. “The Decline of the US Labor Share.” *Brookings Papers on Economic Activity,* 2: 1–63.

European Commission. 2007. The Labour Income Share in the European Union. Chapter 5 of: *Employment in Europe.*

Fabricant, Solomon. 1942. *Employment in Manufacturing, 1899–1939.* NBER: New York.

Feenstra, Robert C., and Gordon H. Hanson. 1997. “Foreign Direct Investment and Relative Wages: Evidence from Mexico’s Maquiladoras.” *Journal of International Economics* 42: 371–393.

Feenstra, R. C., R. Inklaar, and M. P. Timmer. 2015. The Next Generation of the Penn World Table. *American Economic Review* 105(10): 3150–3182.

Fukao, K. and S. Paul. 2017. The Long-Run Dynamics of the Labour Share in Japan, Discussion Paper Series A No.665, Institute of Economic Research, Hitotsubashi University.

Fukao, Kyoji and Christiano Perugini. 2018. The Long-Run Dynamics of the Labour Share in Japan, Discussion Paper Series A No.672, Institute of Economic Research, Hitotsubashi University.

Fukao, K., S. Hamagata, T. Inui, K. Ito, H. Ug Kwon, T. Makino, T. Miyagawa, Y. Nakanishi, and J. Tokui. 2007. Estimation Procedures and TFP Analysis of the JIP Database 2006. RIETI Discussion Paper January 2007 07-E-003.

Goldberg, P. K., and N. Pavcnik. 2007. Distributional Effects of Globalization in Developing Countries. *Journal of Economic Literature*, 45(1): 39–82.

Gollin, D. 2002. Getting income shares right. *Journal of Political Economy*, *110*(2), 458–474.

Grossman, G. M., E. Helpman, E. Oberfield, and T. Sampson. 2017. *The Productivity Slowdown and the Declining Labor Share: A Neoclassical Exploration* (No. w23853). National Bureau of Economic.

Growiec, Jakub. 2008. "Production functions and distributions of unit factor productivities: uncovering the link." *Economics Letters*, 101, 87–90.

Grullon, Gustavo, Yelena Larkin, and Roni Michaely. 2016. "Are US Industries Becoming More Concentrated?" Unpublished Working Paper.

Guerriero, Marta. 2012. The Labour Share of Income Around the World. Evidence from a Panel Dataset. http://piketty.pse.ens.fr/files/Guerriero2012.pdf (accessed 26 November 2018).

Guscina, A. 2006. Effects of Globalization on Labor's Share in National Income, IMF Working Paper no. 294.

Harrison, A. 2005/2002. "Has Globalization Eroded Labor's Share? Some Cross-Country Evidence," Working Paper. University of California at Berkeley.

Harrison, Ann. 2002. "Has Globalization Eroded Labor's Share? Some Cross-Country Evidence." University of California, Berkeley, and National Bureau of Economic Research. http://www.iadb.org/res/publications/pubfiles/pubS-FDI-9.pdf.

Herrendorf, Berthold, Christopher Herrington, and Akos Valentinyi. 2015. "Sectoral Technology and Structural Transformation." *American Economic Journal: Macroeconomics*, 7(4): 104–133.

Hicks, John R. 1932. *Theory of Wages*. London: Macmillan.

ILO. 2017. Key Indicators of the Labour Market (KILM). Available: http://www.ilo.org/ilostat/faces/ilostat-home/home?_adf.ctrlstate=1b2e7htvgk_4&_afrLoop=286517921545847

Jaumotte, Florence, and Irina Tytell. 2007. "How Has the Globalization of Labor Affected the Labor Income Share in Advanced Countries?" IMF Working Paper 07/298, International Monetary Fund, Washington, DC.

Jayadev. 2007. "Capital Account Openness and the Labour Share of Income." *Cambridge Journal of Economics*, 31(3): 423–443.

JIP. 2015. Japan Industrial productivity database http://www.ier.hit-u.ac.jp/English/databases/jip.html

Jones, Charles I. 2005. "The Shape of Production Functions and the Direction of Technical Change." *Quarterly Journal of Economics*, 120(2): 517–549.

Kalecki, M. 1938. "The Determinants of Distribution of National Income," *Econometrica*, April, 6: 97–112.

Kalecki, M. 1954. Theory of Economic Dynamics. Reprinted in J. Osiatynski (ed.), *Collected Works of Michal Kalecki, Vol. 1*, Oxford: Clarendon Press.

Karabarbounis, Loukas, and Brent Neiman. 2014. "The Global Decline of the Labor Share." *Quarterly Journal of Economics* 129 (1): 61–103.

Kehrig, M., and N. Vincent. 2017. Growing Productivity Without Growing Wages: The Micro-Level Anatomy of the Aggregate Labor Share Decline. CESifo Working Paper Series 6454, CESifo Group Munich.

Koh, Dongya, Raul Santaeulalia-Llopis, and Yu Zhang. 2016. Labor Share Decline and Intellectual Property Products Capital," Working Papers 927, Barcelona Graduate School of Economics.

Kortum, Samuel S. 1997. "Research, patenting, and technological change." *Econometrica*, 65, 1389–1419.

Krusell, Per, Lee E. Ohanian, José-Victor Ríos-Rull, and Giovanni L. Violante. 2000. "Capital-skill Complementarity and Inequality: A Macroeconomic Analysis." *Econometrica* 68 (5): 1029–1053.

Lawless, M., and K. T. Whelan. 2011. "Understanding the Dynamics of Labor Shares and Inflation." *Journal of Macroeconomics*, 33(2), 121–136.

Lawrence, Robert Z. 2015. "Recent Declines in Labor's Share in US Income: A Preliminary Neoclassical Account." NBER Working Paper No. 21296, National Bureau of Economic Research.

Leon-Ledesma, M., P. McAdam, and A. Willman, "Identifying the Elasticity of Substitution with Biased Technical Change," *American Economic Review*, 100 (2010), 1330.

Lu, Y and L. B. Fletcher. 1968. "A Generalization of the CES Production Function." *Review of Economics and Statistics*, 50(4), 449–452. (Nov.)

Melitz, M. J. 2003. The Impact of Trade on Intra-industry Reallocations and Aggregate Industry Productivity. *Econometrica* 71(6): 1695–1725.

Melitz, M. J., and G. I. P. Ottaviano. 2008. Market Size, Trade, and Productivity. *Review of Economic Studies* 75(1): 291–316.

O'Mahony, Mary, Catherine Robinson, and Michela Vecchi. 2008. "The Impact of ICT on the Demand for Skilled Labour: A Cross-Country Comparison," *Labour Economics*, 15, 1435–1450.

Oberfield, Ezra, and Devesh Raval. 2014. "Micro Data and Macro Technology." NBER Working Paper No. 20452, National Bureau of Economic Research.

Oishi, Y. and S. Paul. 2018. "Sectoral Labor Income Share Dynamics: Cross-Country Evidence from a Novel Dataset." ADBI Working Paper 875. Tokyo: Asian Development Bank Institute. https://www.adb.org/publications/sectoral-labor-income-share-dynamics.

Organization for Economic Co-operation and Development. 2011. "Special Focus: Inequality in Emerging Economies (EEs)." *Divided We Stand, Why Inequality Keeps Rising*. Paris: OECD.

Paul, S. 2019a. Labor Income Share Dynamics with Variable Elasticity of Substitution, IZA Discussion Paper No. 12418. [June]

Paul, S. 2019b. A Decline in Labor's Share with Capital Accumulation and Complementary Factor Inputs: An Application of the Morishima Elasticity of Substitution, IZA Discussion Paper No. 12219. [March]

Paul, S. 2018. "Capital Skill Substitutability and the Labor Income Share: Identification Using the Morishima Elasticity of Substitution." ADBI Working Paper 839. Tokyo: Asian Development Bank Institute.

Piketty, T. 2014. *Capital in the Twenty-First Century*. Cambridge: Harvard University Press.

Piketty, Thomas, and Gabriel Zucman. 2014. "Capital is Back: Wealth–Income Ratios in Rich Countries 1700–2010." *Quarterly Journal of Economics*, 129(3): 1255–1310.

Rodrigues, Francisco, and Arjun Jayadev. 2010. "The Declining Labor Share of Income." Human Development Research Paper 2010/36, United Nations Development Programme, New York.

Rodrik, Dani. 1997. "*Has Globalization Gone Too Far?*" Washington: Institute of International Economics.

Rognlie, Matthew. 2015. "Deciphering the Fall and Rise in the Net Capital Share: Accumulation or Scarcity?" *Brookings Papers on Economic Activity* 46 (1): 1–69.

Sachs, J. D., and A. Warner. 1995. Economic Reform and the Process of Global Integration. *Brookings Papers on Economic Activity* 1: 1–118.

Slaughter, Matthew J. 2001. "International Trade and Labor-Demand Elasticities." *Journal of International Economics*, 54(1): 27–56.

Smitkova. 2018. Does Openness Matter for Structural Change? Mimeo University of Cambridge.

Stockhammer Engelbert 2013. "Why Have Wage Shares Fallen? A Panel Analysis of the Determinants of Functional Income Distribution" International Labour Office, Conditions of Work and Employment Branch. Geneva: ILO.

Timmer, M. P., E. Dietzenbacher, B. Los, R. Stehrer, and G. de Vries. 2015. An Illustrated User Guide to the World Input Output Database: The Case of Global Automotive Production. *Review of International Economics* 23(3): 575–605.

Trapp, K. 2015. Measuring the Labour Income Share of Developing Countries: Learning from Social Accounting Matrices. UNU-WIDER Working Paper 41.

UN. 2017. United Nations System of National Accounts. Available: http://data.un.org/Explorer.aspx?d=SNA.

UNIDO. 2015. Industrial Statistics Database – 2015 edition. Available: http://www.unido.org/resources/statistics/statistical-databases/indstat2-2015-edition.html.

Valentinyi, A. and B. Herrendorf. 2008. "Measuring Factor Income Shares at the Sectoral Level." *Review of Economic Dynamics* 11: 820–835.

van Treeck, K. 2017. The Labor Income Share of Developing Countries: Data Review and Analysis of International Panel Data. Paper presented at the 5th Conference of the Regulating for Decent Work Network at the International Labour Office Geneva. Switzerland.

Wacziarg, R., and K. H. Welch. 2003. Trade Liberalization and Growth: New Evidence. NBER Working Paper 10152.

Wacziarg, R., and K. H. Welch. 2008. Trade Liberalization and Growth: New Evidence. *The World Bank Economic Review*, 22(2): 187–231.

Young, Andrew T. 2006/2010. "One of The Things We Know That Ain't So: Is US Labor's Share Relatively Stable?," *Journal of Macroeconomics*, 32 (1), 90–102.

Zuleta, Hernando and Andrew T. Young. 2013. "Labor Shares in a Model of Induced Innovation." *Structural Change and Economic Dynamics*, 24(C): 112–122.

CHAPTER 8

Potential Areas of Future Research

8.1 LIS and Personal Income Inequality

The study of factor income shares plays an important role in understanding the relationship between national income and personal income (Atkinson 2009). Figure 8.1 describes the relationship between the labor income share (LIS) and the distribution of personal income in light of a conceptual framework developed by Atkinson and Bourguignon (2000). Consider a standard two-factor (capital and labor) production function, where total income is composed of labor income and capital income. In Fig. 8.1, the Lorenz curve ACD shows the distribution of personal income. The vertical axis AO measures the cumulative share of total income, and α represents the share of income that goes to labor. The horizontal axis measures the cumulative proportion of population and E_L represents the employment share that depends on labor income. The earnings difference between labor income and capital income is the difference between the slopes of line BC and CA. The Gini coefficient of personal income distribution can be directly calculated as $G = E_L - \alpha$ (Atkinson and Bourguignon 2000), which shows a one-to-one relationship between the level of income inequality and the labor income share. When the labor income share increases from α to α', then the personal income distribution becomes more equal (as highlighted by line BD). If $G' = E_L - \alpha'$, then $G' < G$ when $\alpha' > \alpha$.

Figure 8.1 propounds that an increase in the labor income share lowers the inequality of personal income. However, there are several factors act as

S. Paul, *Labor Income Share*,
https://doi.org/10.1007/978-981-15-6860-2_8

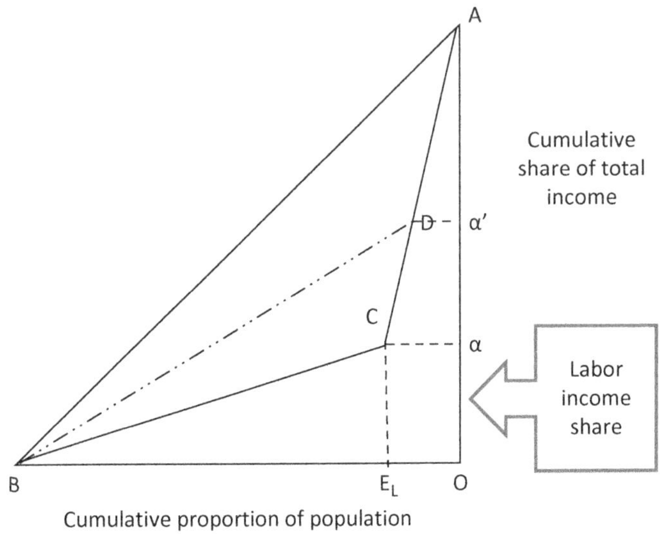

Fig. 8.1 Income distribution (Lorenz curve) in a two-class economy. (Note: Adapted from Atkinson and Bourguignon (2000))

potential confounders to the relationship between the labor income share and distribution of personal income. First, non-labor income is more unevenly distributed than labor income especially in the developed countries. As a result, any transfer from labor income to non-labor income increases the inequality in personal income (Atkinson 2009; Piketty 2014). Such differences in the distribution of income within factor income classes make it difficult to ascertain the causal relationship between the factor income share and the distribution of personal income. Second, mixed sources of personal income contribute to this ambiguity further. If gains from non-labor income compensate for any loss from labor income for wage earners, then a higher labor's share of income does not necessarily lead to a more equal distribution of personal income. Third, the indirect taxes and subsidies constitute a wedge between the factor income shares, and for this reason a fall in the labor income share does not necessarily lead to a rise in the capital income share (Gomme and Rupert 2004). A rise in the capital income share could be driven by a fall in the labor income share as well as by an increase in the share of indirect taxes less subsidies. Fourth, corporate profit is one of the many sources of the capital income, and the use of the terms "capital share" and "profit share" interchangeably is misleading. Barkai (2016) makes a distinction between the evolution of the profit share, the capital income share, and the labor income share. The gains from corporate profits are far less equally distributed than wages, and for the same reason as discussed above, any changes to corporate profits drive the level of inequality in personal income up more easily. The presence of the measurement problems adds to the misery, as it plagues the analysis of the factor income shares.

8.2 LIS and Skilled Emigration

A competitive labor market model has clear and unambiguous implications for a migration-induced reduction in skilled labor supply. A reduction in the supply of skilled labor outflows because of migration should increase the wages of those workers remaining behind, at least in the short run. However, an upward push in wages because of migration-induced skilled labor supply shock holds only if there is no employment demand shock. This can happen if an increased demand for skilled labor in an industry is independent of the emigration that is generated by the higher remittances inflows. Under these circumstances, higher labor demand could reinforce the labor market impact, leading to a further increase in real wages and returning employment back toward its original level. In many developing economies, where resource reallocation is still taking place, several sectors could be contracting where labor shedding occurs. Under these circumstances, the impact on employment is unambiguous, that is it declines. In such cases, the impact of wages would depend on the relative magnitudes of the labor supply and demand shocks in the sector. If the labor supply shock dominates, then wages will go up in that sector (Bouton et al. 2010). The reverse is true if the decline in labor demand dominates.

The simple labor market framework we considered so far in our discussion assumes a single labor market with a homogeneous labor force. This implies the perfect substitutability of workers with different skills. This could be a rare example, since a labor market in most of the cases is highly fragmented and the degree of substitutability between different groups of workers depends on the proximity of skills. Considering these issues in a theoretical model, Card and Lemieux (2001) predict that a group of workers affected by an emigration shock experiences a higher effect on wages than any other group. To prove this, we adopt a simple theoretical model from Docquier et al. (2014), which is based on the labor market (Katz and Murphy 1992; Card and Lemieux 2001) and growth (Caselli and Coleman 2001) literature.

We assume a production function where the labor aggregate is represented as a nested Constant-Elasticity-of-Substitution (CES) function of different types of workers. At time t output (Yt) is produced in a country according to a constant-returns-to-scale Cobb-Douglas production function with two factors, physical capital (Kt), and labor in efficiency units (Lt):

$$Y_t = A_t K_t^{1-\alpha} L_t^{\alpha} \tag{8.1}$$

The term A_t represents the total factor productivity (TFP), and α is the income share of labor. The returns to physical capital are equalized across countries. Also, if R* denotes the net interest rate, then the following arbitrage condition indicates the equilibrium capital to labor ratio

$$R^* = (1-\alpha) A_t K_t^{-\alpha} L_t^{\alpha} \tag{8.2}$$

Substituting (8.2) into (8.1), the aggregate output condition can be expressed as follows, with $\overline{A}_t$ a modified TFP and an increasing function of TFP.

$$Y_t = \overline{A}_t L_t \tag{8.3}$$

Based on Katz and Murphy (1992) and Card and Lemieux (2001) the labor in efficiency unit as a nested-CES function can be expressed as follows:

$$L_t = \left[\theta L_{S,t}^{\frac{\sigma-1}{\sigma}} + (1-\theta) L_{U,t}^{\frac{\sigma-1}{\sigma}} \right]^{\frac{\sigma}{\sigma-1}} \tag{8.4}$$

where $L_{S,t}$ and $L_{U,t}$ can be thought of as skilled and unskilled workers. The relative productivity level of high skilled workers is distinguished by the parameter θ and σ is the elasticity of substitution between two groups of workers. For the sake of simplicity, we assume here that natives and immigrants have the same distribution in both groups. This is to keep the effect of emigration on immigrants across skill groups constant, since our focus is to find the changes in average wages of non-migrant natives. Equation (8.4) provides the changes in average wages of non-migrant natives due to the emigration flow from t-1 to t period, as a function of the changes in wages for high skilled and low-skilled natives.

$$\Delta W_t = \left(W_{S,t} - W_{S,t^*}\right)\frac{N_{S,t}}{N_{S,t} + N_{U,t}} + \left(W_{S,t} - W_{U,t^*}\right)\frac{N_{U,t}}{N_{S,t} + N_{U,t}} \tag{8.5}$$

where $W_{High,t}{}^*$ and $W_{Low,t}{}^*$ are the wages in period t estimated by using the stock of high and low-skilled emigrants from period t-1, respectively. The respective population share weights the differences in the actual wage of non-migrant natives and emigrants for both skill groups. Going one step further, we can link Eq. (8.5) with Eq. (8.6), with skill premium approximated by the differences in the growth rates of skilled and unskilled wages $\omega = \frac{\frac{\partial f}{\partial S} / B_S}{\frac{\partial f}{\partial U} / B_U} \cong \frac{W_{High,t} - W_{High,t^*}}{W_{Low,t} - W_{Low,t^*}}$ Combining these two equations, we get

$$L_S = 1 - \frac{\varnothing}{1-\varnothing}\left(Ak\right)^{\frac{\rho-1}{\rho}}\left[\theta^{\frac{\sigma(\rho-1)}{\rho-\sigma}}\left(1-\varnothing\right)^{\frac{\rho(\sigma-1)}{\rho-\sigma}} + \left(1-\theta\right)^{\frac{\sigma(\rho-1)}{\rho-\sigma}} l^{\frac{\sigma-1}{\rho-\sigma}} \frac{W_{High,t} - W_{High,t^*}}{W_{Low,t} - W_{Low,t^*}}^{\frac{\rho(\sigma-1)}{\rho-\sigma}}\right]^{\frac{\rho-\sigma}{\rho(\sigma-1)}} \tag{8.6}$$

Equation (8.6) suggests that skilled emigration may lower the labor income share through an increase in the skill premium. Ouyang and Paul (2018) in a recent paper show that wage growth for skilled workers is much higher in developing countries (Table 8.1).

For empirical reasons, one can assume that workers with the same level of education are closer substitutes than those with a different education level. Similar strategies have been used to identify the effect of emigration on real wages. One last point to note about the model we have just discussed is important. It has been assumed throughout that capital in this economy is fixed. If capital could fully adjust, migration would probably

Table 8.1 Evolution of monthly wages (% change between 1990 and 2000)

	Developed (%)	*Developing (%)*
Traded skilled worker	12.22	79.40
Traded unskilled worker	11.67	39.47
Nontraded skilled worker	16.00	50.05
Nontraded unskilled worker	14.15	36.85

Source: Ouyang and Paul (2018)

lead to capital outflows, since a decrease in labor supply is likely to decrease the marginal product of capital. It also depends on capital-skill complementarity, as discussed in the first section. Thus, migration can have both direct and indirect effects on labor income share, and the literature has so far been silent on this topic. This remains one of most promising areas of research on the drivers of labor income share.

8.3 LIS, Remittances, and Brain-Gain

According to recent World Bank estimates, the remittance flows to developing countries in 2011 were approximately $351 billion, with a staggering 215 million people living outside their countries of birth. This has enormous implications for economic growth and welfare, as remittances over the past two decades have become more important than the formal, government-sponsored, or international aid to fuel development (GEM 2009; WDI n.d.). The burgeoning literature on migration and development indicates various direct and indirect channels through which remittances affect the aggregate income and welfare in receiving countries (de Haas 2007; Ratha and Shaw 2007). While the direct effects of remittances are manifested through human capital accumulation, better access to health, education, finance, and entrepreneurship, the lost labor outcome due to emigration is likely to impact on wages and households' labor supply decisions in migrant-sending countries.

The impact of remittances from a macroeconomic theoretical point of view can be analyzed by three competing postulates. Based on the Keynesian model, some researchers (El-Sakka and McNabb 1999; Kireyev 2006; Rapoport and Docquier 2006) maintain that remittances provide an increase in income and therefore expand the aggregated demand. In a standard Keynesian macroeconomic model, investment and exports are exogenous and not related to output. Similarly, an increase in a country's income through remittances (R) can also be considered as an increment of export receipts or as further investment. In a recent study, Singer (2010) employs the Mundell Fleming model to explain the impact of remittances. In this modified model, remittances are part of the money supply. The main argument goes that as the money supply is triggered by an inflow of remittances expands, it consequently produces an increase in growth. Kireyev (2006) explores the impact of remittances from the perspective of national accounts theory. He argues that the direct impact of remittances contributes to an expansion of the aggregate demand. Since remittances affect private flows, an increase in consumption is supported either by higher domestic outputs or by higher imports.

The theoretical approach to analyzing the impact of remittances on labor income share through human capital closely corresponds to that of migration, since remittances are a direct consequence of international migration. Theoretical arguments show that migration presents positive as well as negative effects on human capital. On one hand, researchers argue that migration has a negative effect on the local stock of human capital by removing individuals with skills (Grubel and Scott 1966; Bhagwati and Hamada 1974; Kwok and Leland 1982). These studies highlight the negative impact of migration particularly for developing countries; sustaining that migration creates a scarcity of skilled workers (commonly known as brain-drain). On the other hand, Vidal (1998) and Chen (2006) postulate that migration can have positive effects for migrant-sending countries. The general argument in this kind of research is that migration (and the consequently the inflow of remittances) fosters investment in education in migrant-sending countries (brain-gain argument). To this extent, three related studies (Beine et al. 2008; Vidal 1998; Mountford 1997) show that migration prospects have a positive impact on human capital because they increase the expected returns to education, and additionally they may foster education investment in the migrant-sending countries. As a result, the source country could potentially end up with a higher level of human capital. This transforms the classical view of migration from brain-drain to brain-gain. Brain-gain or human capital development has direct bearing on labor income share as argued by Atkinson (2009).

8.4 LIS, Remittances, and Negative Labor Supply

The theoretical approach to analyzing the impact of remittances on labor markets derives from neoclassical models of labor-leisure choice, developed by Barzel and McDonald (1973) and Killingsworth (1983), where remittances are non-labor income. In recent years, interest has grown in using general equilibrium models to analyze the specific transmitting channels through which remittances affect participation in labor markets (Bussolo and Medvedev 2008; Kim 2007). Bussolo and Medvedev (2008) develop a basic model where an increase in remittances is equivalent to a permanent increase in income of the household. They further argue that this increase influences the behavior of tradable and non-tradable goods in the economy: the increase of income in the household represents extra spending on tradable and non-tradable goods (if non-tradable goods are normal goods). The final link in this basic model, which assesses the impact of remittances, comes from a modification of the above model based on work by Annabi (2004), Barzel and McDonald (1973) and most prominently Killingsworth (1983), which introduced a consumption-leisure trade-off in the household utility function. The theoretical model concludes that the labor supply is decreasing in non-labor income, and the sign of the elasticity will depend on the ratio of non-labor income to the total consumption expenditure. Bussolo and Medvedev (2008) further explain that with an increase in non-labor income through remittances, individuals can consume more goods and leisure (i.e., the income effect dominates) and thus their labor supply is reduced. In a general equilibrium setting, wages are set to clear the labor market and reduced labor supply implies raising wages. According to them, this triggers second order effects. They show that higher wages raise the opportunity cost of leisure and the substitution effect can push individuals to increase their labor supply, up to the point where the income effect dominates again like a backward bending labor supply curve. It is difficult to conclude whether a negative labor supply effect through remittances can lower labor income share, as it depends on whether the primary effects dominates the secondary effect or vice versa. As shown in Eq. (8.6), in the absence of effective bargaining, a higher level of reservation wage can also restore a higher share of income for the laborers. Overall, remittance serves as a potential identification mechanism to link the changes in the labor income share to changes in employment or wages.

8.5 LIS and Premature Deindustrialization

The growth of low-skilled service jobs (Autor et al. 2003) could be a threat to already declining labor income share, and this leads to another promising area of research to examine the consequences of "premature deindustrialization" on the labor income share. The employment share in manufacturing typically follows an inverted U-shaped path as countries develop, but as Rodrik (2016) observes the turning point for developing countries arrives sooner and at much lower levels of income than what has been the case for developed countries in the previous decades. He further argues that globalization and labor-saving technological progress in manufacturing play crucial roles in this prematurity of deindustrialization. However, the evidence for premature deindustrialization or even deindustrialization at an aggregate level may not be there. As Haraguchi and Rezonja (2010) argue, industrial production can move from one country to another because of trade liberalization alongside productivity and income growth. For this reason, we may find some countries experiencing a lower industrial production and employment over time, which may not be the case for other countries. As a result, it provides a very interesting identification problem to handle especially among the developing countries. Not to mention, country size also plays a key role here (e.g., the People's Republic of China). Moreover, one needs to be very careful about industry VA and industry employment as they could be very different and follow different growth trajectories. We can use both, but there is no reason to expect that the outcomes would converge. In a recent study, Oishi and Paul (2018) provide some evidence on the relationship between changes in the labor income share in the secondary and the tertiary sectors. They show that the change in the labor income share in the tertiary sector was the highest in Costa Rica and the lowest in the Peru. At the same time, the change in the labor income share in the secondary sector is the highest in Costa Rica and the lowest in Mauritius. Overall, this study finds a positive correlation between changes in the labor income share between tertiary and secondary sectors. One possible extension of this line of research is to compare the drivers of labor income share between manufacturing and services especially in the developing countries (Fig. 8.2).

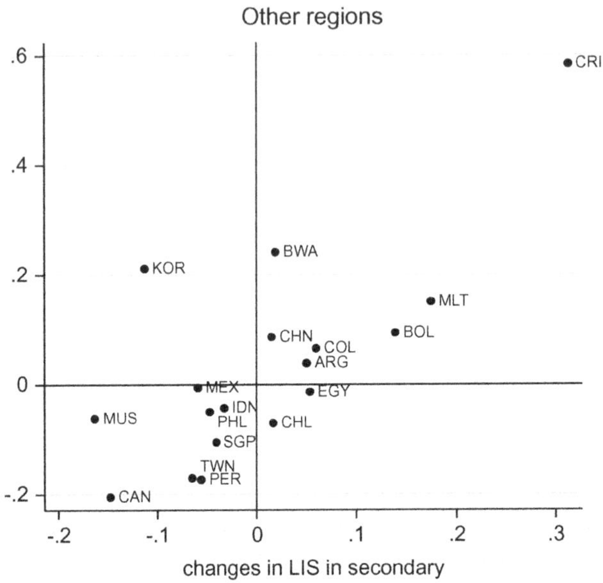

Fig. 8.2 Changes in labor income shares: manufacturing versus services. (Source: Oishi and Paul (2018). Note: Change in the labor income share is based on the starting year and the ending year for each country. For further details please see Oishi and Paul (2018))

8.6 LIS and Firm Restructuring

In this section, we discuss another potential area of research on the drivers of labor income share from the micro perspective. The literature on the effect of the ownership structure of firms, for example, how labor income share differs between state-owned, privately owned and foreign-owned firms has been most mostly silent, except for Decreuse and Maarek (2015), Zhou (2016) and some other studies. Using data from 98 developing countries over the period from 1980 to 2000, Decreuse and Maarek (2015) find a U-shaped relationship between labor income share and the proportion of foreign firms. Furthermore, they argue that the magnitude of the relationship is governed by the technological gap between foreign and local firms. We use a simple model following Decreuse and Maarek (2015). Assume that there are two types of firms. The proportion of the first type of firm is δ, with income level y_1 and the proportion of the second type of firm is 1 − δ with income level y_2, and the first group of firms is more productive than the second group of firms, that is, $y_1 > y_2$. This could be because type 1 firms use better technology, insertional set up, or unobserved factors related to ownership structures. We maintain the homogeneity assumption of labor to keep the model simple. Firm 2 enters the market first, and firm 1 sets a wage with a markup over firm 2's wage assuming $w_1 > w_2$, in the following manner:

$$w_1 = \frac{\left[\delta y_1 + (1-\delta)y_2\right]w_2}{y_2} > w_2 \tag{8.7}$$

Plugging this into the labor income share formula, we can write expressions for the labor income share for both types of firms as follows:

$$LIS_1 = \frac{W_1}{y_1} = \frac{\left[\delta y_1 + (1-\delta)y_2\right]W_2}{y_1 y_2} \text{ and } LIS_2 = \frac{W_2}{y_2} \tag{8.8}$$

Combining LIS_1 and LIS_2, we get the aggregate labor income share as follows:

$$LIS = \frac{w_1}{y_1} = \frac{\delta w_1 + (1-\delta)w_2}{\delta y_1 + (1-\delta)y_2} = \frac{\delta\frac{\left[\delta y_1 + (1-\delta)y_2\right]w_2}{y_2} + (1-\delta)w_2}{\delta y_1 + (1-\delta)y_2} \tag{8.9}$$

Differentiating the aggregate labor income share with respect to δ, we find a non-linear (convex) relationship between the aggregate labor income share and the share of productive firms as depicted in Fig. 8.3.

$$LIS = \frac{dLIS}{d\delta} = \delta^2 y_1 - (1-\delta)^2 y_2; \frac{d^2 LIS}{d\delta^2} > 0 \tag{8.10}$$

Equation (8.10) shows that in a frictional labor market with productive heterogeneity, and shock such as foreign direct investment (FDI) can have two opposite effects on the labor income share. The first is a negative effect originated by technological advancement and then a positive effect

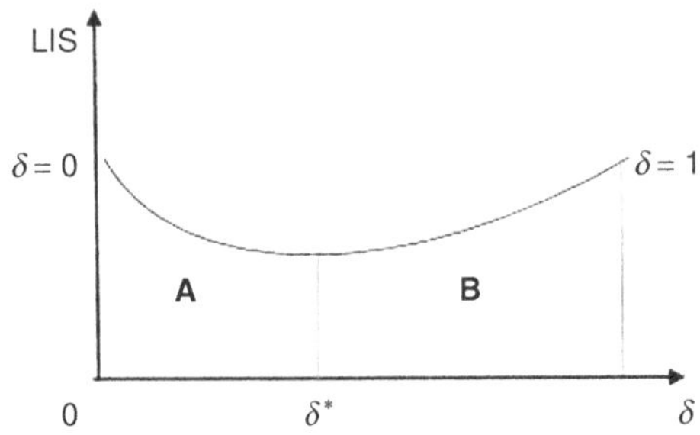

Fig. 8.3 Labor income share and the ownership structure of the firm. (Source: The authors, following Zhou (2016). The enterprise survey data http://www.enterprisesurveys.org/data./ could be an effective tool to conduct empirical studies on labor income share by comparing firms of different ownership types, as well as for using information about the size and the age of the firm across countries)

due to an increasing labor market (wage) competition between firms. As evident from Fig. 8.3, the technological effect dominates the wage coopetition effect when LIS is downward sloping (the region marked by A), whereas the wage coopetition effect dominates the technological effect when the LIS is upward sloping (the region marked by B).

8.7 LIS and Globalization at the Sectoral Level

In Sect. 3.3, we discussed various channels that connect globalization to movements in the labor income share at the national level. The study of labor income shares at the sectoral level play an important role in understanding the relationship between sectoral value-added and personal income. However, the empirical studies on the effect of globalization on the labor income share are limited to the country-level analysis mainly because at the sectoral level, data on labor income share is available only for the advanced countries. In a recent study, Oishi and Paul (2018) construct a novel data set on labor income share at the 10-sector level[1] following the classification of Groningen Growth Data Centre (GGDC). This new data allows us to estimate sectoral labor income shares for 54 countries across five regions (9 from East Asia and the Pacific, 28 from Europe

[1]We follow the Groningen Growth Data Center (GGDC) classification of 10 sectors (AGR, MIN, MAN, PU, CON, WRT, TRA, FIRE, GOV, and OTH).

and Central Asia, 8 from Latin America and the Caribbean, 2 from the Middle East and North Africa, 2 from North America, and 5 from sub-Saharan Africa). Out of 54 countries, 20 countries are developing countries (based on the World Bank classification). They found that on average, the labor income shares in developing countries are slightly lower than that in the developed countries. They also find considerable variation in the labor income share estimates within each region and within each broad category of sectors, measured at the level and changes over time. For example, labor receives the lowest share of income in primary sectors in all regions except in the Middle East and North Africa (MENA) and the sub-Saharan Africa (SSA). In East Asia and the Pacific (EAP) and North America, the labor income share is the highest in the tertiary sector, whereas in the Europe and Central Asia region, the secondary sector shows the most favorable returns to labor. On the other hand, data on tariff rates at the sectoral are available from various data sources including COMTRADE https://comtrade.un.org/ and UNCTRADE https://unctad.org/en/Pages/statistics.aspx. Analyzing the cross-country sectoral patterns of labor income share in conjunction with the trade reforms can help us closely identify the drivers of the labor income share.

References

Annabi, N. 2004. *Modeling Labor Markets in CGE Models: Endogenous Labor Supply, Unions, and Efficiency Wages. Poverty and Economic Policy (PEP).* Network Working Paper, May.

Atkinson, A. B. 2009. "Factor Shares: The Principal Problem of Political Economy?" *Oxford Review of Economic Policy* 25 (1): 3–16.

Atkinson, A. B. and F. Bourguignon. 2000. "Introduction: Income Distribution and Economics", in A.B. Atkinson and F. Bourguignon (eds), *Handbook of Income Distribution*, Geneva, Elsevier Science.

Autor, D., F. Levy, and R. Murnane. 2003. "The Skill Content of Recent Technical Change: An Empirical Exploration." *Quarterly Journal of Economics* 118: 1279–1334.

Barkai, S. 2016. *Declining Labor and Capital Shares.* University of Chicago, November.

Barzel, Y., and R. J. McDonald. 1973. Assets, Subsistence, and the Supply Curve of Labor. *The American Economic Review*, 63(4): 621–633.

Beine, M., F. Docquier, and H. Rapoport. 2008. Brain Drain and Human Capital Formation in Developing Countries: Winners and Losers. *The Economic Journal*, 118(528): 631–652.

Bhagwati, J., and K. Hamada. 1974. "The Brain-Drain, International Integration of Markets for Professionals and Unemployment: A Theoretical Analysis." *Journal of Development Economics*, 1(1): 19–42.

Bouton, L., S. Paul, and E. Tiongson. 2010. "The Impact of Emigration on Source Country Wages: Evidence from the Republic of Moldova." Policy Research Working Paper 5764, The World Bank.

Bussolo, M., and D. Medvedev. 2008. "Do Remittances Have a Flip Side? A General Equilibrium Analysis of Remittances, Labor Supply Responses and Policy Options for Jamaica." *Journal of Economic Integration*, 23(3): 734–764.

Card, David, and Thomas Lemieux 2001. "Can Falling Supply Explain the Rising Return to College for Younger Men? A Cohort-Based Analysis," *Quarterly Journal of Economics*, CXVI, 705–746.

Caselli, Francesco, and Wilbur John Coleman. 2001. "The U.S. Structural Transformation and Regional Convergence: A Reinterpretation," *Journal of Political Economy* 109: 584–616.

Chen, H. J. 2006. "International Migration and Economic Growth: A Source Country Perspective." *Journal of Population Economics*, 19(4), 725–748.

de Haas, H. 2007. *Remittances and Social Development: A Conceptual Review of the Literature*. Geneva: UNRISD.

Decreuse, B., and P. Maarek. 2015. "FDI and the Labor Share in Developing Countries: A Theory and Some Evidence." *Annals of Economics and Statistics/ Annales d'Économie et de Statistique*, 119/120: 289–319.

Docquier, F., C. Özden., and G. Peri. 2014. "The Labor Market Impact of Immigration and Emigration in OECD Countries," *Economic Journal*, 124 (579): 1106–1145.

El-Sakka, M. I. T., and R. McNabb. 1999. "The Macroeconomic Determinants of Emigrant Remittances." *World Development*, 27(8): 1493–1502.

GEM. 2009. *Global Entrepreneurship Monitor Global Report*, Babson College.

Gomme, P. and P. Rupert. 2004. *Measuring Labor's Share of Income. Policy Discussion Paper* 7. Federal Reserve Bank of Cleveland.

Grubel, H. B., and A. D. Scott. 1966. "The International Flow of Human Capital." *The American Economic Review*, 56(1/2), 268–274.

Haraguchi, N., and G. Rezonja. 2010. "In Search of General Patterns of Manufacturing Development." Development Policy and Strategic Research Branch Working Paper 02/2010. Vienna: United Nations Industrial Development Organization.

Katz, Lawrence F., and Kevin M. Murphy 1992. "Changes in the Wage Structure, 1963–1987: Supply and Demand Factors," *Quarterly Journal of Economics* CVII, 35–78.

Killingsworth, M. R. 1983. *Labour Supply*. Cambridge: Cambridge University Press.

Kim, N. 2007. "The Impact of Remittances on Labor Supply: The Case of Jamaica", Policy Research Working Paper Series 4120, World Bank, Washington, DC.

Kireyev, A. 2006. The Macroeconomics of Remittances: The Case of Tajikistan. IMF Working Paper No. 06/2.

Kwok, V., and Leland, H. 1982. An Economic Model of the Brain-Drain. *The American Economic Review*, 72(1), 91–100.

Mountford, A. 1997. "Can a Brain Drain Be Good for Growth in the Source Economy?" *Journal of Development Economics*, 53(2), 287–303.

Oishi, Y. and S. Paul. 2018. "Sectoral Labor Income Share Dynamics: Cross-Country Evidence from a Novel Dataset." ADBI Working Paper 875. Tokyo: Asian Development Bank Institute. https://www.adb.org/publications/sectoral-labor-income-share-dynamics.

Ouyang, A, and S. Paul. 2018. The Effect of Skilled Emigration on Real Exchange Rates Through the Wage Channel. *Journal of International Money and Finance* 89: 139–153.

Piketty, T. 2014. *Capital in the Twenty-First Century*. Cambridge: Harvard University Press.

Rapoport, H., and F. Docquier. 2006. "The Economics of Migrants' Remittances." *Handbook on the Economics of Giving, Reciprocity and Altruism*, 2, 1135–1198.

Ratha, D., and W. Shaw. 2007. "South-South Migration and Remittances." World Bank Working Paper, No. 102, The World Bank.

Rodrik, Dani. 2016. "Premature Deindustrialization" *Journal of Economic Growth* 21: 1–33.

Singer, D. A. 2010. "Migrant Remittances and Exchange Rate Regimes in the Developing World." *American Political Science Review*, 104(2), 307–323.

Vidal, J. P. 1998. The Effect of Emigration on Human Capital Formation. *Journal of Population Economics*, 11(4), 589–600.

World Bank World Development Indicators (WDI). n.d. http://data.worldbank.org/datacatalog/world-development-indicators

Zhou, Minghai. 2016. *Labor's Share of Income: Another Key to Understand China's Income Inequality*. Singapore: Springer. https://www.springer.com/kr/book/9789811001727 (accessed 26 November 2018).

CHAPTER 9

Concluding Remarks

The study of factor income shares plays an important role in understanding the relationship between national income and personal income and the relationship between wage inequality and wealth inequality. In recent years, a large body of research has documented a global decline in the labor income share. The literature offers several explanations but there is little consensus on the drivers of the decline in the labor income share. This book critically evaluates the role of capital accumulation, capital-skill complementarity, and globalization as potential drivers of this phenomenon. It also highlights issues related to measurement of the labor income share and discusses some policy frameworks to benefit low-skilled workers.

This book refines our understanding of the global decline in labor income share by emphasizing the significance of the skill composition of the labor market. It shows that a fraction of the labor market can alone produce a decline in the aggregate labor income share. This can be explained in the context of the changing skill composition of the labor force and in the variation in the elasticity of substitution between capital and labor at all skill levels. This happens particularly when a decrease in the labor income share for the unskilled labor force outweighs an increase in the labor income share for skilled labor, which could occur if wages do not immediately change due to the changing composition of skills in the market. The relevance of capital-skill complementarity for the labor share of income can also be drawn using a two-stage production structure. In the first stage, skilled workers adopt new technologies and efficiently use

S. Paul, *Labor Income Share*,
https://doi.org/10.1007/978-981-15-6860-2_9

capital, thus showing high capital-skill complementarity. In the second stage, unskilled workers continue the mechanical process of machine maintenance indicating a relatively low level of capital-skill complementarity. Such practices are common across both developing and developed countries and provide an important link between capital-skill substitutability and factor income shares.

This book provides a unique opportunity to compare the labor income share trends at the country, sector, and firm level. At the country level, income and trade measures are positively correlated with the average labor income share, whereas the informal sector share of GDP, self-employment show a negative correlation with the average labor income share. On the other hand, sectoral data confirms a fall in the average rate of change in the labor income share in the secondary sector and the primary sector and a rise in the same in the tertiary sector. Finally, the labor income share estimates at the firm level average around 0.45, with considerable variations across regions and firm characteristics. Manufacturing firms tend to have a lower labor income share compared to firms in the services sectors.

Globalization does not provide a clear answer as a driver of the labor income share fall. An analysis of countries before and after their liberalization shows the labor income declining in countries throughout the period, making it difficult to trace the source of labor income share fall to globalization. Similar pattern is found at sector level, where there is a negative correlation between the volume of trade (as a share of GDP) and labor income share. The negative correlation in the manufacturing sector is somewhat weaker than in other sectors. However, we find a positive association between changes in the labor income shares in agriculture and changes in the trade share of GDP. Regression results at the sector level do not allow us to claim any strong causal relationship between trade and labor income share. We find support for a negative correlation between trade openness and sectoral labor income share; however, the evidence on the relationship between the process of structural transformation and labor income share is at best mixed. Skill-biased structural transformation is likely to be positively correlated with the share of labor income predominantly in the service sectors.

The global decline in labor income share at the aggregate level hides more than it reveals, as outcomes at disaggregated levels are quite diverse. As shown in this book, analysis of the labor income shares by skill and sectors remains a promising area of future research. Growing skill premium with capital complementing higher skills, greater exposure to routinization, and participation in global value chains lead to polarization of wages and employment across the skill spectrum. This points to the need for policies that promote skill deepening for medium- and low-skilled workers. Short-term policies that aim to create jobs for low-skilled workers in this transitioning phase should be implemented, alongside medium- to long-term redistributive measures to prevent welfare losses in well-being resulting from further decline in low-skilled workers' share of total income.

The key findings of this book also highlight the role of social and economic policies that have also led to reductions in the labor income share, especially for unskilled workers. If unions can raise wages, then this can have a positive impact on the labor income share by increasing the gap between growth in real wages and labor productivity growth. The role of institutional forces becomes imperative when wage gains come at the expense of profits, because otherwise labor income share will continue to decline as the share of profit and capital income grows.

References

Acemoglu, Daron. 2002. "Technical Change, Inequality and the Labor Market." *Journal of Economic Literature* 40: 7–72.

Acemoglu, D., and D. H. Autor. 2011. Skills, Tasks and Technologies: Implications for Employment and Earnings. In Handbook of Labor Economics Volume 4, Orley Ashenfelter and David E. Card (eds.), Amsterdam: Elsevier.

Aghion, Philippe, and Peter Howitt. 2006. Appropriate Growth Policy: A Unifying Framework. *Journal of the European Economic Association* 4(2–3): 269–314.

Allen, R.G.D. 1938. *Mathematical Analysis for Economists.* London: Macmillan.

Alvarez-Cuadrado, F., N. V. Long, and M. Poschke. 2015. *Capital–Labor Substitution, Structural Change and the Labor Income Share.* IZA Discussion Paper No. 8941.

Anderson, R. K. and J. R. Moroney. 1993. "Morishima Elasticities of Substitution with Nested Production Functions." *Economics Letters* 42: 159–166.

Annabi, N. 2004. *Modeling Labor Markets in CGE Models: Endogenous Labor Supply, Unions, and Efficiency Wages. Poverty and Economic Policy (PEP).* Network Working Paper, May.

Antras, P. 2001. Is the U.S. Aggregate Production Function Cobb-Douglas? New Estimates of the Elasticity of Substitution. Contributions to Macroeconomics 4 (1): Article 4.

Arpaia, Alfonso, Esther Perez, and Karl Pichelmann. 2009. "Understanding Labour's Income Share Dynamics in Europe." European Economy Economics Paper No. 379, European Commission.

Atkinson, A. B. 2009. "Factor Shares: The Principal Problem of Political Economy?" *Oxford Review of Economic Policy* 25 (1): 3–16.

S. Paul, *Labor Income Share*,
https://doi.org/10.1007/978-981-15-6860-2

Atkinson, A. B. and F. Bourguignon. 2000. "Introduction: Income Distribution and Economics", in A.B. Atkinson and F. Bourguignon (eds), *Handbook of Income Distribution*, Geneva, Elsevier Science.

Autor, D., F. Levy, and R. Murnane. 2003. "The Skill Content of Recent Technical Change: An Empirical Exploration." *Quarterly Journal of Economics* 118: 1279–1334.

Autor, David H., David Dorn, Lawrence F. Katz, Christina Patterson, and John Van Reenen. 2017. "Concentrating on the Fall of the Labor Share." NBER Working Paper 23108, National Bureau of Economic Research, Cambridge, MA.

Barkai, S. 2016. *Declining Labor and Capital Shares.* University of Chicago, November.

Barzel, Y., and R. J. McDonald. 1973. Assets, Subsistence, and the Supply Curve of Labor. *The American Economic Review*, 63(4): 621–633.

Beine, M., F. Docquier, and H. Rapoport. 2008. Brain Drain and Human Capital Formation in Developing Countries: Winners and Losers. *The Economic Journal*, 118(528): 631–652.

Bentolila, Samuel and Saint-Paul, Gilles. 2003. Explaining Movements in the Labor Share. *The B.E. Journal of Macroeconomics*, 3(1), 1–33.

Berman, Eli, John Bound, and Zvi Griliches. 1994. "Changes in the Demand for Skilled Labor within U.S. Manufacturing Industries: Evidence from the Annual Survey of Manufacturing." *Quarterly Journal of Economics* 109(2): 367–397.

Bernard, Andrew and Jensen, J. 2004. Why Some Firms Export. *The Review of Economics and Statistics*, 86(2), 561–569.

Bhagwati, J., and K. Hamada. 1974. "The Brain-Drain, International Integration of Markets for Professionals and Unemployment: A Theoretical Analysis." *Journal of Development Economics*, 1(1): 19–42.

Blackorby C. and R. R. Russell. 1989. "Will the Real Elasticity of Substitution Please Stand Up? (A Comparison of the Allen/Uzawa and Morishima Elasticities)." *American Economic Review* 79: 882–888.

Blanchard, O., and Giavazzi, F. 2003. "Macroeconomic Effects of Regulation and Deregulation in Goods and Labor Markets." *The Quarterly Journal of Economics*, 118(3): 879–907.

Blanchard, O., W. Nordhaus, and E. Phelps. 1997. "The Medium Run." *Brookings Papers on Economic Activity*, 2: 89–158.

Blaug, M. 1996. *Economic Theory in Retrospect*, 3rd ed., Cambridge, Cambridge University Press.

Böckerman, Petri, and Mika Maliranta, 2012. Globalization, Creative Destruction, and Labour Share Change: Evidence on the Determinants and Mechanisms from Longitudinal Plant-Level Data. *Oxford Economic Papers* 64(2): 259–280.

Bouton, L., S. Paul, and E. Tiongson. 2010. "The Impact of Emigration on Source Country Wages: Evidence from the Republic of Moldova." Policy Research Working Paper 5764, The World Bank.

Bridgman, B. 2014. *Is Labor's Loss Capital's Gain?: Gross Versus Net Labor Shares.* BEA.

Buera, F. J., and J. P. Kaboski. 2012. The Rise of the Service Economy. *American Economic Review*, 102 (6): 2540–69.

Buera, F. J., J. P. Kaboski, and R. Rogerson. 2015. *Skill Biased Structural Change.* NBER Working Paper No. 21165.

Bussolo, M., and D. Medvedev. 2008. "Do Remittances Have a Flip Side? A General Equilibrium Analysis of Remittances, Labor Supply Responses and Policy Options for Jamaica." *Journal of Economic Integration*, 23(3): 734–764.

Card, David, and Thomas Lemieux 2001. "Can Falling Supply Explain the Rising Return to College for Younger Men? A Cohort-Based Analysis," *Quarterly Journal of Economics*, CXVI, 705–746.

Caselli, F. 1999. Technological Revolutions. *American Economic Review* 89, 78–102.

Caselli, Francesco, and Wilbur John Coleman. 2001. "The U.S. Structural Transformation and Regional Convergence: A Reinterpretation," *Journal of Political Economy* 109: 584–616.

Charpe, M., S. Lee, D. Arias, and S. Bridji. 2014. Does income distribution matter for development? Trends in labour share of income and their economic impacts in developing countries. World of Work Report: ILO, Chap. 8.

Chen, H. J. 2006. "International Migration and Economic Growth: A Source Country Perspective." *Journal of Population Economics*, 19(4), 725–748.

Chirinko, Robert S. 2008. "The Long and Short of It." *Journal of Macroeconomics* 30: 671–686.

Chirinko, Robert S., and Debdulal Mallick. 2017. "The Substitution Elasticity, Factor Shares, and the Low-Frequency Panel Model." *American Economic Journal: Macroeconomics*, 9(4): 225–253.

Cooley, T. F. and E. C. Prescott. 1995. "Economic Growth and Business Cycles," in *Frontiers of Business Cycle Research*, pp. 1–38, ed. Princeton: Princeton University Press.

Dao, M. C., M. M. Das, Z. Koczan, and W. Lian. 2017. *Why is Labor Receiving a Smaller Share of Global Income? Theory and Empirical Evidence.* International Monetary Fund.

de Haas, H. 2007. *Remittances and Social Development: A Conceptual Review of the Literature.* Geneva: UNRISD.

de Serres, Alain, Stefano Scarpetta, and Christine de la Maisonneuve. 2002. "Sectoral Shifts in Europe and the United States: How They Affect Aggregate Labour Shares and the Properties of Wage Equations," OECD Economics Department Working Papers 326, OECD Publishing, April.

de Vries, Gaaitzen J., Marcel P. Timmer, and Klaas de Vries. 2013. "Structural Transformation in Africa: Static Gains, Dynamic Losses." *Groningen Growth and Development Centre Research Memorandum* GD-136.

Decreuse, B., and P. Maarek. 2015. "FDI and the Labor Share in Developing Countries: A Theory and Some Evidence." *Annals of Economics and Statistics/ Annales d'Économie et de Statistique*, 119/120: 289–319.

Diwan, I. 2001. "*Debt as Sweat: Labor, Financial Crises, and the Globalization of Capital*", The World Bank, Mimeo.

Doan, H. T. T. and G. Wan. 2017. *Globalization and the Labor Share in National Income*. ADBI Working Paper 639. Tokyo: Asian Development Bank Institute.

Docquier, F., C. Özden., and G. Peri. 2014. "The Labor Market Impact of Immigration and Emigration in OECD Countries," *Economic Journal*, 124 (579): 1106–1145.

Duarte, M. and D. Restuccia. 2010. "The Role of the Structural Transformation in Aggregate Productivity." *Quarterly Journal of Economics* 125: 129–173.

Eden, M., & Gaggl, P. 2015. *On the Welfare Implications of Automation*. The World Bank.

El-Sakka, M. I. T., and R. McNabb. 1999. "The Macroeconomic Determinants of Emigrant Remittances." *World Development*, 27(8): 1493–1502.

Elsby, Michael W., Bart Hobijn, and Ayşegül Şahin. 2013. "The Decline of the US Labor Share." *Brookings Papers on Economic Activity*, 2: 1–63.

EU KLEMS Consortium. 2007. EU KLEMS Growth and Productivity Accounts Version 1. http://www.euklems.net/data/EUKLEMS_Growth_and_Productivity_Accounts_Part_II_Sources.pdf (accessed 26 September 2018).

European Commission. 2007. The Labour Income Share in the European Union. Chapter 5 of: *Employment in Europe*.

Fabricant, Solomon. 1942. *Employment in Manufacturing, 1899–1939*. NBER: New York.

Fallon, P. R., and P. R. G. Layard, "Capital-Skill Complementarity, Income Distribution, and Output Accounting," *Journal of Political Economy* 83 (1975), 279–302.

Feenstra, Robert C., and Gordon H. Hanson. 1997. "Foreign Direct Investment and Relative Wages: Evidence from Mexico's Maquiladoras." *Journal of International Economics* 42: 371–393.

Feenstra, R. C., R. Inklaar, and M. P. Timmer. 2015. The Next Generation of the Penn World Table. *American Economic Review 105*(10): 3150–3182.

Fields, G. and S. Paul 2019. (eds.) *Labor Income Share in Asia: Measurement, Drivers and Policy*, Springer—ADBI Series, Springer.

Fukao, K. and S. Paul. 2017. The Long-Run Dynamics of the Labour Share in Japan, Discussion Paper Series A No.665, Institute of Economic Research, Hitotsubashi University.

Fukao, Kyoji and Christiano Perugini. 2018. The Long-Run Dynamics of the Labour Share in Japan, Discussion Paper Series A No.672, Institute of Economic Research, Hitotsubashi University.

Fukao, K., S. Hamagata, T. Inui, K. Ito, H. Ug Kwon, T. Makino, T. Miyagawa, Y. Nakanishi, and J. Tokui. 2007. Estimation Procedures and TFP Analysis of the JIP Database 2006. RIETI Discussion Paper January 2007 07-E-003.

Gammarano, R. 2018. Paid employment vs vulnerable employment: a brief study of employment patterns by status in employment.

GEM. 2009. *Global Entrepreneurship Monitor Global Report*, Babson College.

Glyn, A. 2009. "Functional Distribution and Inequality." In W. Salverda, B. Nolan, and T. M. Smeeding (eds.), *Oxford Handbook of Economic Inequality*. Oxford: Oxford University Press. 101–126.

Goldberg, P. K., and N. Pavcnik. 2007. Distributional Effects of Globalization in Developing Countries. *Journal of Economic Literature*, 45(1): 39–82.

Goldin, Claudia, and Lawrence F. Katz. 1998. "The Origins of Technology-Skill Complementarity." *Quarterly Journal of Economics*, 113 (3): 693–732.

Gollin, D. 2002. Getting income shares right. *Journal of Political Economy*, *110*(2), 458–474.

Gollin, D., D. Lagakos, and M. E. Waugh. 2014. The agricultural productivity gap. *The Quarterly Journal of Economics*, 129(2): 939–993.

Gomme, P. and P. Rupert. 2004. *Measuring Labor's Share of Income. Policy Discussion Paper* 7. Federal Reserve Bank of Cleveland.

Gomme, P., & Greenwood, J. 1995. On the Cyclical Allocation of Risk. *Journal of Economic Dynamics and Control*, *19*(1–2), 91–124.

Griliches, Z. 1969. "Capital–Skill Complementarity." *Review of Economics and Statistics*, 5: 465–468.

Grossman, G. M., E. Helpman, E. Oberfield, and T. Sampson. 2017. *The Productivity Slowdown and the Declining Labor Share: A Neoclassical Exploration* (No. w23853). National Bureau of Economic.

Growiec, Jakub. 2008. "Production functions and distributions of unit factor productivities: uncovering the link." *Economics Letters*, 101, 87–90.

Grubel, H. B., and A. D. Scott. 1966. "The International Flow of Human Capital." *The American Economic Review*, 56(1/2), 268–274.

Grullon, Gustavo, Yelena Larkin, and Roni Michaely. 2016. "Are US Industries Becoming More Concentrated?" Unpublished Working Paper.

Guerriero, Marta. 2012. The Labour Share of Income Around the World. Evidence from a Panel Dataset. http://piketty.pse.ens.fr/files/Guerriero2012.pdf (accessed 26 November 2018).

Guscina, A. 2006. Effects of Globalization on Labor's Share in National Income, IMF Working Paper no. 294.

Hamermesh, D. 1993. *Labor Demand*. Princeton, NJ: Princeton University Press.

Haraguchi, N., and G. Rezonja. 2010. "In Search of General Patterns of Manufacturing Development." Development Policy and Strategic Research Branch Working Paper 02/2010. Vienna: United Nations Industrial Development Organization.

Harrison, A. 2005/2002. "Has Globalization Eroded Labor's Share? Some Cross-Country Evidence," Working Paper. University of California at Berkeley.

Harrison, Ann. 2002. "Has Globalization Eroded Labor's Share? Some Cross-Country Evidence." University of California, Berkeley, and National Bureau of Economic Research. http://www.iadb.org/res/publications/pubfiles/pubS-FDI-9.pdf.

Harrod, R. F. 1942. *Towards A Dynamic Economics: Some Recent Developments of Economic Theory and Their Application to Policy*. London: Macmillan.

Herrendorf, B., R. Rogerson, and Á. Valentinyi. 2014. "Growth and Structural Transformation." In *Handbook of Economic Growth*, Vol. 2B, pp. 855–941 (Chapter 6). North Holland, Amsterdam and New York.

Herrendorf, B., R. Rogerson, and A. Valentinyi. 2015a. Growth and Structural Transformation. In *Handbook of Economic Growth* (Vol. 2, pp. 855–941). Elsevier.

Herrendorf, Berthold, Christopher Herrington, and Akos Valentinyi. 2015b. "Sectoral Technology and Structural Transformation." *American Economic Journal: Macroeconomics*, 7(4): 104–133.

Hicks J. R., and R. G. D. Allen. 1934. "A Reconsideration of the Theory of Value, Part II." *Economica* 1: 196–219.

Hicks, John R. 1932. *Theory of Wages*. London: Macmillan.

ILO. 2017. Key Indicators of the Labour Market (KILM). Available: http://www.ilo.org/ilostat/faces/ilostat-home/home?_adf.ctrlstate=1b2e7htvgk_4&_afr-Loop=286517921545847

ILO. 2018. *World Employment Social Outlook 2018*. Geneva: International Labour Organization.

ILO Department of Statistics Data and Protection Analysis Unit. 2019. *The Global Labour Income Share and Distribution*. International Labour Organization.

Jaumotte, Florence, and Irina Tytell. 2007. "How Has the Globalization of Labor Affected the Labor Income Share in Advanced Countries?" IMF Working Paper 07/298, International Monetary Fund, Washington, DC.

Jayadev. 2007. "Capital Account Openness and the Labour Share of Income." *Cambridge Journal of Economics*, 31(3): 423–443.

JIP. 2015. Japan Industrial productivity database http://www.ier.hit-u.ac.jp/English/databases/jip.html

Jones, Charles I. 2005. "The Shape of Production Functions and the Direction of Technical Change." *Quarterly Journal of Economics*, 120(2): 517–549.

Kaldor, N. 1956. "Alternative Theories of Distribution." *The Review of Economic Studies* 23 (2): 83–100.

Kalecki, M. 1938. "The Determinants of Distribution of National Income," *Econometrica*, April, 6: 97–112.

Kalecki, M. 1954. Theory of Economic Dynamics. Reprinted in J. Osiatynski (ed.), *Collected Works of Michal Kalecki, Vol. 1*, Oxford: Clarendon Press.

Kapsos, S., & Bourmpoula, E. 2013. *Employment and Economic Class in the Developing World*. Geneva: ILO.

Karabarbounis, Loukas, and Brent Neiman. 2014. "The Global Decline of the Labor Share." *Quarterly Journal of Economics* 129 (1): 61–103.

Katz, Lawrence F., and Kevin M. Murphy 1992. "Changes in the Wage Structure, 1963–1987: Supply and Demand Factors," *Quarterly Journal of Economics* CVII, 35–78.

Kehrig, M., and N. Vincent. 2017. Growing Productivity Without Growing Wages: The Micro-Level Anatomy of the Aggregate Labor Share Decline. CESifo Working Paper Series 6454, CESifo Group Munich.

Keynes, J. M. 1939. "Relative Movements of Real Wages and Output." *The Economic Journal* 49 (193): 34–35.

Killingsworth, M. R. 1983. *Labour Supply*. Cambridge: Cambridge University Press.

Kim, N. 2007. "The Impact of Remittances on Labor Supply: The Case of Jamaica", Policy Research Working Paper Series 4120, World Bank, Washington, DC.

Kireyev, A. 2006. The Macroeconomics of Remittances: The Case of Tajikistan. IMF Working Paper No. 06/2.

Koh, Dongya, Raul Santaeulalia-Llopis, and Yu Zhang. 2016. Labor Share Decline and Intellectual Property Products Capital," Working Papers 927, Barcelona Graduate School of Economics.

Kortum, Samuel S. 1997. "Research, patenting, and technological change." *Econometrica*, 65, 1389–1419.

Kraemer, Hagen, 2010. "The Alleged Stability of the Labour Share of Income in Macroeconomic Theories of Income Distribution," IMK Working Paper (11).

Krueger, Alan B. 1998. Measuring Labor's Share. *American Economic Review* 89(2): 45–51.

Krusell, Per, Lee E. Ohanian, José-Victor Ríos-Rull, and Giovanni L. Violante. 2000. "Capital-skill Complementarity and Inequality: A Macroeconomic Analysis." *Econometrica* 68 (5): 1029–1053.

Kwok, V., and Leland, H. 1982. An Economic Model of the Brain-Drain. *The American Economic Review*, 72(1), 91–100.

Lagakos, and Waugh. 2013. Selection, Agriculture, and Cross-Country Productivity Differences. *American Economic Review*, 103(2): 948–980.

LaPorta, Rafael and Andrei Shleifer. 2014. Informality and Development. *Journal of Economic Perspectives*, 28(3): 109–126.

Lawless, M., and K. T. Whelan. 2011. "Understanding the Dynamics of Labor Shares and Inflation." *Journal of Macroeconomics*, 33(2), 121–136.

Lawrence, Robert Z. 2015. "Recent Declines in Labor's Share in US Income: A Preliminary Neoclassical Account." NBER Working Paper No. 21296, National Bureau of Economic Research.

Leon-Ledesma, M., P. McAdam, and A. Willman, "Identifying the Elasticity of Substitution with Biased Technical Change," *American Economic Review*, 100 (2010), 1330.

León-Ledesma, Miguel, Peter McAdam, and Alpo Willman. 2015. "Production Technology Estimates and Balanced Growth." *Oxford Bulletin of Economics and Statistics* 77 (1): 40–65.

Life in Transition Survey. 2010. European Bank for Reconstruction and Development. <https://www.ebrd.com/what-we-do/economic-researchand-data/data/lits.html>

Lu, Y and L. B. Fletcher. 1968. "A Generalization of the CES Production Function." *Review of Economics and Statistics*, 50(4), 449–452. (Nov.)

Lübker, M. 2007. "Labour Shares." *Technical Brief* No. 1. Geneva: ILO, P. I. Department.

Marshall, Alfred. 1920. *Principles of Economics*, 8th ed., New York: Macmillan.

Mas, M. 2005. "Public Capital, Internal Rate of Return and Growth Accounting." EU KLEMS Note. https://mpra.ub.uni-muenchen.de/15821/. (accessed 1 March 2018).

McFadden D. 1963. "Constant Elasticity of Substitution Production Functions." *Review of Economic Studies* 31: 73–83.

McMillan, Margaret, Dani Rodrik, and Inigo Verduzc-Gallo. 2014. "Globalization, Structural Change, and Productivity Growth, with an Update on Africa," *World Development* 63: 11–32.

Melitz, M. J. 2003. The Impact of Trade on Intra-industry Reallocations and Aggregate Industry Productivity. *Econometrica* 71(6): 1695–1725.

Melitz, M. J., and G. I. P. Ottaviano. 2008. Market Size, Trade, and Productivity. *Review of Economic Studies* 75(1): 291–316.

Morishima M. 1967. "A Few Suggestions on the Theory of Elasticity (in Japanese)." *Keizai Hyoron (Economic Review)*, 16:144–150.

Mountford, A. 1997. "Can a Brain Drain Be Good for Growth in the Source Economy?" *Journal of Development Economics*, 53(2), 287–303.

Mućk, J., McAdam, P., & Growiec, J. 2018. Will the "True" Labor Share Stand Up? An Applied Survey on Labor Share Measures. *Journal of Economic Surveys*, *32*(4), 961–984.

Mundlak Y. 1968. "Elasticities of Substitution and the Theory of Derived Demand." *Review of Economic Studies*, 35: 225–236.

O'Mahony, Mary and Marcel P. Timmer. 2009. "Output, Input, Productivity Measures at the Industry Level: The EU KLEMS Database." *Economic Journal*, 374–403.

O'Mahony, Mary, Catherine Robinson, and Michela Vecchi. 2008. "The Impact of ICT on the Demand for Skilled Labour: A Cross-Country Comparison," *Labour Economics*, 15, 1435–1450.

Oberfield, Ezra, and Devesh Raval. 2014. "Micro Data and Macro Technology." NBER Working Paper No. 20452, National Bureau of Economic Research.

OECD. 2009. "Compensation of Employees," National Accounts at a Glance.

Oishi, Y. and S. Paul. 2018. "Sectoral Labor Income Share Dynamics: Cross-Country Evidence from a Novel Dataset." ADBI Working Paper 875. Tokyo: Asian Development Bank Institute. https://www.adb.org/publications/sectoral-labor-income-share-dynamics.

Organization for Economic Co-operation and Development. 2011. "Special Focus: Inequality in Emerging Economies (EEs)." *Divided We Stand, Why Inequality Keeps Rising*. Paris: OECD.

Ouyang, A, and S. Paul. 2018. The Effect of Skilled Emigration on Real Exchange Rates Through the Wage Channel. *Journal of International Money and Finance* 89: 139–153.

Paul, S. 2020. 'Understanding the Global Decline in the Labor Income Share', IZA World of Labor, 472.

Paul, S. 2019a. Labor Income Share Dynamics with Variable Elasticity of Substitution, IZA Discussion Paper No. 12418. [June]

Paul, S. 2019b. A Decline in Labor's Share with Capital Accumulation and Complementary Factor Inputs: An Application of the Morishima Elasticity of Substitution, IZA Discussion Paper No. 12219. [March]

Paul, S. and H. Isaka 2019. Labor Income Share at the Firm Level: Global Trends, IZA Discussion Paper No. 12852. [December].

Paul, S. 2018. "Capital Skill Substitutability and the Labor Income Share: Identification Using the Morishima Elasticity of Substitution." ADBI Working Paper 839. Tokyo: Asian Development Bank Institute.

Piketty, T. 2014. *Capital in the Twenty-First Century*. Cambridge: Harvard University Press.

Piketty, Thomas, and Gabriel Zucman. 2014. "Capital is Back: Wealth–Income Ratios in Rich Countries 1700–2010." *Quarterly Journal of Economics*, 129(3): 1255–1310.

Rapoport, H., and F. Docquier. 2006. "The Economics of Migrants' Remittances." *Handbook on the Economics of Giving, Reciprocity and Altruism*, 2, 1135–1198.

Ratha, D., and W. Shaw. 2007. "South-South Migration and Remittances." World Bank Working Paper, No. 102, The World Bank.

Ricardo, David. 1821 [1971]. *Principles of Political Economy*, 3rd ed., ed. R. M. Hartwell. Harmondsworth: Pelican Classics.

Ricardo, David. 1911. *Principles of Political Economy*, First Published 1817. London: Dent.

Robinson, Joan. 1933. *The Economics of Imperfect Competition*. London: Macmillan.

Rodrigues, Francisco, and Arjun Jayadev. 2010. "The Declining Labor Share of Income." Human Development Research Paper 2010/36, United Nations Development Programme, New York.

Rodrik, Dani. 1997. "*Has Globalization Gone Too Far?*" Washington: Institute of International Economics.

Rodrik, Dani. 1998. "Globalization, Social Conflict and Economic Growth." *World Economy* 21: 143–158.

Rodrik, Dani. 2016. "Premature Deindustrialization" *Journal of Economic Growth* 21: 1–33.

Rognlie, M. 2016. Deciphering the Fall and Rise in the Net Capital Share: Accumulation or Scarcity?. *Brookings Papers on Economic Activity*, *2015*(1), 1–69.

Rognlie, Matthew. 2015. "Deciphering the Fall and Rise in the Net Capital Share: Accumulation or Scarcity?" *Brookings Papers on Economic Activity* 46 (1): 1–69.

Sachs, J. D., and A. Warner. 1995. Economic Reform and the Process of Global Integration. *Brookings Papers on Economic Activity* 1: 1–118.

Sato, R. 1975. "The Most General Class of CES Functions," *Econometrica*, 43, 999–1003.

Schneider, D. 2011. "Bargaining, Openness and the Labor Share," Tech. rep., SFB 649 Discussion Paper.

Singer, D. A. 2010. "Migrant Remittances and Exchange Rate Regimes in the Developing World." *American Political Science Review*, 104(2), 307–323.

Slaughter, Matthew J. 2001. "International Trade and Labor-Demand Elasticities." *Journal of International Economics*, 54(1): 27–56.

Smitkova. 2018. *Does Openness Matter for Structural Change?* Mimeo University of Cambridge.

Solow, Robert M. 1958. "A Skeptical Note on the Constancy of Relative Shares." *American Economic Review* 48(4): 618–631.

Stockhammer Engelbert 2013. "Why Have Wage Shares Fallen? A Panel Analysis of the Determinants of Functional Income Distribution" International Labour Office, Conditions of Work and Employment Branch. Geneva: ILO.

Stockhammer, E. 2004. "Financialization and the Slowdown of Accumulation." *Cambridge Journal of Economics*, 28(5): 719–741.

Timmer, M. P., E. Dietzenbacher, B. Los, R. Stehrer, and G. de Vries. 2015. An Illustrated User Guide to the World Input Output Database: The Case of Global Automotive Production. *Review of International Economics* 23(3): 575–605.

Trapp, K. 2015. Measuring the Labour Income Share of Developing Countries: Learning from Social Accounting Matrices. UNU-WIDER Working Paper 41.

UN. 2017. United Nations System of National Accounts. Available: http://data.un.org/Explorer.aspx?d=SNA.

UNIDO. 2015. Industrial Statistics Database – 2015 edition. Available: http://www.unido.org/resources/statistics/statistical-databases/indstat2-2015-edition.html.

Uzawa, H. 1962. "Production Functions with Constant Elasticities of Substitution." *Review of Economic Studies* 30: 291–299.

Valentinyi, A. and B. Herrendorf. 2008. "Measuring Factor Income Shares at the Sectoral Level." *Review of Economic Dynamics* 11: 820–835.

van Treeck, K. 2017. The Labor Income Share of Developing Countries: Data Review and Analysis of International Panel Data. Paper presented at the 5th Conference of the Regulating for Decent Work Network at the International Labour Office Geneva. Switzerland.

Vidal, J. P. 1998. The Effect of Emigration on Human Capital Formation. *Journal of Population Economics*, 11(4), 589–600.

Wacziarg, R., and K. H. Welch. 2003. Trade Liberalization and Growth: New Evidence. NBER Working Paper 10152.

Wacziarg, R., and K. H. Welch. 2008. Trade Liberalization and Growth: New Evidence. *The World Bank Economic Review*, 22(2): 187–231.

Wakita, S. 2006. The Lost Decade in the Japanese Labor Market: Labor's share and Okun's Law. *Public Policy Review*, *2*(1), 77.

World Bank World Development Indicators (WDI). n.d. http://data.worldbank.org/datacatalog/world-development-indicators

World Enterprise Analysis Unit. 2018. Firm Level Productivity Estimates. World Bank.

Young, A.T. 2004. "Labour's Share Fluctuations, Biased Technological Change, and the Business Cycle." *Review of Economic Dynamics* (7): 916–931.

Young, Andrew T. 2006/2010. "One of The Things We Know That Ain't So: Is US Labor's Share Relatively Stable?," *Journal of Macroeconomics*, 32 (1), 90–102.

Zhou, Minghai. 2016. *Labor's Share of Income: Another Key to Understand China's Income Inequality*. Singapore: Springer. https://www.springer.com/kr/book/9789811001727 (accessed 26 November 2018).

Zuleta, H., and Young, A. T. 2007. Labor's Shares—Aggregate and Industry: Accounting for both in a Model of Unbalanced Growth with Induced Innovation. *Documentos de trabajo* 003105, Universidad del Rosario, Facultad de Economia.

Zuleta, Hernando and Andrew T. Young. 2013. "Labor Shares in a Model of Induced Innovation." *Structural Change and Economic Dynamics*, 24(C): 112–122.

The manufacturer's authorised representative in the EU is Springer Nature Customer Service Centre GmbH, Europaplatz 3, 69115 Heidelberg, Germany. If you have any concerns regarding our products, please contact ProductSafety@springernature.com

Printed and bound by CPI Group (UK) Ltd, Croydon, CR0 4YY
30/09/2026
02225497-0001